P9-CQM-994

Understanding
Social Science

Understanding Social Science

*A Philosophical Introduction
to the
Social Sciences*

ROGER TRIGG

Basil Blackwell

© Roger Trigg 1985

First published 1985

Basil Blackwell Publisher Ltd
108 Cowley Road, Oxford OX4 1JF, UK

Basil Blackwell Inc.
432 Park Avenue South, Suite 1505,
New York, NY 10016, USA

British Library Cataloguing in Publication Data
Trigg, Roger
    Understanding social science: a philosophical
    introduction to the social sciences.
    1. Social sciences—Philosophy
    I. Title
    300'.1   H61
    ISBN 0-631-13365-8
    ISBN 0-631-14161-8 Pbk

Library of Congress Cataloging in Publication Data
Trigg, Roger.
    Understanding social science.
    Bibliography: p.
    Includes index.
    1. Social sciences—Philosophy.   I. Title.
H61.T72   1985   300'.1   84-28280
ISBN 0-631-13365-8
ISBN 0-631-14161-8 (pbk.)

Typeset by DMB (Typesetting), Oxford
Printed in Great Britain by Page Bros (Norwich) Ltd

Contents

74483

Acknowledgement

The writing of this book was aided by a research grant from the British Academy. I am most grateful for this support.

Some of the material on sociobiology in chapters 8 and 9 is derived from two lectures given in 1983. I spoke on 'The Social Sciences and Biology' at the 7th International Congress of Logic, Methodology and Philosophy of Science in Salzburg, Austria. I also lectured on 'Human Sociobiology' to the Annual Meeting of the British Association for the Advancement of Science at the University of Sussex.

1

The Nature of Science

What is social science? This is a characteristically philosophical question, examining the assumptions and presuppositions of an area of human activity. It seems easy to give a list of would-be social sciences. Sociology and social anthropology would inevitably be on it, as would such subjects as politics and economics. History has a claim to be there too, although it is often not thought of as a social science. It certainly studies the interactions of humans in society. The main difference between it and the others is that it confines itself to the past. Psychology, even social psychology, should probably not be there as it concentrates on the individual rather than on his or her place in the wider group.

It is already obvious that the notion of social science is not as clear-cut as might be first imagined. Most people would accept psychology as a science, but would wonder about its qualifications as a *social* one. History deals with societies, as well as individuals, but perhaps it is often more like literature, and ought not to be classified as a science. Its imaginative reconstruction of individuals' motives may sometimes appear more like writing a novel than like the repeated experiments of a chemist in a laboratory.

All this assumes that 'social' qualifies 'science' in the same way that 'physical' or 'natural' do. A contrast is often drawn between physical and social sciences which takes it for granted that both sets of disciplines are sciences. Physicists study the natural world while sociologists study the social world. It would follow that social sciences are not different kinds of sciences from the physical ones. The same scientific method is being used in a different area. This could not be the case for, say, theology, if that were classified as a science. It has sometimes been described as one and has on occasions even claimed to be 'the queen of the sciences'. Yet no one has ever suggested that it proceeds in the way that a physicist does. It may attempt to study the nature of God in a systematic way, but it is not an empirical science. Much of its function lies in studying what, if anything, transcends human experience.

Social sciences claim to be empirical. The enormous success of modern physical science in manipulating the world has made it appear that its methods provide the key for the extension of human knowledge in all areas. Any intellectual discipline is thus put under immense pressure to appear 'scientific' in precisely the manner in which physics is; otherwise it may be deemed not to produce any contributions to genuine knowledge.

The question whether the social sciences are 'proper' sciences is not a terminological quibble. Given that modern governments provide money for scientific research, there is a political question whether social scientists should be treated on a par with physicists and engineers. Some social scientists are very eager to show scientific credentials, while governments intent on controlling public expenditure will query how far social science is 'real' science. In 1983 the Social Science Research Council in the United Kingdom decided to change its name to the Economic and Social Research Council. This was apparently after pressure from government ministers, and they were presumably not merely interested in the philosophical issues involved. The public view of the social 'sciences' will determine decisions about public spending.

Nevertheless the pressure to make all disciplines conform to the one model begins to lessen as cynicism increases about the ability of science to further human welfare. The bright hopes for human progress which were once pinned on science already seem childishly optimistic. It is now easier to re-examine the presuppositions of a scientific world-view. All science may not be like physics, and physics itself may not provide a very good example of an empirical science, at least as understood by empiricism. Empiricism in fact has been put on trial and in many philosophers' opinion has to be discarded.

There has already been considerable disagreement over whether the social sciences should follow the methods of the natural sciences and share their assumptions. Are they to uncover the laws governing human behaviour and explain its causes? This is to assume that the social world is indistinguishable from the natural world in important respects and may even be reducible to it. Many philosophers, particularly if they have been influenced by the European hermeneutical tradition, point out that the social world is constituted by the meanings and purposes of rational agents. The function of a social science is then to interpret and render intelligible rather than to invoke causes. People are different from physical objects and must be understood differently. This approach has been dubbed 'humanist', as opposed to the 'naturalist' approach of those taking natural science as a model. It has been alleged that each side focuses on part of the truth. For instance two writers about the social sciences say:

> These sciences are *social*, which is to say that the phenomena they study are intentional phenomena, and so must be identified in terms of their meanings. Secondly, these sciences are *sciences*, in the sense that they try to develop systematic theories to explain the underlying causal interactions among phenomena of a widely divergent sort. Because they each fasten on only one of these features, humanism and naturalism fail to provide an adequate account of social science.[1]

Naturalism, in various guises, has had the most influence on the social sciences. Its assumptions may be increasingly questioned, but any survey of the social sciences must start with them. The scientific character of the social sciences is emphasized, and anything that cannot be subsumed under scientific laws is excluded. This can be part of an empiricist outlook, according to which human experience provides the standard by which anything can be tested. What is beyond experience is discarded. Perhaps the most notable group of philosophers expressing this position in this century was the Vienna Circle. Meeting in Vienna in the 1920s and the 1930s, they championed what they termed the 'scientific world-conception'. They claimed this was empiricist and positivist and explained these terms in a pamphlet by claiming: 'There is knowledge only from experience, which rests on what is immediately given. This sets the limits for the content of legitimate science.' They were empiricists because they rested knowledge on human experience, and positivists because they considered that scientific method was the only path to truth. They continued:

> The aim of scientific effort is to reach the goal, unified science, by applying logical analysis to the empirical material. Since the meaning of every statement of science must be statable by reduction to a statement about the given, likewise the meaning of any concept, whatever branch of science it may belong to, must be statable by step-wise reduction to other concepts, down to the concepts of the lowest level which refer directly to the given.[2]

The Vienna Circle explicitly dealt with the social sciences as branches of science and mentioned history and economics as examples.[3] They had a view of the unity of science, according to which all sciences fitted harmoniously together, and in which the social sciences were included. Science rested on the firm foundation of what was given in experience.

'Sense-data' is a term often used in this connection. Such data were supposed to be intersubjective, in that different people could grasp the same ones. This meant that science could apparently appeal to a fixed standard, and could repeat experiments to obtain the data according to which theories could be assessed. The data were independent of particular theories, since they were 'raw', in the sense that they contained no element of interpretation. Any theory had to fit them to be empirically adequate, and the meaning of observation terms was the same, whatever theory was adopted.

The details of this approach have been modified, but the shadow of the Vienna Circle still falls over the philosophy of science, even when philosophers are reacting against their views. The emphasis is often still on the empirical content of a theory. An empiricist will make no distinction between the empirical information it gives and its ability to explain. The description and prediction of observable facts becomes the aim of science. *Why* observed regularities should be as they are is not thought to be the most fundamental question. The reality of theoretical entities, unobservable but posited by the demands of theory, becomes a problem for the empiricist. A consistent empiricism must maintain that they are not really there but are a convenient fiction which helps in the prediction of what is observable. This problem becomes particularly acute when electrons and other sub-atomic particles are being dealt with. What is quantum mechanics about, if there can in principle be no unobservable entities? An empiricist can only conclude that it is attempting to describe and predict observations and measurements made on sub-atomic systems, rather than refer to any intrinsic properties of the systems. There can be no intrinsic properties beyond the scope of measurement, since what cannot be observed cannot be there. As a result the emphasis must move from the nature of reality to questions about scientists and their operations.[4] Sub-atomic particles can be talked of only in the terms of classical mechanics, and that means that the entity measured cannot in principle be separated from the act of measurement. The observation made provides the foundation for the theory, even though that involves a necessary reference to a human observer. What started by being a description of the basic constituents of matter apparently ends by being about an episode of human observation.

Its emphasis on experience lays empiricism open to the charge of being anthropocentric. It switches attention from what is or can be experienced to the mere fact of experience itself. By definition, what lies beyond human experience can be conveniently dismissed. The consistent empiricist cannot talk of the other side of the universe, the interior of a black hole, the position *and* the momentum of an electron, or a myriad other possible states of affairs which science may need to envisage. It is hardly surprising that realists who insist that what exists does so independently of human conceptions see idealist echoes in empiricism. Idealists make existence depend logically on its being perceived by a mind, usually a human one. Although empiricists may say that *what* is experienced does not depend on being experienced for its reality, they still limit reality to what can be experienced. Unobservable entities are thus contradictions in terms. This radically changes the character of scientific explanation. Theoretical entities cannot explain what we perceive. Perceptions themselves become the bedrock on which theory rests. Actual and possible observations become ends in themselves. Science may predict them but is left with no resources with which to explain them. Nothing else of a more fundamental nature can be invoked.

Many may object to a picture of the world in which reality is made to depend logically on the possibility of human observation. Another major criticism of empiricism has concentrated on the fact of observation. 'Raw' sense-data have been seen as the brute facts on which our knowledge of the world rested. For this reason empiricist epistemology is often termed a 'foundationalist' one. Such an epistemology is only as reliable as its foundations. Although much effort was expended by empiricists in showing how sense-data were experiences stripped of all interpretation, such as simple colour patches, there has been increasing scepticism about this. The view implied that the mind was a passive receptacle for experience, rather than an active searcher. Yet expectation can govern what we see. So far from experience governing how we interpret it, our interpretation can affect what we experience. If we are waiting for a red bus, the fluttering of reddish leaves can be mistaken for the approach of the bus. When we recognize the leaves for what they are, we may even find that we see the colour differently. The leaves may look more orange than before.

One of the most influential philosophers of this century, Ludwig Wittgenstein, was much exercised by questions about this kind of change of aspect.[5] One of the most famous examples is the 'duck-rabbit', the drawing that can be seen as a duck or a rabbit. One can see the beak of a duck, but one can also interpret the same lines as the ears of a rabbit. Wittgenstein could not finally decide whether the visual impression altered along with our interpretation.[6] Yet the very fact the question could intelligibly be raised spelt the end of the sense-data theory. Passive experience, according to that, would always be the grounding for the mind's interpretation, so that the latter could not alter the former. Any theory about the empirical foundations of knowledge was in jeopardy once it was accepted that what we thought we were seeing could influence what we saw. 'Sense-data' were supposed to be given to us and not created or altered by us. Our knowledge of them was supposed to be infallible, with any errors coming in our interpretation. Once it was accepted that our interpretation could govern the nature of the data, however, any error in interpretation was seen to be liable to infect the data. The 'rock-solid' foundations of empirical knowledge are revealed as being in as much a quagmire as other parts of human reasoning.

One major tenet of empiricist thought was the total separation of fact from value. Sense-data are what they are, and facts are just what we know is the case as a result of them. Human evaluation is a totally distinct matter. The empiricist philosopher, David Hume, had, in the eighteenth century, sternly forbade sliding from assertions about what *is* the case to some about what *ought* to be so.[7] Descriptions and evaluations are still distinguished, as for instance in the moral philosophy of the Oxford philosopher, R. M. Hare. The result is that a privileged status is accorded to facts, which are thought, in a typically empiricist manner, to be true or false in a way that evaluations cannot be. It has become something of a challenge to empiricists to rescue evaluations from the charge of arbitrariness, and to demonstrate how there can still be rational constraints on what we may value. Having suggested that values cannot be empirically verified in the way that facts can be, they are faced with the possibility that humans can logically value anything, without the possibility of error.

The importance of the idea of a 'value-free' science for the social sciences is clear. Social scientists want to be seen to establish 'facts' about society in the same way that they think that a physicist or a chemist uncovers 'facts'. They do not want to appear to be in the grip of an ideology or particular view of the world, which would make their results suspect to those who do not share it. The idea, for example, of a 'conservative' or 'liberal' social science seems to undermine the notion of a social science. Yet it is perhaps significant that Marxists find nothing surprising about the notion of Marxist social science. Most Marxists do not share the philosophical presuppositions of empiricists about the distinction between facts and values. This is a problem of major importance to which I shall return. For the moment, it is merely relevant to stress that any distinction between 'facts' and 'values' rests on empiricist assumptions, giving a privileged status to the idea of a scientifically verifiable fact.

THE ROLE OF THEORIES

Empiricism laid great emphasis on the possibility of testing through experience, and this constituted its conception of objectivity. Carl Hempel, the American philosopher of science, says of science that 'it is concerned to develop a conception of the world that has a clear logical bearing on our experience and is thus capable of objective test'.[8] We have already seen that this approach depends on a notion of 'neutral' experience, which does not already presuppose the holding of a particular theory. Hempel developed a notion of scientific explanation which involves fitting an isolated phenomenon into an overall pattern. Scientific laws are then to be understood as mere observable regularities under which we can subsume whatever we wish to explain. This view is derived from Hume's analysis of causation as constant conjunction. Perceived regularities thus form the basis of our idea of cause, and explanation involves fitting our experiences into a pattern of such regularities. Hempel says: 'The explanation fits the phenomenon to be explained into a pattern of uniformities and shows that its occurrence was to be expected, given the specified laws and the pertinent particular circumstances.'[9]

Hempel proposes as a model what he terms 'deductive-nomological' explanation. This takes the form of a deductive argument, whose premisses include general laws as well as statements about particular observations. One example of a deductively valid inference which he gives is the following:

> Any sodium salt, when put into the flame of a Bunsen burner, turns the flame yellow.
> This piece of rock salt is a sodium salt.
> Therefore, this piece of rock salt, when put into the flame of a Bunsen burner, will turn the flame yellow.[10]

One acknowledged difficulty of this form of explanation is that not all generalizations can have the status of general causal laws. It may well be true that the barometer falls when it gets windier, but it would not be right to say that the wind makes the barometer fall. The wind and the fall of the barometer each have the same underlying cause. In other cases there is no genuine connection at all. The sounding of a factory hooter in one city has no effect on workers in a factory a hundred miles away, even if the latter always stop work when the former sounds. The importation of counterfactuals (concerning what would happen if certain facts were different) can help to distinguish between accidental generalizations and causal laws. The issue is then whether the same apparent connection continues if one of the factories changes its hours of work.

Sometimes it is far from clear whether something is a coincidence or whether there is a causal connection. It used to be a joke in one English city afflicted with particularly bad traffic congestion that there was always a policeman on point duty in the middle of the worst traffic jams. It was a joke because everyone assumed that the situation would be worse if the police were not there. Yet, when they were withdrawn as an experiment, the traffic flowed more freely and there was less congestion. There proved to be a causal link in what appeared to be a mere empirical regularity.

Fitting particular instances into a network of regularities which are established empirically conforms to some ideal of explanation. Yet problems remain. The difficulty of sifting out 'real' empirical regularities from the coincidences arises only because empiricists wish to stop at the level of observation. Their ideal of explanation is the association of different experiences on different occasions. Yet *why* should these be associated? Even the appeal to counterfactuals so as to discover genuine causal connections merely pushes the question back a stage. What makes a connection a genuine causal one? Many philosophers still follow the eighteenth-century philosopher, Hume, in wishing to deny the existence of hidden powers and necessary connections. It is impossible to *experience* the way two events are causally related. One can merely observe that one typically follows the other. Anything more requires a theory which may need to posit unobservable entities as the source of the relevant causal power. That seems irredeemably metaphysical, and therefore bad to genuine empiricists. They would not see the point of postulating mysterious causes behind observable effects but would be content to be successful in predicting observations. Yet this is done at a cost. Explanation becomes merely a summary of actual and possible observations, and the reason why events are linked as they are can never be given.

Another source of worry for empiricism is shown in the example given by Hempel of a deductive inference. How can one observe that 'this piece of rock salt is a sodium salt'? We are already a long way from the level of simple sense-data. If the simplest colour patches cannot be disentangled from interpretation, the making of complicated observations in a scientific laboratory is certainly going to be 'theory-laden'. The recognition of a substance as 'rock salt', let alone its classification as a 'sodium salt', is in no sense a 'raw' experience, uncomplicated by interpretation. A trained chemist may well see at a glance what the substance is, but it is naïve to imagine that a schoolboy could immediately see a substance as 'rock salt' without being told. Reference to a 'sodium salt' goes further and presupposes a scientific theory.

Classification is the outcome of theory, even at fairly simple levels. It is not a question of neutral observations forming the basis for theory. The observations we make, the way we classify them, and even what counts as a relevant observation, may be governed by the theory we hold. Once this was understood, the emphasis inevitably swung away from sense-data to the role of theory or, more generally, of our conceptual scheme in making sense of the world around us. Of course, much depends on what is meant by 'theory', and it may be that, within our overall scheme, different theories will still compete with each other. Nevertheless, a theory seen as a whole claims priority, instead of each level in it being ultimately reducible to statements about what the Vienna Circle saw as the given. This means that at every level, whether at that of the observation of colour or of the study of complex social phenomena, the 'facts' become secondary. They cannot be read off without a theory to guide classification and selection.

One writer on Marxism says, in a manner reminiscent of those attacking sense-data:

> There are no 'brute' facts, descriptions which describe facts but independently of any interest in terms of which they are relevant. . . . The objects of knowledge are objects only in relation to some knowledge-generating inquiry. For 'objects', being 'facts *for*' some inquiry, are classes of events or states of affairs *under some description*, the descriptions in question being determined by the controlling interest of the inquiry.[11]

He mentions for illustration that there are many possible descriptions of the kind of society which Marx classified as capitalist:

> Any society which is capitalist is also, necessarily, an 'industrial' society, and any modern industrial society which is capitalist is modelled, at any rate fundamentally, on market relations, and so can be called a 'market' society. Most market societies are politically 'liberal-democratic'.[12]

It appears that, instead of facts being discovered in the world, our descriptions are governed as much by our interests and purposes as by what is there. Human knowledge is then not just the passive reflection of reality but is itself partly constituted by human interests. This move in the social sciences was inevitable once the physical sciences were partially detached from empirical phenomena. Contemporary philosophers of science have themselves emphasized the crucial role of theories more and more, dismissing the notion that experience can be neutral. It seems that everything is 'theory-laden'. Even the contemporary American philosopher, W. V. Quine, who attended meetings of the Vienna Circle, and still stresses the importance of sensory stimuli as a starting-point for theory, shows how our most ordinary experiences already include an element of interpretation. To take one of his most famous examples, a linguist in a foreign country confronted by a native saying 'Gavagai' when a rabbit scurried by would have difficulties translating this unknown word.[13] Quine would assume that the native and the linguist had the same 'ocular irradiations', but these are physical states, far removed from sense-data, which were supposed to be mental ones. On this sensory base, Quine thinks, we have to build our theories, but there can be no guarantee that the native and the linguist possess exactly the same theory. When we see a rabbit, the native may see 'rabbit stages' or 'rabbit parts'. Quine insists that there will always be a certain indeterminacy of translation, even given the same sensory input. Interpretations of the most basic experience may differ, and indeed the very notion of a basic experience is exposed as an empiricist prejudice. What we say about the world always goes beyond available data, so that all theories are underdetermined. Quine writes:

> The truths that can be said even in common-sense terms about ordinary things are themselves, in turn, far in excess of any available data. The incompleteness of determination of molecular behavior of ordinary things is hence only incidental to this more basic indeterminacy: *both* sorts of events are less than determined by our surface irritations.[14]

The ghost of empiricism lives on in Quine, with his insistence on 'surface irritations'. They still provide the starting-point for all theory. Yet the very fact that even our ordinary experience of the world is itself the result of theory places, he says, ordinary physical objects on a par with the most theoretical of entities. Tables and chairs have no privileged status over electrons and protons. They are all posits of a theory. Quine says: 'Everything to which we concede existence is a posit from the standpoint of a description of the theory-building process.'[15] Yet, if theories are underdetermined by data, alternative theories can in their own terms be equally valid. One example he has given is seeing a procession of three lumps moving along at the surface of the water. We may posit a school of dolphins or a single Loch Ness monster. We choose our theory in such cases, he thinks, by preferring the simpler or more familiar explanation.

Further observations may sometimes settle the matter, but, even if all possible observations have been made, Quine holds that alternative theories are always possible. Empirically equivalent theories may still be significantly different. In this and in his wholehearted acceptance of theoretical entities, he shows himself as no empiricist.

Quine's acceptance of theoretical entities as posits does not raise them to the level of familiar objects. Rather, he appears to question the objective reality of the latter. He would insist that 'to call a posit a posit is not to patronize it'.[16] He says that 'we can never do better than occupy the standpoint of some theory or other, the best we can muster at the time'. It is perhaps fruitless to complain that theoretical entites are 'only' theoretical if all entities are. Insisting, though, on the complete priority of theory like this is bound to raise some misgivings. According to Quine, we can only talk about what our theory counts as real. He would deny that there is any sense in which we can further refer to reality. We can only conceive of what we can conceive.[17] The notion of objective reality thus becomes what our current theory says is real. Quine's view demands that 'world', 'reality' and all such concepts are theoretical, and that theories cannot be simply understood as attempts to describe an independently existing world. The world becomes the reflection of theory, rather than theories mirroring the world, more or less well. This is why translation becomes such a problem for him, since he cannot assume that different theories are *about* the same world. He has to attempt to correlate the words of one theory with those of another without assuming that each refers to the same entities. He cannot assume that the native sees a rabbit and he certainly cannot dogmatically assert that there just are rabbits and the native is wrong if he does not recognize the fact. That is only so from the standpoint of *our* current theory. For Quine the fundamental relationship has to be between word and word, and not between word and object. There are no such things as objects viewed outside the mediation of any particular theory. There is no possibility, therefore of a unique description of the world. Alternatives are always possible, because theories are underdetermined by data.

If theories are not merely means of predicting phenomena, nor are deducible from them, the importance of the empirical content of a theory has somehow been downgraded. It is not just that we are now free to posit unobservable entities to explain experience. The loosening of experience as a constraint on our choice of theory raises the question of what other influences there might be. The foundationalist epistemology of empiricism provided a curb on what could be rationally adopted. If the possibility of such an epistemology is an illusion, the status of rationality itself must be queried. There may seem something highly suspicious about asking for reasons for being rational, but we have to ask where our theories come from and on what they are based. Just how desperate the situation could be is illustrated by the way in which Richard Rorty can talk of 'the cultural space left by the demise of epistemology'.[18]

The same problem arises at a multiplicity of levels. Epistemology as a discipline flounders once the tight constraints of empiricism are loosened. It seems that we do not know where to look for justification, whether it is of our most general theory about the external world, for the practice of science, for the holding of particular theories within science, or for social theory. The same applies to the myriad other forms of belief which we may fondly imagine constitute knowledge.

The practice of physical science has come under particular scrutiny, because empiricism laid such store by observation, and modern science has appeared to be built on the results of observation and experiment. It was part of the received doctrine about science that the history of science was logically distinct from the philosophy of science. The rational justification of a theory may not coincide with the way the theory was actually arrived at. Philosophy laid bare the philosophical foundations of science, while history showed what actually happened. Such an outlook presupposed that science *had* epistemological foundations. Once, however, scientific theory is cut loose from its empirical base, it becomes unclear whether the philosopher can any longer stand aloof from history. Maybe there is no way of distinguishing between what ought to have happened in the development of science from what actually did happen. Insistent questions, however, remain to be answered. What is the purpose of science if it is no longer understood as the search for greater accuracy in empirical observation and prediction? Why should scientists ever change their theories? What, in fact, constitutes scientific progress?

THE VIEWS OF KUHN AND FEYERABEND

One of the major influences in the cataclysmic changes that have affected modern philosophy of science has been the work of T. S. Kuhn. Significantly, he is a historian of science. He introduced the notion of a scientific 'paradigm' which governs a scientist's view of the world. A major change in scientific thinking involves a change in paradigm and the switch from classical to quantum mechanics would provide one example. Kuhn's thesis is that, when scientists work under a paradigm, they take part in what he calls 'normal science', trying to solve the problems thrown up by the theory they hold. Every so often, however, a scientific revolution occurs when the existing paradigm proves unable to cope with what appear to be anomalous situations. Kuhn's views are particularly interesting as regards what happens when a scientific community shifts from one paradigm to another:

> The historian of science may be tempted to exclaim that when paradigms change, the world itself changes with them. Led by a new paradigm, scientists adopt new instruments and look in new places. Even more important, during revolutions scientists see new and different things when looking with familiar instruments in places they have looked before.[19]

The inversion of the empiricist scheme of things is clear. The theory determines the observations, according to Kuhn, instead of observations determining the theory. Indeed, he seems to be going further than saying that a new theory shows us how to notice what we did not notice before. He appears to be asserting that the world is actually different for different theories. What counts as real under one paradigm does not under another. Scientists once believed there was a substance called phlogiston and now do not. They once believed the atom could not be split, whereas now they continue to search for new sub-atomic particles. There is a continuing ambiguity, though, in illustrations like this. Everyone accepts that scientific theories change our conceptions of reality, but the question is whether there is a sense in which they actually change reality. Perhaps the way the issue is posed begs the question, since it presupposes that we can sensibly talk of a reality which is independent of our conceptions of it. Yet this is what Quine denied, and Kuhn seems merely to be taking this a step further by saying that the world might itself change. The world as conceived by scientists does change, but does that mean the world itself changes? The distinction between these two positions is of major philosophical importance. Arguments rage over whether such a distinction can be made. Kuhn poses the question of what scientific theories are about. Can they be measured against anything external to themselves, and therefore at least in principle be judged correct or mistaken, true or false? The alternative is that we are left with a succession of different theories, or conceptions of the world, with no means of determining which is better than the others.

Kuhn uses the 'duck-rabbit' drawing as an analogy to illustrate the way in which a scientist's vision can change after a switch of paradigms. He draws attention to the way in which theories can govern what we see.

A student, he says, may only see confused and broken lines when looking at a bubble-chamber photograph, whereas a trained physicist will actually *see* a record of sub-nuclear events. He says:

> It is as elementary prototypes for these transformations of the scientist's world that the familar demonstrations of a switch in visual gestalt prove so suggestive. What were ducks in the scientific world before the revolution are rabbits afterwards.[20]

One consequence of these radical shifts in a scientist's vision is that scientists working under different paradigms possess different concepts and make different observations. They cannot appeal to any theory-neutral observation, and Kuhn removes the possibility of referring to the same objective world underpinning all paradigms. Since 'the world' is seen only through a paradigm, there is a problem as to how those with allegiance to different paradigms can discuss their theories with each other. Empiricists could argue with those they disagreed with, by appealing to the experience they all shared. Kuhn cannot do that and considers the introduction of a neutral language of observation 'hopeless'.[21] He has to talk instead of the 'incommensurability' of different scientific theories. At a time of revolution a scientist will find the world of his research here and there 'incommensurable with the one he had inhabited before'.[22] This has an important and worrying consequence. Since scientists will each see a world constituted by their own paradigm, those with allegiance to different paradigms will be talking at cross-purposes to each other. They will actually be referring to different entities and their theories will not rest on a common base, nor apparently even be about the same world. Kuhn does not even use the physical impact of the world on our senses as a starting-point, as Quine does. There is instead a competition between different visions of the world, some of which may overlap, but which cannot formulate their disagreements in any common language.

Why, then, should scientists change their paradigms? The history of science shows that this has often happened and Kuhn attempts to describe that process. At what point do the strains of an existing theory become unbearable? Kuhn has left himself with few resources to answer that. It cannot be because of an appeal to experience, since that is governed by a paradigm. It cannot be because we discover basic errors, since the paradigm controls what is to count as correct. Discovering basic 'errors' is, in fact, tantamount to changing the way we choose to see the world. Kuhn points out that individual scientists embrace a new paradigm 'for all sorts of reasons and usually for several at once'. He continues:

Some of these reasons – for example the sun worship that helped make Kepler a Copernican – lie outside the apparent sphere of science entirely. Others must depend upon idiosyncrasies of autobiography and personality. Even the nationality or the prior reputation of the innovator and his teachers can sometimes play a significant role.[23]

This is not a very encouraging summary of the rational processes of scientists, and Kuhn goes on to stress that his interest is mainly in the sort of community that re-emerges after a time of scientific crisis. He mentions that those who resist the new paradigm cannot be said to be wrong, and indeed he could have no criterion by which they could be judged wrong. He says of the historian: 'At most he may wish to say that the man who continues to resist after his whole profession has been converted has *ipso facto* ceased to be a scientist.'[24]

The philosophy of science can thus no longer provide a rational reconstruction of the way theories logically depend on each other and can justify each other. There is nothing left but the question how science has actually developed. The philosophy of science has to become the history of science, since there is no way left in which what has happened can be rationally criticized. Science is what particular communities happen to do, rather than being an impressive rational creation of the human mind. It is hardly surprising that Kuhn's views have paved the way to a growing interest in the sociology of science. The account he gives of paradigm shifts cries out for a sociological explanation for them. Sociologists must feel confident that they can contribute to our understanding of a sudden change in the behaviour of a community, particularly if there is no possibility of its having occurred on rational grounds. By talking of the interaction of scientists with each other, Kuhn focuses on the idea of a community, and he explores the idea of standards enforced by the community. The very fact that a particular social group can accept one solution to a problem but not another, or can see one argument as a justification but not another, cries out for sociological analysis. So at least a sociologist of science would argue. The conventional character of scientific judgement has seemingly been exposed, and it is the sociologist's concern to show us how the conventions operate and change. One such sociologist writes:

Scientific standards themselves are a part of a specific form of culture; authority and control are essential to maintain a sense of the reasonableness of the specific form. Thus, if Kuhn is correct, science should be amenable to sociological study in fundamentally the same way any other form of knowledge or culture.[25]

Kuhn's attack on the rational foundations of science (for that is in effect what it is) has not been a solitary one. Its anti-empiricism has been in tune with the mood of the times and has found a ready following. There is no doubt, though, that at times the reaction from the idea that knowledge has firm foundations in experience has been very extreme. It is one thing to say that theories can govern how we see and experience the world, but quite another to make it impossible any longer to refer to the world. It is one thing to question whether experience is the only source of human knowledge, but quite another to say that knowledge is conventional. The latter is to say that societies or traditions determine what we count as knowledge. Our grasp on reality becomes exceedingly tenuous, if that is so. What we believe or claim to know is merely the product of social forces of which we may be utterly ignorant.

The philosopher of science, P. Feyerabend makes it explicit that reality in some sense actually depends on our choice. He says flatly: 'We decide to regard those things as real which play an important role in the kind of life we prefer.'[26] He considers that there is no more ultimate way of referring to reality than through the particular tradition we belong to. Instead of reality controlling our beliefs, at least to some extent, it seems as if the beliefs of a tradition determine what is to count as real. There are countless traditions, each of which has firm teaching on what is real. Within any one of them, we can gain the illusion that knowledge can be and has been attained. Yet, once we see that many conflicting traditions have the same conceit, we realize, it is alleged, that judgements of truth only have relative validity. They hold for our colleagues in the tradition to which we are attached, but not for those outside.

Feyerabend's unsettling view is that this kind of argument can be applied in any sphere. The practice of science, and even the exercise of reason, can be revealed as themselves historical traditions. He says:

> Scientific practice, even the practice of the natural sciences, is a tightly woven net of historical traditions. . . . This means that general statements *about* science, statements of logic included, cannot without further ado be taken to agree with scientific practice.[27]

The notion of a philosophy of science with an ideal of rational justification is again under attack. What is left is merely what scientists happened to have done, or are doing, and that forms suitable material for sociological study. Scientific standards are 'not imposed upon science from the outside'.[28] Instead Feyerabend insists that they are produced by scientists in the course of their research. He particularly stresses the importance of being able to choose between competing alternatives, and advocates the principle (or anti-principle) of 'anything goes' as a basis for scientific method. Because he sees Western science as one tradition among many, he wants freedom of choice between that and its alternatives. He also talks of the exercise of reason itself (or 'rationalism', as he puts it) as a tradition:

> Each tradition, each form of life, has its own standards of judging human behaviour and these standards change in accordance with the problems that the tradition is constrained to solve. Rationalism is not a boundary condition for traditions: it is itself a tradition, and not always a successful one. There exists, therefore, a plurality of standards just as there is a plurality of individuals. In a free society, however, a citizen will use the standards to which (s)he belongs: Hopi standards, if he is a Hopi: fundamentalist Protestant standards, if he is a fundamentalist.[29]

This is a classic statement of relativism. There are different, self-contained traditions and ways of life. Each generates its own standards. None can be understood, let alone judged, by means of criteria rooted in a different tradition. Many have found this an attractive doctrine when applied to human customs or even morality. It is perhaps a philosophical version of the saying, 'When in Rome, do as the Romans do'. Different societies have different ways of doing things, and sometimes at least there is mere difference, without one set of practices being better or worse than another. An obvious example is which side of the road we drive on. No one can say that driving on the left is better than driving on the right, or vice versa. We naturally tend to prefer what we are used to, but as long as everyone in one country conforms to the same convention that is enough. There is a story of a newly independent nation which decided to change from driving on the left to driving on the right, but to do so gradually. That is clearly the speedy route to chaos. So it is with many social conventions. Conformity to particular ones in a given society is necessary for the functioning of that society, but a different society can conform to totally different ones.

Questions about this kind of relativity in the case of moral standards become much more controversial. Feyerabend, however, goes even further.

So far from accepting scientific method as the very model of rationality, or indeed considering rationality itself as a universal ideal, he belittles each as being one tradition among many. He says of scientists that they are 'salesmen of ideas and gadgets, they are not judges of truth and falsehood'.[30] This is not the raving of a crank but is the inevitable outcome of the attacks on empiricism which removed the foundations of our empirical knowledge without putting anything in its place. As a result, questions of knowledge, truth, reality and reason are all discarded. We step back from knowledge to belief, from what is true to what is held true, from reality to people's beliefs about it, and from questions of rational standards to all the peculiar ways in which humans do actually purport to reason. We step from justification to description, and from philosophy, or, at least, epistemology, to sociology. The emphasis laid on the incommensurability of theories by Feyerabend, as well as Kuhn, develops into a position where theories or traditions set their own standards of rationality and are immune to criticism from outside.

Feyerabend eagerly seizes on Wittgenstein's view that the meaning of concepts is given by their use in a practice.[31] Concepts are not labels for things but are grounded in ways of acting. I shall return to this later, but Feyerabend draws out one very important consequence. If we understand what a word means by using it in connection with a particular activity, the only way to learn it is by participating in that activity. Instead of words referring to an objective world or an experience which can be shared intersubjectively, they are rooted in what Wittgenstein refers to as a 'language-game' or a 'form of life'. The purpose of both expressions is to drawn attention to the fact that language is intimately connected with activities. It cannot, it is suggested, be peeled off and understood apart from the life of which it is a part. Yet this means that non-participants cannot understand what is being said in any practice. This doctrine, if true, has tremendous consequences for the social sciences, and the problem of *Verstehen* (understanding) is indeed one of the most venerable topics for the philosophy of social science. Clearly, though, on Feyerabend's view, all the sciences face the same difficulty. So far from the social sciences finding it difficult to live up to the exacting standards of the natural sciences, the latter seem to be dissolving into social groupings posing problems of understanding and interpretation for the social scientist.

This might seem an argument against Feyerabend's position, but unfortunately it is a consequence that he embraces. He has rejected the idea that philosophy can uncover basic rational principles according to which science proceeds. He rejects the idea of an objective, extratheoretical reality, so that as a result everything is valid only within the confines of a particular theory. The practices of a science are valid only for the practitioners of the science. Feyerabend explicitly mentions the position of traditional methodologists of science who have held 'that a historian studies a distant culture by trying to "understand" it while a physicist who deals with explicit abstract notions "explains"'.[32]

He will have none of this dichotomy between the interpretation of a social scientist and the explanation of a natural scientist. In fact, he has left the latter without any materials with which to explain in a manner that can be either intelligible or relevant to a non-physicist. Explanation can only satisfy those who are physicists. By insisting that physics is itself a social practice or tradition, Feyerabend has removed its claims to have any ultimate answers, or to be in a privileged position compared with other disciplines. He explicitly follows in Kuhn's footsteps and says with approval: 'Kuhn makes the highly interesting and revolutionary suggestion that *physics is a historical tradition and therefore as much in need of* Verstehen *as history proper.*'[33] The theories of a contemporary physicist, therefore, may stand in as much need of interpretation and understanding as those of an ancient Greek. Physics is no longer seen as the base to which other sciences can be reduced, but as one tradition out of many; it can be investigated only by means of the methods of the social sciences.

We have arrived at a bewildering conclusion. According to a dominant trend in contemporary philosophy of science, science is not a path to truth at all, let alone the only one. It sometimes looks as if some philosophers are saying that there is no such thing as truth. The incoherence of that is revealed if we realize that they are asserting *as true* the proposition that there is no such thing as truth. Feyerabend himself realizes that he may appear to be giving reasons for his view that reason 'is a tradition in its own right with as much (or as little) claim to the centre of the stage as any other tradition.'[34] There are times when it looks as if he views the opportunity of choice between different traditions and theories as a good stratagem in the pursuit of truth. Refusal to be bound by a rigid methodology may itself be the last of all methodologies. At other times, it seems as if his advocacy of relativism is leading us perilously close to denying that any view is better than any other, or any reason more valid than any other. The problem that remains is whether it is possible to dethrone the natural sciences without undermining the possibility of human reason. Can the social sciences step in with new modes of explanation?

NOTES

1 B. Fay and J. D. Moon, 'What Would an Adequate Philosophy of Social Science Look Like?', *Philosophy of the Social Sciences*, 7, 1977, p. 227.
2 'The Scientific Conception of the World: the Vienna Circle', in M. Neurath and R. S. Cohen (eds), *Otto Neurath: Empiricism and Sociology*, 1973, p. 309.
3 Ibid., p. 315.
4 For a further discussion of quantum mechanics and reality, see my *Reality at Risk*, 1980, ch. 6.
5 Ludwig Wittgenstein, *Philosophical Investigations*, 1958, II, xi.
6 See my *Pain and Emotion*, 1970, pp. 81 ff.
7 David Hume, *A Treatise of Human Nature*, Book III, reprinted in *Hume's Ethical Writings*, ed. A Macintyre, 1965, p. 196.
8 Carl Hempel, *Philosophy of Natural Science*, 1968, p. 47.
9 Ibid., p. 50.
10 Ibid., p. 10.
11 D. Turner, *Marxism and Christianity*, 1983, p. 104.
12 Ibid., p. 104.
13 W. V. Quine, *Word and Object*, 1964, p. 29.
14 Ibid., p. 22.
15 Ibid.
16 Ibid.
17 For a longer discussion of Quine, see my *Reality at Risk*.
18 Richard Rorty, *Philosophy and the Mirror of Nature*, 1980, p. 315.
19 T. S. Kuhn, *The Structure of Scientific Revolutions*, 1962, p. 110.
20 Ibid., p. 110.
21 Ibid., p. 125.
22 Ibid., p. 111.
23 Ibid., p. 151.
24 Ibid., p. 150.
25 Barry Barnes, *T. S. Kuhn and Social Science*, 1982, p. 10.
26 P. Feyerabend, *Philosophical Papers*, Vol. I, *Realism, Rationalism and Scientific Method*, 1981, p. xiii.
27 Ibid., p. 4.
28 Feyerabend, *Philosophical Papers*, Vol. II, *Problems of Empiricism*, p. 27.
29 Ibid.
30 Feyerabend, Philosophical Papers, Vol. II, p. 31.
31 Ibid., p. 129.
32 Ibid., p. 237.
33 Ibid.
34 Feyerabend, *Science in a Free Society*, 1978, p. 8.

2

Objectivity and the Sociology of Knowledge

Traditional philosophy of science has always made a firm distinction between what it termed 'internal' and 'external' reasons for holding theories. The success of a relevant experiment would be an internal reason, while the rejection, say, of evolutionary theory because of a funda- mentalist belief that the book of Genesis was true would count as an external one. In other words, some reasons would be properly grounded in scientific method, in the building of theories on repeated observations, while others would cut across it. The presumption has been that scientific method set the standard for the pursuit of knowledge, and indeed positivism has insisted that it is the only standard.

Once the possibility of scientific method is challenged, and it is sug- gested that we can only study what scientists actually do, any distinction between internal and external reasons is removed. We can no longer assume that the Protestant fundamentalist is wrong in rejecting one of the theories of modern science. As Feyerabend pointed out, the fun- damentalist just belongs to a different tradition from the scientist, with different standards.

There are some very odd consequences of putting different outlooks into self-contained compartments like this. Things are more complicated in real life; the distinctions between the compartments are blurred. One can be both a scientist and a fundamentalist, and it would be curious to have one set of beliefs on Sunday and another in the laboratory in the week. One will inevitably have to face the question which set of standards are right. Relativists would have us believe that such a question cannot arise. They claim that the whole edifice of Western science is a mere sociological fact, which cannot be judged better or worse than astrology, witchcraft, or any other set of practices. It is significant how the adjective

'Western' can easily be attached to the word 'science'. That already locates it in a particular time and place and suggests that it is merely a particular kind of social practice.

Science has often been extolled as the basic source of knowledge, and scientific method has been held up as an example of objectivity, detached from the interests and prejudices of its practitioners. As a result scientists have perhaps gained an inflated reputation for wisdom. They appear to be good at manipulating the world, and giving us such things as non-stick frying pans and colour television. Yet now we are told their activities are to be investigated on a par with, say, the rain-dances of a primitive tribe. Are we then to conclude that scientists do not make discoveries about the world or extend our knowledge of it? The genuine relativist would always say, at this point, that notions such as those of 'the world' are already theoretic. They can only be understood in the context of someone holding beliefs. 'Reality' has no meaning apart from what is believed real by some group. The very concept of an objective world, independent of all points of view, is dissipated. It may be a convenient idea *within* science, but it cannot be used to adjudicate between science and other activities. Ontology has thus to become dependent on epistemology. What there is is seen as the product of our strategies for finding things out. If our epistemology changes, as when we move from one world-view to another, so do our beliefs about what is real.

Feyerabend sums up his advocacy of this position when he says:

> We no longer assume an objective world that remains unaffected by our epistemic activities, except when moving within the confines of a particular point of view. We concede that our epistemic activities may have a decisive influence even upon the most sordid piece of cosmological furniture – they may make gods disappear and replace them by heaps of atoms in empty space.[1]

This view may be an affront to common sense. It is also an explicit denial of the philosophical doctrine of realism which insists on the objectivity of reality in the sense that it is independent of all beliefs about it. For the realist there is, at least in principle, a standard by which all human societies and their beliefs can be judged: they can all have beliefs about the world which turn out to be mistaken.

The denial of realism makes us turn our attention to the fact of belief and away from what is believed. It invites us to replace the traditional attempts of epistemology to show *the* path to reality with the empirical descriptions of the sociologist of knowledge. Instead of trying to find out timeless, abstract principles, we look at the strategies that are actually adopted in different times and places. Philosophy and the natural sciences themselves become objects of study for the social scientist. The social sciences no longer need to appear respectable through being 'scientific', but instead seem to be putting the natural sciences in their place.

One of the major reasons for this is the increasing emphasis on the *social* character of knowledge in general, and science in particular. The very fact that science has been seen as a social institution, in which the notion of objectivity is determined by the structure of the institution, means that it is a fit object of study for the social scientist. It is in this context that the attacks on empiricism have been so important. If knowledge was obtained through the senses, it was clearly an individual matter. Each person could obtain knowledge in isolation. If, on the other hand, it is a product of a community, it is by definition attainable only through education in the ways of that community. Similarly, empiricism seemed to suggest that knowledge came in bits and pieces. Its approach was atomistic, in contrast to the view of knowledge which suggests that it is deeply embedded in the way of life of which it is a part. Thus particular strands cannot be torn away from the wider whole. Marjorie Grene expresses this type of view when she writes:

> Science is a family of practices. . . . And practices are by their nature rooted in community, and permit communication only on that ground. Each science requires from its initiates a long and arduous apprenticeship. . . . Thus it is only a philosophical approach which accepts the sociality of human nature from the very beginning that can begin to deal adequately with the cognitive claims of science, let alone its relation to other commitments of the culture to which it belongs.[2]

WITTGENSTEIN AND RULES

Wittgenstein provides an example of this kind of philosophical approach, at least in his later work. He emphasized the rule-governed nature of our practices. Human activity is not to be understood as the isolated actions of individuals, and we cannot make sense of what anyone does except in the context of a wider whole. For this reason, this kind of view has sometimes been dubbed 'contextualist', particularly in, say, social anthropology. It stems naturally from Wittgenstein's equation of meaning and use. Words mean what they do because of the context in which they are used. Meaning cannot be privately conferred, and is not, for instance, to be correlated with internal sense-impressions. Wittgenstein's arguments against the possibility of a 'private language' are well known,[3] although much of the discussion about them has occurred in the philosophy of mind. How do we learn the word 'pain'? We can all communicate with each other about pain and teach the word, but it apparently refers to a private sensation. Wittgenstein was concerned to show how the meaning of such a word can only be rooted in a public language, with public checks that it is being used correctly. He was looking for a 'criterion of correctness',[4] and argued that one cannot have a private rule for using a word. In that case there would be no distinction between my having a rule which I kept, and my having a rule which I thought I was keeping even when I was not. The rules of the private language could not be *impressions* of rules.[5]

This apparently applies merely to problems about communicating the nature of our sensations, but Wittgenstein is making a point which concerns *all* concepts and the way they are used. The discussion about private language comes after a long discussion about following rules, in which he stresses how all rules have to be rooted in public practices. He asks at one point: 'Is what we call "obeying a rule" something that it would be possible for only *one* man to do, and to do only *once* in his life?'[6] His answer is that it would not be, since all practices, whether linguistic or not, are rooted in ways of life and cannot be understood in isolation. They gain their meaning from their context and are passed on by means of shared, public criteria. He says: 'To obey a rule, to make a report, to give an order, to play a game of chess, are *customs.*'[7] He makes a logical link between the use of a word, the custom of a people and the institution of a society. Words cannot be understood apart from the practices in which they are embedded, and these practices are social institutions.

In a paragraph which clearly anticipates the 'private language' argument, he says:

> And hence also 'obeying a rule' is a practice. And to *think* one is obeying a rule is not to obey a rule. Hence it is not possible to obey a rule 'privately': otherwise thinking one was obeying a rule would be the same thing as obeying it.[8]

I cannot be said to be obeying a rule if there is no way any mistake I made could be uncovered. I may even be changing the rules unconsciously as I go on. If there is no distinction between doing that and accurately keeping to the rule I set myself, we cannot talk of rules.

Wittgenstein is very fond of analogies with games, as his famous phrase 'language-games' indicates. A group of boys are not playing cricket if each plays according to his own personal rules. Someone who decides to play 'hit and run' and then refuses to run even though he has hit the ball cannot defend himself by saying that he has changed his rule for that ball. There would then be no distinction between his having a rule and playing in a totally arbitrary fashion. What is the difference between his changing the rule without telling anyone, and forgetting to keep to the rule? Rules are of their very nature public, or so Wittgenstein would argue. One may wonder how far Wittgenstein was himself still influenced by the strictures of the Vienna Circle on the importance of verifiability. Even though he himself had abandoned any trust in experience as a source of knowledge, his stress on the importance of public checking apparently has its roots in the verification theory of meaning. According to that theory the ascription of meaning depends on the possibility of public checking, so that what is unverifiable is meaningless. It could be argued from this that the private mental processes of individuals are themselves unverifiable and that language purporting to be about 'them' must be rooted in public criteria. Private processes are, then, irrelevant for meaning.

This seems to be precisely Wittgenstein's conclusion, although it is somewhat ironic that his argument against private languages itself has appeared to be a challenge to the empiricism of the Vienna Circle. The latter relied heavily on the incorrigibility of private experience, and Wittgenstein replaces that with the public rules of social practices. His quest for public criteria as a basis for meaningfulness leads him to stress the social origins of thought and experience. We are what we are largely because of the practices and institutions in which we are immersed. Knowledge does not come from the atomistic experience of individuals but is the product of rule-governed activities, which must be public and social. A game of cricket cannot be understood in terms of the private intentions of individual players. What they are doing can gain its sense from the rules of the game in which they are participating. Boys banging a ball around a field with a bat are not necessarily playing cricket. Unless their activities are governed by rules, they are just banging a ball with a bat.

Where, then, do rules come from? They are embedded in society and indeed constitute a society. Rules make a society what it is. Different rules and institutions will by definition produce a different society. Wittgensteins' views provide an invitation to the sociologist to describe the practices and rules of a society. Once again, it looks as if epistemological foundations have been repudiated and only sociological investigation will throw light on the nature of society.

It is hardly surprising that Wittgenstein's views have provided inspiration for sociologists of knowledge, wishing to emphasize the social character of knowledge. Although of very different origin, his notions fit very easily with those of Kuhn. What is at stake, however, is not just a question about epistemology or sociology of knowledge. Wittgenstein's opinions can apparently give support to all who stress the priority of the society over the individual. If the activities of individuals only gain sense through participation in social practices, we have to look at the latter as sources of explanation.

Embedding rules in societies does not finally answer questions about their origin. Much controversy has raged over whether Wittgenstein's later views lead to relativism. If rules can be justified only in the context of a particular society, what happens when we come to the question whether societies as a whole can be judged right or wrong, correct or mistaken? A genuine relativism ensues when everything is 'contextual', with consequences I shall later investigate.

In saying that the individual does not choose a rule but obeys it 'blindly',[9] Wittgenstein shows how rules are a starting-point. We have no resources with which to choose or discard rules, since the rules themselves provide the context for choice. This leads Wittgenstein to conclude that asking for justification is impossible: 'If I have exhausted the justifications, I have reached bedrock, and my spade is turned. Then I am inclined to say: "This is simply what I do".'[10] This leaves unanswered what constitutes the bedrock. It is easy to find instances where Wittgenstein seems to be suggesting that the bedrock will be different in different societies or systems of thought.[11] He seems to think, for example, that it is impossible for a physicist to give any rational justification for physics to people who trust in oracles rather than science.[12] Yet in the course of his discussion of rules he also asks a question of fundamental difficulty to the relativist, and gives an answer that is apparently totally at odds with relativism:

Suppose you came as an explorer into an unknown country with a language quite strange to you. In what circumstances would you say that the people there gave orders, understood them, obeyed them, rebelled against them, and so on?

The common behaviour of mankind is the system of reference by means of which we interpret an unknown language.[13]

Wittgenstein is intent on showing the way in which language is rooted in activities, so that there must be a regular connection between the sounds people make and what they do. The striking point he raises, at least in this passage, is that, despite their multiplicity, language-games have a common base in the 'common behaviour of mankind'. The problem of understanding other societies is acute, without some such reference point. Elsewhere he talks of 'the correspondence between concepts and very general facts of nature', and seems to be tracing human ways of acting back to the most general facts about human nature.[14] This is markedly different from stressing the ultimate nature of language-games or forms of life, so that everything has to be understood only in its social context, which may itself vary radically. What is at issue is whether the social context is itself rooted in anything more fundamental. When Wittgenstein says that what has to be accepted – the given – is forms of life,[15] this looks like a charter for relativism. Indeed it must be if the phrase 'forms of life' is taken to refer to different social institutions. At times, though, it looks as if he may regard such forms of life as grounded in human nature. They are what they are, not because of any social context, but because of what he terms 'the natural history of human beings'.[16] Certainly what he says about pain, for example, would seem to be linked to the most general features of human behaviour, rather than to the particular facts about particular institutions.

Whatever Wittgenstein's own position, he has been interpreted in many different ways. The issue is clear enough. Are human institutions to be studied in their own terms or traced back to a common base? Wittgenstein's emphasis on the priority of the social has certainly been a spur to many who consider that sociological understanding is of prime importance.

THE SOCIOLOGY OF KNOWLEDGE

Science can be regarded as a rule-governed social practice, and so its institutions are obvious candidates for sociological investigation and explanation. Because scientists work in groups and enforce communal standards, the sociologist may have much of interest to tell us. Yet how much can be explained in this manner? Perhaps science can be regarded merely as a social institution. It is significant that Peter Winch specifically refers to science as a 'mode of social life' in contrast to religion, which he considers to be a different mode. He says that 'each has criteria of intelligibility peculiar to itself'.[17] This has obvious echoes of Wittgenstein, but it raises an important problem. A clear corollary of this view is that the rules of a particular practice determine what is to count as real. Science may be concerned with electrons, while religion deals with God. The reality of each is an internal matter for the mode of social life concerned. There is no neutral language in which the respective claims of each can be discussed, and neither can ever contradict the other. Yet this means that reality is not what belief-systems are about, but is what is expressed in them. There is not one reality against which all putative knowledge can be measured, even if only in principle: there are as many realities as there are different institutions of belief. Kuhn's readiness to admit of different worlds for different paradigms involves a similar position. It tends to lapse into incoherence since it is difficult to talk of there *being* different realities, without inviting the charge that one is still in some sense talking about reality. It seems that any statement about reality can only be made from the standpoint of a particular social practice. It is an illusion on this view that there is any way of transcending all practices and talking about them meaningfully.

The conclusion can easily follow that 'reality' is given sense only by the rules of a particular social institution. Science forms one such institution, and its notions of reality can be studied, it seems, from a sociological standpoint, as can all human conceptions of reality. The sociology of knowledge tells us that knowledge is a human construct, grounded in the facts of our social life. It denies traditional definitions of knowledge which insist that knowledge must involve *true* belief, and reflect reality. For the sociologist of knowledge, reality is what is reflected by the beliefs of a society. Some have suggested that the sociology of knowledge is misnamed, since it is in fact concerned with explaining the social context of *beliefs*. This trades on a distinction between knowledge and belief which depends on the assumption that reality is independent of human conceptions. The sociology of knowledge often appears to attack this view head-on. One of its exponents, David Bloor, says:

> Knowledge for the sociologist is whatever men take to be knowledge. It consists of the beliefs which men confidently hold to and live by. In particular, the sociologist will be concerned with beliefs which are taken for granted or institutionalized or invested with authority by groups of men.[18]

Far from looking at the content of knowledge and trying to assess its worth through reason, the sociologist of knowledge will refuse to abstract what is known from its social setting. Any remaining contrast between knowledge and belief would have to be between what is socially accepted and what is individually held. The sociologist will wish to investigate the 'agreement in judgements' which Wittgenstein held to constitute a social practice. Individual deviations from this would not affect the general social setting. The social sources of authority and the institutional basis for what is counted knowledge are the focus of sociological concern. Implicit, of course, is the assumption that social rules and public practices are not merely the product of individual decisions. The sociologist of knowledge needs the priority of the social as a starting-point. The judgements of the individual gain their sense from a public framework. Reality is the product of social agreement.

The sociologist of knowledge can locate objectivity in the public practices of an institution. Individual deviations from this standard provide the possibility for error. It is, however, an odd kind of error, since it is error within a context. Any Christian who denied the divinity of Christ would appear to be making an error according to the rules of the institutional Church. In this sense, he or she is objectively wrong, but it is tempting to raise the further question whether the Church is right. Was Christ really the son of God? This type of question is forbidden us by the sociologist of knowledge. To ask it, let alone answer it, we have to step outside all institutional frameworks and social practices, and try to discover the truth without their aid.

Yet even this example shows that any sociological idea of rigid practices is misleading, since many theologians do wish to debate the divinity of Christ and the meaning of the 'Incarnation'. Some who would claim to be Christians and have an influence within the Church seem to be suggesting that Christ was not uniquely divine, as traditional orthodoxy insisted. How can they do this when they are challenging the 'objective' or at least public standards of their institution? It seems as if they should acknowledge those standards or leave the institution. There are doubtless many orthodox believers in the Christian Church who would say precisely that. Yet if what is claimed is objective truth, in a non-contextual sense, belief must be susceptible to justification and be subject to criticism. The possibility of justification is, of course, normally ignored in the sociological account, where the mere fact that beliefs are held is taken to be sufficient. Without that possibility, the question must arise why the standards of any institution should ever be challenged from within. Institutions do, of course, change through time, but the sociological account has to rule out any justification for change or for questioning existing standards. At the most, it can map the causes of change. However, if it follows that all practices can only be judged in accordance with their own existing standards, sociologists of knowledge lay themselves open to the charge of conservatism: each practice must be accepted as it is, and no reasons can be given for changing it.

Bloor contrasts the belief in progress championed by spokesmen of the Enlightenment with the appeal a conservative makes to history: 'In opposition to the appeal to the individual reason, conservatives appealed to the wisdom of tradition. In opposition to the rights of the individual, conservatives stressed our dependence on culture, nation and institution.'[19] Given the way in which Wittgenstein stresses the importance of 'forms of life', it is not surprising that Bloor classifies him as a 'conservative thinker'. This is perhaps paradoxical, since Marxists also tend to find affinities with him, particularly because of his emphasis on the priority of society over the individual. Yet, whereas conservatives will take custom and tradition as their authority, Marxists will be eager for radical social change. Wittgenstein himself certainly accepted that social practices can alter through time. Language-games could change or lose their point. If rational justification for such change had been ruled out, the sociologist will look to other influences. In fact, since rational justification is simply whatever a particular community takes it to be, sociologists may argue that they alone are in a position to chart the currents of social change. Questions about the divinity of Christ cease to be questions about a purported fact, or even merely questions about the existing rules of an institution. They are transposed by the sociologist of knowledge into questions about the character of the institution which produces such beliefs. Reason becomes merely the product of social arrangements, and, as they are put under pressure by alterations in their environment, so standards of rationality themselves change.

In the example given about arguments concerning the divinity of Christ, a sociologist of knowledge would find it easy to point to the impact of other religions on Christians. Immigration into England, for instance, by Muslims and others, has meant that the problem of living side by side with adherents of other religions has literally been brought home to English theologians. As social pressures increase pressures on the institutional Church to moderate its claims to absolute truth also grow. The roots of an apparently theological argument lie, the sociologist might claim, not so much in eternal truth, but in the changing social patterns of a particular place and time. Reason is thus the product of social arrangements.

OBJECTIVITY AND REFLEXIVITY

The views implicit in the sociology of knowledge are gaining increasing currency within and beyond the social sciences. They affect every intel lectual discipline from theology to physics and even mathematics. The views of such diverse thinkers as Wittgenstein and Kuhn are applied in a manner which seems to undermine traditional conceptions of knowledge. The writings of David Bloor provide one illustration of this approach. For example, he argues that objectivity is social. He holds that the impersonal and stable character of some of our beliefs has its origins in the existence of social institutions. The emphasis must be moved from the reality we believe in to the social causes which incline us to accept that (whatever it may be) as real. Echoing Wittgenstein, he holds that 'what counts as obeying a rule is a matter of convention'. Different societies may then have different 'objective' beliefs:

> Suppose the tribe on this side of the river worship one god, and the tribe on the other side of the river worship another god. If the worship of the gods is a stable feature of tribal practice, if they are spoken of routinely, if courses of action are justified by reference to them, then I would say both beliefs are objective.[20]

This is a far cry from notions of objectivity linked with truth. At least one tribe must be mistaken in its beliefs, if an 'objectivist' view of truth is invoked. That is ruled out by Bloor. 'Reality' is not the focus of his interest, but he holds instead that 'variations in objectivity ought to be locatable as variations in the institutions that embody knowledge.' He tells us that 'we know reality *with* our conventions, not in spite of them'. This suggests that he still wishes himself to retain some idea of a reality independent of our conceptions of it. His brand of sociology of knowledge, however, pushes any such reality for ever beyond our reach. Whatever we 'know' is socially conditioned, and is apparently explicable wholly in terms of the social institutions in which we find ourselves. The only interesting question remaining can be why we trust something as real. Whether it is real is a question that can never be answered, since any answer is itself the product of social convention. Claims to knowledge will be the outcome of group interests rather than the way the world is.

An example of Bloor's approach is his treatment of the increasing professionalization of science over the years in Britain. He argues that, in order to claim a special expertise, independent of, say, the authority of the Church, scientists were led to champion the idea that knowledge gained by experiment comprised the whole of knowledge: 'One way of ensuring that it was to be all was to deny any reality over and above that revealed by "experience" – where experience was defined to mean just those things one which the scientific expert can pronounce.'[21] Thus, he says, 'empiricism functioned as the ideology of scientific professionalism'.

Bloor has put forward what he terms 'the strong programme' of the sociology of knowledge.[22] He sketches its main characteristics by saying that it is causal, and concerned with the conditions bringing about knowledge. It is also impartial and symmetrical in its style of explanation. In other words, it treats true and false beliefs in identical fashion, and in so doing ultimately removes all distinction between truth and falsity. Bloor also hopes that it will be reflexive, so that, 'in principle, its patterns of explanation would have to be applicable to sociology itself'.

Just how strong a programme is envisaged can be judged by the fact that Bloor thinks that even the 'truths' of logic and mathematics are susceptible to sociological explanation. Since he is interested in the social origins of belief, he is immediately suspicious of appeals to self-evidence or to authority of any kind. What makes us treat certain statements as self-evident? What is the social grounding even of intellectual authority? Writing with Barry Barnes, he says:

> As a body of conventions and esoteric conditions the compelling character of logic, such as it is, derives from certain narrowly defined purposes and from custom and institutionalized usage. Its authority is moral and social, and as such it is admirable material for sociological investigation and explanation. In particular, the credibility of logical conventions, just like the everyday practices which deviate from them, will be of an entirely local character.[23]

Far from logic being an indispensable presupposition of all thought, it is thus demoted to being a custom or convention. The result is that the fact of contradiction matters less than that one should feel it wrong to contradict oneself. Yet, although society enforces this kind of norm, we are still left wondering why its authority should be used in this way. The answer to this might appear to lie in the province of sociology, but at this point the sociology of knowledge overreaches itself. It cannot be a matter of purely local convention that it is undesirable for someone both to assert and to deny the same thing, since the speaker is then saying absolutely nothing. He is withdrawing what he is also putting forward. It is not an accident the societies disapprove of contradiction. The law of non-contradiction is an example of a logical law providing an indispensable framework for rational thought and for language. The alternative is not a different kind of society. It is silence.

Bloor accepts that there will be 'other types of causes apart from social ones which will cooperate in bringing about belief'.[24] This is an interesting admission which raises a question about the scope of the sociology of knowledge. It can be a very imperialistic discipline. Not content with disposing of epistemology, it aspires to explain the whole of science too. Presumably it would wish to explain the practice of psychology or of neurophysiology in sociological terms. Yet these disciplines themselves have ambitions of explaining the origins of human belief. Psychological causes might be very potent in inclining an individual to one set of beliefs rather than another. Research into the workings of the brain has barely begun. The sociology of knowledge has to decide whether such causes are genuine. Bloor's admission seems to accept this. On the other hand, why should we not say that social influences incline psychologists to accept psychological causes as genuine? If we do, the sociology of knowledge apparently becomes a crucial discipline, able to interpret the functioning of all other intellectual disciplines. If we do not, its significance depends on how important a role we ascribe to society and its influences. The impact of Wittgenstein's views, together with those of Kuhn, have led some to consider that the role of society is predominant, and perhaps all-pervasive.

The sociology of knowledge appears to be locked in a battle for supremacy with other intellectual disciplines. Looked at from a sociological point of view, such a battle itself provides plenty of material for study. That very fact, however, raises an insoluble problem. Bloor mentioned the requirement of reflexivity. The sociology of knowledge is itself a social practice with its own rules. Sociologists are themselves subject to the influences of the influences of the society to which they belong. The idea, therefore, of a sociology of the sociology of knowledge is not ludicrous: it is essential. Yet an infinite regress beckons at this point. Sociological explanations may be given for the sociology of knowledge. There may be something about the conditions of our society at this time which gives rise to such a discipline. The ease with which it can attack the previously revered portals of physical science itself invites sociological explanation. Why should sociologists find it plausible to suggest that science is not the discovery of truth but merely one rule-governed social activity among others? Sensible answers can no doubt be given to these questions, but if they are given we face the next one. Why do they seem sensible to us now, when they may not have to intellectuals fifty years ago? Thus we get sucked into a sociology of the sociology of the sociology of knowledge.

This process is not an interesting curiosity like the Cotswold village which includes a model village portraying itself. In the model, at the appropriate place there is a model of the model and in that a model of the model of the model. The regress in sociology is a vicious one, since the sociology of knowledge purports to offer *explanations* of why beliefs are ' held. Yet each explanation turns out not to be valid at all, but only what a particular group holds valid. The reason they do can itself be 'explained', but that, it turns out, is itself only an explanation held by a particular group. In each case, the explanation may be accepted because of social conditions and group interests which have nothing to do with the explanation. There can be no reason why any such sociology should be accepted by other groups who may have their own interests. Psychologists, or even philosophers, can reject the grandiose claims of the sociology of knowledge if they choose, and on the premises of the latter they will inevitably do so. Each group can only operate according to its own rules.

Unless sociologists are prepared to assert certain things as *true* and to maintain that certain types of social conditions *are* causes, there is no reason why non-sociolgists should accept anything they say. The trouble is that, if sociologists of knowledge do this, they undermine their own thesis. If the strong programme of the sociology of knowledge is true, it is thereby shown to be false. Its whole purpose is to shift attention from what is the case to what people hold is the case. Since this appears to involve the denial of objective truth, the basic distinction between what is and what is not the case is removed. Without it the linguistic acts of assertion and denial seem pointless. It is hard to avoid the conclusion that anyone presenting rational arguments for the sociology of knowledge to those beyond the discipline cannot in consistency believe what he or she is saying.

No one would deny that social influences on belief can be very powerful, but the question is whether they tell the *whole* story. Reflexivity only becomes a logical problem if they are held to do so. Otherwise we still appear to have access to whatever the beliefs are about. We are on the verge of unutterable bewilderment when *any* reality is repudiated. It seems then that we have beliefs, which are the product of our society, but that they are not really *about* anything. Language then floats free and science becomes pointless. Indeed, even an assertion that we have beliefs seems a claim about part of the reality that is prescribed.

Barnes and Bloor realize the incongruity of all this. Apparently they do not wish to deny the existence of objective reality so much as to question its relevance: 'Reality is a common factor in all the vastly different cognitive responses that men produce to it. Being a common factor it is not a promising candidate to field as an explanation of that variation.'[25] This, they think, gives them *carte blanche* to investigate the social causes operating locally which enable many different beliefs to seem credible.

There is undoubtedly a problem why mankind has produced so many different systems of belief if confronted by the same objective reality. It seems inescapable that many have been mistaken. Perhaps even many of our own most firmly held beliefs may be wrong. Saying, though, that there is no such thing as a mistake, or even that questions of truth and falsity are irrelevant, not only removes the motive for any further intellectual effort on our part. More important, it fundamentally distorts many of the activities which sociologists may wish to study.

TRUTH AND FALSE CONSCIOUSNESS

Viewing a body of belief as a social practice may be illuminating, since it enables us to see social influences which we may have previously ignored. Suggesting, though, that we have then given an adequate explanation for the belief misrepresents the belief. I touched on this when remarking how sociologists can concentrate on the fact of belief rather than the content. The sociology of science may have interesting discoveries to make about the conduct of science, but that cannot be all there is to science. Scientists themselves are presumably often unaware of the social influences on their work. Yet someone cannot play cricket without having some idea of the rules, and similarly the rules of science cannot be totally hidden from the participants. This is the beginning of a major issue concerning the relationship between sociological explanation and the understanding of participants which I shall pursue later. Suffice it to say at the moment that scientists obviously think that they are acquiring knowledge of the world. Even the empiricist stress on observations carried with it the assumption that the world was being observed. Being told by sociologists that they are not really doing what they think they are doing is bound to be unsettling. Instead of discovering truth, scientists are, they will be told, merely engaging in a complex social activity. It does not matter that sociologists only need to be listened to if they are claiming the kind of truth for their theories that they are denying to branches of the physical sciences. The fact remains that, if any group of people are told that they are not doing what they imagine they are, this may itself influence their actions. They may even stop what they are doing.

This comes out more clearly if we examine the sociology of religion. Religious institutions, such as denominations of the Christian church, are prime targets for sociological investigation. Their organizations and their impact on society, not to mention the secularizing influences of Western society on them, will be of consuming interest. Even the impact of different beliefs on societies can be studied. One can, for example, examine the respective impact of Catholic and Protestant versions of Christianity on different countries. Does Protestantism really encourage greater self-reliance and enterprise so that the 'Protestant work ethic' contributes to the prosperity of nations? Does Catholicism, with its opposition to contraception and its traditional emphasis on large families, contribute to the poverty of others? These are hotly debated issues which are of legitimate sociological concern.

The impact of society on belief can also be studied. There has been a marked tendency for some theologians to revise Christian belief to make it more acceptable to those around them. They themselves may have been influenced by complex currents in society which a sociologist can chart. Yet this does not face the underlying question: is Christianity true? Sociologists would immediately say that it was illegitimate for them to deal with such a question. Some of them would reject the idea of objective truth, with the consequences we have already sketched. Others would say that they wished to 'bracket off' the question of truth, and merely look at the fact of belief, together with its causes and influences. This position may seem more acceptable, but it too has its dangers. By trying to ignore questions about the content of a belief, it fails to take seriously the fact that to the person holding it the most important aspect is that *it is true*. The religious believer, rightly or wrongly, considers that he or she possesses knowledge. Any sociological interpretation which undercuts this falsifies what it is interpreting. 'Bracketing off' questions of truth may be the inevitable function of the sociologist, but it must not result in the view that questions of truth are of no importance.

The central feature of religious belief, as of theories in science, may well lie in its claim to be about an objective reality. It has this feature, even if it is mistaken. It is not a mere body of practices or rituals, because these are themselves based on assumptions about the kind of reality that confronts mankind. As a result, religious believers may quite justifiably feel threatened by sociological attempts to 'explain' their religion. Accepting the sociology may mean that they can no longer retain their beliefs. That is a curious state of affairs, since sociology should not undermine any such beliefs unless it is willing to proclaim the falsity of religion. What has happened is that the essential nature of religious belief has been ignored. By side-stepping issues of truth and falsity, sociology has often forgotten the importance of claims to truth. Ignoring that can appear tantamount to assuming their falsity.

Since any denial of objective reality as such must be self-defeating, it is prudent for sociologists of knowledge to take seriously the fact that those they are studying to make claims about reality. Their own discipline thereby becomes less important, because they cannot adjudicate between different claims about reality. That is irrelevant. The very fact that they are willing to participate in an intellectual discipline in a rational manner shows that they are committed to the rational pursuit of truth. Whatever the social influences at work, we do have access to the real world, and can uncover real social influences at work. Sociologists are themselves in the business of studying reality and must accept that others do the same. Sociology has to claim objectivity so as to be taken seriously, and must note the similar claims of others.

Two sociologists, writing about the problem of reflexivity which haunts the sociologist, say the following:

> It is important to re-iterate that the sociologist does not interpret 'reality' but rather interprets various interpretations of 'reality' (or 'reality defini-tion'). 'False consciousness' as a concept implies 'correct consciousness', which in turn implies a direct access to reality which the sociologist cannot supply.[26]

The term 'false consciousness' is in fact often used in sociology. Must sociology be neutral towards different world-views and does that suggest that the term is illegitimate? I have warned against the dangers of sociological scepticism about the possibility of objectivity, understood as the grasping of objective reality. That view can produce the conclusion that no beliefs could be true because truth is unattainable. Another approach, however, could start from the assumption that it already possesses knowledge, and attack beliefs it considered false. If it not only proclaimed the possibility of objective truth but said that it pos-sessed it, is this a coherent position? Since I have already implied that the striving for truth is an important feature of scientific disciplines, there would seem to be nothing in principle wrong with it. We might, though, be suspicious of such arrogance, given the fallibility of mankind. An important consequence of stressing the objectivity of truth and denying that it is context-dependent is the realization that we may ourselves always be mistaken.

Berger and Kellner imply that sociologists have no access to reality. That is certainly so if it means that sociologists have no privileged position from which to judge which of several rival interpretations of reality is correct. They cannot properly use the prestige of sociology to tell us that Christianity is or is not true. They have strayed beyond their professional competence if they do so. What, though, is the position if a sociologist does not assess the worth of beliefs, but refers to the functioning of 'social reality'. If sociology cannot tell us anything about that and has no direct access to it, we might well wonder what is the supposed scientific value of the subject. It is at least plausible that, just as physics can investigate one level of reality, sociology and the other social sciences can discover laws about the functioning of a different level.

If there is such a thing as social reality, over and above the reality perceived by the individuals participating in a society, then participants may perhaps not properly understand it. Sociology may be able to uncover facts about societies of which their members may be totally unaware. It may even show why participants persistently misunderstand what is occurring in that society at the social level. It could, for instance, show how the class structure of a society has a pervasive and misleading influence on the way its members see themselves and their roles in society. On the other hand, it might be able to assert that some groups are in a favoured position to see society as it is. Georg Lukács thought that the proletariat was able to do this: 'It was necessary for the proletariat to be born for social reality to become fully conscious.'[27] We might wonder how Lukács himself was in a position to assert this. How had he obtained knowledge of social reality so as to endorse the beliefs of the proletariat? He seems to be saying that all beliefs are conditioned by the social background, and yet that means that his own views are bound merely to be the product of *his* background. Sociologists must be wary of claiming knowledge unless they can show some basis for it. If there is no independent way of establishing the truth of a belief, the mere fact that they endorse it themselves is irrelevant. Yet we must be careful that this does not immediately drive us to the conclusion that sociology is not concerned with reality but only interpretations of it.

Berger and Kellner are well aware that they hold a controversial position about the function of the social sciences. Sociology, they believe, does not discover laws about social reality, but investigates the different ways humans give meaning to the world. In their view, the sociologist 'presents a spectrum of meanings and values' but 'cannot tell people whether they should or should not adopt these meanings and values as their own.'[28] In other words, the main object of sociology is the understanding of meaning, or the different ways in which people can construct social reality. The focus of attention is the making of social reality and not the nature of social reality. Different forms of consciousness have to be accepted at face value, since there is no sociological standard by which they can be assessed. Any belief in reality is the product of consciousness, and sociologists must recognize that, if, like Lukács, they try to set up a standard of truth, they are merely setting up the constructs of their own consciousness over those of other people.

There is some force in this view, but it is a position which can undercut itself. Anyone claiming knowledge has to give reasons to justify the claim. The retort that 'that is just your opinion' can make all truth unattainable and induces the very paralysis which the strong programme of the sociology of knowledge brings on. We cannot always reduce the notion of a reason to 'what someone thinks is a reason'. Sociology and the other social sciences may claim that social reality is distinctive and cannot be adequately understood by those immersed in it. Such a belief is not just the product of the consciousness of sociologists. It may have much to commend it, but this has to be shown. Its truth depends on whether there is such a thing as social reality.

NOTES

1 Feyerabend, *Science in a Free Society*, p. 70.
2 M. Grene, 'Dogmas of Empiricism', in R. S. Cohen and M. W. Wartofsky (eds), *Epistemology, Methodology and the Social Sciences*, 1983, p. 104.
3 See Wittgenstein, *Philosophical Investigations*, I, § 243 ff.
4 § 258.
5 Ibid., § 259.
6 Ibid., § 199.
7 Ibid., § 199.
8 Ibid., § 202.
9 Ibid., § 219.
10 Ibid., § 217.
11 See my *Reason and Commitment*, 1973, p. 94 ff.
12 Wittgenstein, *On Certainty*, 1969, § 609 ff.
13 Wittgenstein, *Philosophical Investigations*, I, § 206.
14 Ibid., II, xii, p. 230.
15 Ibid., II, xi, p. 226.
16 Ibid., I., § 415.
17 Peter Winch, *The Idea of a Social Science*, 1958, p. 100.
18 David Bloor, *Knowledge and Social Imagery*, 1976, II, p. 2.
19 Bloor, *Wittgenstein: a Social Theory of Knowledge*, 1983, p. 160.
20 Bloor, 'A Sociological Theory of Objectivity', in S. C. Brown (ed.), *Objectivity and Cultural Divergence*, 1984, p. 236.
21 Ibid., p. 243.
22 Bloor, *Knowledge and Social Imagery*, pp. 4–5.
23 D. Bloor and B. Barnes, 'Relativism, Rationalism and the Sociology of Knowledge', in M. Hollis and S. Lukes (eds), *Rationality and Relativism*, 1982, p. 45.

24 Bloor, *Knowledge and Social Imagery*, p. 5.
25 Bloor and Barnes, 'Relativism, Rationalism and the Sociology of Knowledge', p. 34.
26 P. Berger and H. Kellner, *Sociology Reinterpreted*, 1982, p. 74.
27 G. Lukács, *History and Class Consciousness*, 1971, p. 19.
28 Berger and Kellner, *Sociology Reinterpreted*, p. 74.

3

Individuals and Society

The idea that all standards are embedded in particular social practices and that 'objective' claims only have validity against a particular social background is self-defeating. It destroys itself, since it can no longer claim the kind of truth it needs if others are to take notice of it. It also seems to undermine the possibility of comparing different societies. There would be nothing in common to facilitate comparison, if each could only be understood in its own terms. Social scientists would be immersed in their own society and would inevitably judge other societies in the terms of their own. Their views would be ethnocentric and parochial, merely assuming the concepts of their own background, although we might well wonder what else they could do.

Social science is distinct from physical science in that it studies human society rather than inanimate objects. Positivism may well have inclined some social scientists to treat social interactions as if they were the colliding of physical objects. The emphasis on obtaining neutral observations and measurements as the basis for theory led to the exclusion of whatever could not be conveniently observed or measured. Behaviourism in psychology, for example, led to the systematic exclusion of whatever could not be scientifically tested in a laboratory. Pain behaviour, rather than the feeling of pain, would be the focus of attention. The same approach could lead to the exclusion of all questions concerning human consciousness. The important question would be what actually happened rather than how it was viewed by the participants. The latter was not testable from a scientific point of view.

This all begs a basic question, since it is assumed that we can distinguish what happened from what the participants thought. One of the issues, indeed, is just how important human consciousness is. Does it constitute human social activity by the meaning it bestows on it, or is it irrelevant? One of the problems of dismissing consciousness and its products as perhaps an interesting, but irrelevant, appendage to human activity, is that this must be done through arguments emanating from human consciousness. The extreme materialist who says that ideas are unimportant is, in fact, in the grip of an idea. Those who believe that society functions at a level untouched by human understanding have to come to terms with the irrelevance of their own understanding of this fact. Yet those who believe that society is constituted by human consciousness also have their problems. Since the repudiation of empiricism has removed the possibility of 'raw data', the problem of understanding different societies becomes acute, if all that is left is the different ways the world is perceived in them. Interpretation becomes the sole aim of the social sciences, although it is sometimes unclear on what basis this can be achieved.

Even before the demise of positivism, there were strong voices in the social sciences urging concentration on human consciousness rather than human behaviour. The very vigour of the positivist approach created a reaction away from it. Instead of looking to the natural sciences as models for a social-scientific methodology, many have urged that the social sciences must be distinct. The reasons for this are not hard to find. Any would-be science of human behaviour, modelled on a positivist conception of the natural sciences, is not just appealing to neutral observations to provide the raw data on which theories can be based. It is restricting its attention to what can be observed or, better still measured. Its prejudice for what is public and verifiable means that anything which is apparently subjective can be ignored. What is subjective is denigrated precisely because it is out of reach of controlled scientific observation. The viewpoint of an individual is left out of account, since science, according to the positivist, can only take hold of what is viewed inter-subjectively. The objectivity of science sometimes appears to consist precisely in this abstraction from all points of view. The scientist believes that an experiment can be repeated by anyone else and still give the same results; the fact that a particular person is conducting it must be irrelevant. Yet that means that scientists abstract from the objects of their study all traces of anyone's point of view and conception of the situation. This is quite proper when they are experimenting on physical objects. What is measured is distinct from the person measuring, and what is observed is distinct from the observer. There are difficulties in quantum mechanics, but the basic view that reality is logically independent of anyone investigating it is crucial.

Problems arise when the reality to be investigated includes human beings. They can be studied as if they are mere physical objects; their movements can be charted and their behaviour noted. Studies of animal behaviour can do this without any speculation about how far animals understand what they are doing. That is a further question. They may be acting intentionally, but it is still possible to question how far they are conscious of what they are doing and why they are doing it, or how far they have been programmed by evolution to act *as if* they know what they are about. Animals can certainly learn through imitation, so that patterns of behaviour are passed on from generation to generation. One of the most famous examples is that of a group of Japanese macaques.[1] One female monkey began washing the sand off potatoes with which she was fed on a beach. Others followed her example, and most of the monkeys there now wash them in the sea. The tradition is passed on to infants, who imitate their mothers. Apart from cleaning the potatoes, the sea-water presumably leaves a salty taste. All this can be observed without taking into account how the monkeys conceive of the situation. Their behaviour can be recorded even if we leave aside questions about such subjective aspects. My reference to a salty taste is itself perhaps a piece of needless speculation, by positivist standards. Even talk of 'tradition' is perhaps unnecessary. Baby monkeys imitate their elders, and we need only refer to the way individuals behave, apparently copying others. Suggesting that teaching occurs is unnecessary, since that could imply the deliberate transmission of conscious knowledge. Richard Passingham says: 'We have little evidence that any animal does teach. In almost all instances there is a more parsimonious description of what the animal is doing.'[2] He points out that young lions certainly learn to hunt by being taken on expeditions with their mothers. He considers it likely that the mothers happen to allow the infants to go on the hunt, rather than set out with the deliberate intention of training them. They do not appear, for instance, to make any effort to demonstrate the relevant techniques.

Whether cases of animals intentionally teaching others can be produced or not, animal behaviour can be adequately studied without assumptions being made about animal culture, tradition or consciousness. Even here there is a danger. Because the mental states of animals are inaccessible to scientists, it is easy to conclude that they do not have any. It would not be surprising to discover that empiricist prejudice had led us to underrate the abilities of animals to feel or even to think. Nevertheless their mental life can only be rudimentary, and there is no way it could be reasonably suggested that an animal's understanding of what it was doing actually changed the character of its behaviour. The monkeys washing potatoes could do so whether they have any views about the matter or not. Questions about the interpretation of actions do not arise. It may be suggested that 'washing potatoes' is itself a human classification of an action. This, however, merely demonstrates that animal behaviour is understood by reference to human categories and not animal ones.

It is not as easy to discount the concepts which human agents possess. Human beings do not just *behave*. They *act*, and their actions occur with an understanding of their significance in a wider social context. Human actions are endowed with meaning, and it may appear that they cannot be properly understood unless that meaning is grasped. Human behaviour, viewed as a mere succession of bodily movements, and human actions performed with definite motives and intentions may not be the same. The bodily movements involved in signing a cheque, for instance, can never by themselves explain what is occurring. We would have in addition to understand the agent's reasons for wishing to transfer money – to buy a house, give a present, pay a bribe, or perform countless other actions. All these actions presuppose a wider social setting; indeed the whole notion of paying by cheque itself presupposes an elaborate background of banking institutions.

Once we venture on explaining human action, we cannot treat humans as physical objects. The abstraction of what is occurring from all points of view, including those of the agent and of the observer, does not allow for any consideration of the individual's, or other people's, understanding of what he or she is doing. All psychological and social aspects of behaviour are excluded. Founding the social sciences on a positivist methodology will inevitably draw criticism from those who see human action in terms of the meaning given to it, whether by the agent, the whole society, or even the observer trying to make sense of what is observed.

THE GOAL OF SOCIAL SCIENCE

Any attempt to exclude from the study of society whatever the positivist might view as unscientific 'subjective' elements would appear to many to evacuate human society of all that is essential to it. The very term 'subjective' means something different to positivists and to their opponents. Positivists might use it to refer to what should be excluded because it is private and unverifiable. Others do not use it in the pejorative sense. Alfred Schutz, who was influenced in his work on social science by the phenomenology of Edmund Husserl, puts the matter in this way:

The critics of understanding call it subjective, because they hold that understanding the motives of another man's action depends upon the private, uncontrollable and unverifiable intuition of the observer or refers to his private value system. The social scientists, such as Max Weber, however, call *Verstehen* subjective because its goal is to find out what the actor 'means' in his action, in contrast to the meaning which this action has for the actor's partner or a neutral observer.[3]

We are at the point of a major divide in the understanding of the social sciences. There are several strands to the argument. At the root is the question whether the natural and social sciences should have the same methodology, if that methodology stems from positivism. The stand taken on that issue also has implications for other arguments. For instance, if the goal of social science is to discover 'meanings', the direct conclusion must be that it is not concerned with causal explanation but has a different aim. Social reality would then appear to be different from physical reality, and the question must arise about its relationship with the individual. The controversy over whether there is such a thing as social reality is a recurring one. A positivist view of human behaviour denies it.

Schutz referred to Weber, whose concept of *Verstehen* provided an alternative to the positivist ideal of causal explanation. By *Verstehen* is meant something like interpretive understanding. Weber insisted that what we had to understand was the subjective meaning attached by an individual to his or her behaviour. There was, then, no question of imposing any framework of explanation which the agent would not accept. One had to get into his mind and look at his actions through his eyes. Weber defined sociology as a 'science which attempts the interpretive understanding of social action'.[4] Behaviour is action in so far as 'the acting individual attaches a subjective meaning to it' and social in so far as the individual takes account of the behaviour of others.

Both Weber and Schutz were anxious to differentiate the kind of explanation they were seeking in the social sciences from the 'external observation' which they believed characterized explanation in the natural sciences. While accepting that this kind of subjective understanding delivered results which possessed a 'mere hypothetical and fragmentary character', Weber emphasized that 'subjective understanding is the specific characteristic of social knowledge.' Schutz, whose views have also been highly influential, puts the matter this way:

> We cannot deal with phenomena in the social world as we do with phenomena belonging to the natural sphere. . . . We want to understand

social phenomena, and we cannot understand them apart from their place-ment within the scheme of human motives, human means and ends, human planning – in short – within the categories of human action. The social scientist must therefore ask . . . what happens in the mind of an individual actor whose act has led to the phenomena in question.[5]

Ethologists do not have to ask what is going on in the minds of monkeys washing potatoes; the monkeys' behaviour requires no further inter-pretation. Human action, however, can only be understood, it is sug-gested, in terms of human concepts. This inevitably raises the question of interpretation, since, if the nature of an action is determined by the con-sciousness of an agent, there is a difficult question how far an observer can become attuned to that consciousness. Similar problems arise when we wonder about any aspect of the private mental life of another. Positivism was naturally accompanied by behaviourist views, which would, for example, countenance motives only in so far as they were understood as dispositions to behave in particular ways. Social theories which emphasize the importance of the contents of individual minds are also often linked to philosophical presuppositions about the status of mind – for example, the dualist position, which distinguishes between bodily movements and mental activity. Mind and body are regarded as distinct, the mind giving meaning to bodily behaviour. In that way, reflex actions, such as the involuntary jerk of one's knee, can be dis-tinguished from meaningful activity. The notorious problem then arising is how to gain access to the contents of another's mind. The argument from analogy is normally invoked here: I know the kind of pain you are feeling because I know what I feel in similar circumstances. Nevertheless philosophers are always aware of the dangers of scepticism. We find it easy enough to imagine that animals do not have minds, and perhaps conclude that too easily. Why should we not assume that because other minds are inaccessible 'they' are non-existent? In essence, this is the verificationist or 'anti-realist' position. Because we cannot verify the existence of other minds, we just have to deal with public ways of behav-ing. Yet one curious feature of some versions of empiricism, defending doctrines about sense-data, is that they stress the importance of what is publicly accessible through the concept of intersubjective experience. The sense-data themselves, however, which form the foundations of empirical knowledge, are archetypal instances of what is private and sub-jective. Wittgenstein's emphasis on the public and social led him to repudiate any such basis for knowledge.

The dualist conception of mind makes it private and subjective in the sense that it is accessible only to the subject of the experiences and thoughts. In another sense, it is not subjective at all, since the contents of mind are real enough if dualists are right. It is objectively true that someone is, or is not, in pain. There is sometimes an unfortunate slide from the notion of what is accessible only to a particular subject, to what is subjectively valid or true only for that person. The positivist attack on the subjectivity of experience makes what is private and hence not susceptible to scientific investigation not an objective matter in any sense. The objectively true becomes synonymous with the scientifically accessible.

Phenomenological views of social action explicitly challenge positivism in matters of this kind. Far from considering it a virtue to be bound by the standards of physical science, they consider that this empties society of all that is distinctively human. By basing society on the products of individual minds, they are not merely taking a position on the privacy of the mental, they also stress the primacy of the individual as the source of society. The social is thus created by the individual thoughts of individuals. Society is not a 'thing' coercing individuals, and social explanation is not at a different level from that of the explanation of the understanding of individuals. *Verstehen*, in Weber's sense, is not groping for the concepts of one society from the standpoint of an alien system. It is one individual trying to understand another.

The argument about the relationship between individuals and society is of basic importance for social science, and the significance of the social sciences as a whole is tied up with this question. Sociology, for example, is going to be of much greater interest and relevance if it uncovers structures in society to which no other discipline has access. If, however, society can be adequately explained in terms of the individual contents of individual minds, psychology might perhaps seem of more vital importance for the understanding of society. Sociology would then have to become a branch of social psychology which concentrates on the small-scale interactions of individuals. A basic issue is whether it is possible to gain insights into politics or economics, say, through concentration on individuals. Can individual actions throw light on social currents flowing through whole societies? According to one sociologist, David Rubinstein,

The belief that the intentional actions of concrete individuals are the exclusive concern of social science produces a seriously limited kind of sociology, a sociology that is programmatically unable to deal with issues encompassing entire societies.[6]

The question is well illustrated by economics. Is economics to be concerned with the cumulative effects of individuals interacting with each other, or are there economic laws operating beyond the consciousness of any individual agent? This is one more instance where a social science might wish to give explanations of behaviour which would not have been conscious to an agent and which indeed that agent may vehemently reject. Any position locating the origin of the social world in the individual consciousness may be restricted to explanations that individuals would accept. Otherwise the social world is treated as if it were independent of its origin in the individual mind.

A complication in all this is that the actions of individuals very often have unintended social consequences. The combined effect of these may itself be worthy of study, even when the individual agent is unaware of them. Even if the working of the market depends on many individual decisions, it might itself function in a way that seems independent of them. If everyone decides simultaneously to buy the same kinds of goods, shortages will develop, even though no one deliberately tried to create them. It might appear that, once created by individuals, social reality has a life of its own. Those who emphasize the role of individual consciousness are not saying that, but insist that any social-scientific understanding has to be in accord with the agents' commonsense understanding of their society. The everyday world of agents cannot then differ from the social world as studied by social scientists. There is no other reality for them to investigate. They may bring their own categories to bear on it, but they must remember that social reality is dependent on the minds of the agents.

This theory thereby betrays its idealist origins. For idealists, reality is dependent on mind: what exists does so because it is being perceived by a mind. Such a theory goes against common sense when applied to physical reality. However much we may debate the reality of the 'external' world, we know that tables and chairs are there, whether they are perceived or not. Perhaps slightly more dubiously we assume that a clock goes on ticking even when there is no one in the room to hear it. The theory, however, does seem more congenial when applied to social reality. Is society an abstract force that goes on working regardless of the thought process of its members? Perhaps this is another way of asking whether a whole is more than the sum of its parts. A jigsaw puzzle may form a striking picture when put together, but it is still merely a collection of different pieces. It is more plausible to think of a car as more than that, since when assembled it seems to form a new entity able to function as one complex piece of machinery. The question is whether society is a collection of individuals or whether it is a new kind of entity, depending for its existence on its parts but not reducible to them.

SOCIAL REALITY AND THE INDIVIDUAL

The notion that society or particular social patterns are entities with an existence independent of human minds has often been attacked. It is said to be *reification*, a process which treats essential human characteristics as if they were non-human *things*. Berger and Luckmann give as an example the ways in which human marriage can be reified:

> Marriage may be reified as an imitation of divine acts of creativity, as a universal mandate of natural laws, as the necessary consequence of biological or psychological forces, or for that matter, as a functional imperative of the social system. What all these reifications have in common is their obfuscation of marriage as a human production.[7]

Stress on individual consciousness as the source of society certainly reminds us that society is a human creation, and that the way humans live together is the result of human decisions. It is possible to go too far, however, since a completely idealist emphasis on consciousness inevitably removes any notion of an objective, or independently existing, reality. The only way, then, of understanding a society is to look into the minds of its members. It will not help to look at the reality confronting those minds. From holding that social reality is a human creation, some theorists can easily get drawn into treating all reality in the same way.

Berger and Luckmann say: 'All symbolic universes and all legitimations are human products: their existence has its base in the lives of concrete individuals, and has no empirical status apart from those lives.'[8] This is a reiteration of the importance of the individual as the source of society. Yet it can lead not just to a view of social reality as a human creation, but also to an undue extension of what is regarded as within the scope of human creation. It may seem obvious that, if all social arrangements are the product of human minds, everything social must be the result of mental categories. This in turn leads to the impression that they might have been created otherwise. Indeed, different societies seem actually to possess different categories. Yet all this precludes the possibility that some arrangements might have been imposed on society, and on the minds creating it, by external contingencies.

Berger and Luckmann show how an institutional world can be experienced as an objective reality by an individual. We feel that we are placed in something that constrains us. It seems objective, because it has been created by other minds. Yet they say: 'Despite the objectivity that marks the social world in human experience, it does not thereby acquire an ontological status apart from the human activity that produced it.'[9] A university, for example, may seem to be as objectively there as its buildings. Different participants in the life of the institution come and go, but it remains recognizably the same institution. It is possible to look at an ancient college and see the way its life continues through many generations of students. Similarly the Christian Church, even if viewed merely as a social institution, without any supernatural overtones, continues through history. Popes, bishops and clergy all change, yet the same Church lives on into new generations. It is, of course, possible to identify such institutions with the buildings they inhabit, but that would be an obvious mistake. The question is whether they have an ontological status apart from the activity of those producing them. They appear to influence their members, and that might indicate that they do, despite the danger of reification. It is easy to see why some are tempted to insist that an institution does have an existence of a different order from that of the individuals participating in it.

It may nevertheless seem plausible to deny that what is created by humans can exist apart from them. The more, though, that we focus our attention on the active role of the human mind in the creation of such institutions, the more we are in danger of ignoring the way in which the mind might itself be constrained by external factors. For example, taboos are rules enforced by societies, sometimes with great ferocity. They are in one sense the creation of minds, and yet that leaves open the question why they were created. Berger and Luckmann refer to the incest taboo and say that it is 'nothing but the negative side of an assemblage of typifications, which define in the first place which sexual conduct is incestuous and which is not.'[10] This could suggest that such definitions are merely products of the human mind, and are arbitrary ways of categorizing social behaviour. Yet *why* have minds produced just those definitions? The incest taboo appears to be universal. Why is this so? A phenomenological approach concentrates on minds as the source of society. Even if we accept the individualist emphasis, there remains the question: what makes them produce the kinds of society that they do?

One answer would refer to human nature, however that is to be explained. It is significant, however, that the more that individual consciousness is asserted to be the source of conceptual schemes and of society, the less room is left for any such general notion. Indeed, the concept of human nature, like all concepts, could itself be portrayed as a product of consciousness. Stress on the active role of consciousness seems to leave little beyond the scope of its creation. Luckmann explicitly denies that human life possesses any 'elementary structures' which could constitute 'anything like an immutable human nature'. He sweepingly asserts: 'Modern philosophical and social anthropology cured us of this illusion.'[11] His position is explained more fully as follows:

> No doubt both human consciousness and social organization have a phylogeny which goes far back into our primate and even mammal ancestry. Yet human society structures have become historical; in part they have become emancipated from simple phylogenetic determination. They are the result of purposive as well as blind, of individual as well as collective, human *action*.[12]

This is the edge of a major controversy to which I shall return. The strength of this type of approach is its recognition of the distinctiveness of *human* society as a *human* creation. This may paradoxically also be a weakness, but emphasizing the role of consciousness certainly distinguishes humans from animals, or mere physical objects. Understanding the significance of what is being done distinguishes human action from animal behaviour or the movements of objects.

Writers such as Weber and Schutz do not so much concentrate on the significance of the human as deal with the priority of the individual. Yet the social sciences do not merely need to differentiate themselves from the physical sciences. It is not sufficient for them to show that social reality cannot be studied by the physicist or biologist. Unless society possesses 'emergent properties' the social sciences will tell us little more than we can understand through the study of individuals. An emphasis on human consciousness in an idealist manner can easily be combined with beliefs about society as a 'thing'. Combinations of individuals may, for instance, form a collectivity with its own forms of consciousness which transcend the individual. References to the 'spirit of a nation' or the 'spirit of an age' perhaps suggest something like this.

Weber would have none of that kind of theory. He is very emphatic that apparent collectivities are merely combinations of individuals, and reducible to them. It is easy to talk about all kinds of human social units as agents. We may say about a mother that the family were concerned about her health. This means nothing more than that the individual members were severally concerned about it. Matters are perhaps less clear-cut if we talk of vast multinational business corporations or even states. They can certainly be party to legal agreements, and there is often a definite distinction between the liabilities of a corporation and those of its employees. Weber grants that the law may see things differently but insists that sociology cannot make this kind of distinction. He says of such social institutions as states and corporations:

> For the subjective interpretation of action in sociological work these collec-
> tivities must be treated as solely the resultants and modes of organization of
> the particular acts of individual persons, since these alone can be treated as
> agents in a course of subjectively understandable action.[13]

This approach must lead to the search for an empathy with individual members of a society, so that sociology involves the understanding of people's motives. It does not then uncover laws of human behaviour or of the functioning of social structures. There would thus appear to be little room for any misunderstanding by agents of the social significance of what they were doing (although even many opposed to holism might accept that the unintended social consequences of individual action were a proper subject for study). The concept of false consciousness would have no application. Individual self-deception may be possible, but the social analogue of this is ruled out. Whole groups cannot misunderstand the nature of their actions, and one class could not, it seems, exploit another, while being unaware of the fact. Since, on this view, groups are combinations of individuals, reference to the agency of classes as such, rather than merely of their members, is prohibited.

Weber gives as an example the working of a socialist economy, the members of which may perhaps have a belief in the importance of 'society' and the 'social'. He says that any sociological understanding would have to proceed in terms of the actions of individuals. It could, for example, refer to the types of officials found in it. He continues:

> The real empirical sociological investigation begins with the question: What
> motives determine and lead the individual members and participants in this
> socialistic community to behave in such a way that the community came
> into being in the first place and that it continues to exist?[14]

Sociology, on this understanding, is built on what Schutz calls 'the thought objects constructed by the common-sense thinking of men',[15] and it is in no position to repudiate its foundation. It elucidates the ways ordinary individuals see themselves as interacting in society. These cannot be contrasted with what is actually going on. Because individual consciousness is regarded as the source of society, it cannot be detached from it and be judged by it. Social reality is as it is seen by common sense, since that is what made it. Schutz made this very clear when he wrote:

> By the term 'social reality', I wish to be understood the sum total of objects and occurrences within the social, cultural world as experienced by the common-sense thinking of men living their daily lives among their fellowmen, connected with them in manifold relations of interaction.[16]

Once it is suggested that social reality goes beyond what individuals conceive, the whole function of the social sciences has to change. It always seemed implausible that they were only concerned with understanding individual motives, since this left out of account the sheer complexity of society. Individualist accounts are atomistic. The meaning of actions becomes the meaning given separately to them by individuals acting in isolation from each other. Each separate social happening can then be understood even when it is wrenched from its social setting. This, though, is an impossible view for anyone to take to extremes, since human beings are born into societies and are made by them, as well as making them. Berger and Luckmann themselves can admit, in the same breath as saying that society is a human product, that man is a social product.[17] They argue that we can participate in a social world by playing 'roles'.[18] Just as we expect certain behaviour of a waiter in a restaurant, and a good waiter will fulfil these expectations, all of us fill roles expected of us by others. This is still consonant with individualism, but a strong feeling that society is exerting pressures on us can easily lead to the view that the social cannot be reduced to the individual. The complex reality of society might appear visible only in its entirety. This approach is termed 'holistic', and would be connected with the contextualist view which demands that proper understanding must see the part played by agents in a wider social pattern. Social explanation is then made irreducible to psychological explanation, so that what happens at the one level cannot be understood merely in terms of what happens at another.

CONSTRAINTS ON SUBJECTIVITY

Durkheim provides a good example of someone putting forward a view of society which does indeed explicitly reify it, treating it as totally separate from the minds of its members. He takes as his starting point the feeling that each of us is confronted by something apart from ourselves when we are immersed in society. We are faced with demands and claims that are created by social conditions and are not of our own making. As individuals we are introduced to traditions and ways of living which are seemingly 'there', confronting us as much as the physical world does. The complexity of individual interactions entails that any individual has to cope with a system of demands and expectations. The problem is whether the system can ultimately be understood in terms of the choices and ways of acting of countless individuals, or whether social phenomena can be explained in other terms without changing the subject.

Many dualists vehemently object to individual actions being explained totally in neurophysiological terms. While recognizing that brains are indispensable, they refuse to accept that as the whole story: reference to the brain is necessary but not sufficient for the explanation of human action. Dualists would argue that the mental is irreducible to the physical, and an understanding of, say, the intentions of someone getting married could not be explained in terms of electrical activity in the brain. This is analogous to the argument about society and individuals. Indeed, it is a continuation of it, since there are those (as we shall see) who would like to explain the complex arrangements of society in terms of the activity of individual brains. To do so they have to ignore both the protests of the dualists, and the arguments of those who do not in the first place wish to reduce the social level to that of the individual. The latter would argue that questions about the significance of marriage are not simply questions about the attitude of individuals to marriage, because marriage is a social institution with its own rules and functions and, as such, cannot be fully explained in terms of the motives and thoughts of individuals.

Indeed, the role played by an institution in society may be so complex that it is not fully understood by any individual. Individuals are introduced to the institution, rather than perpetually re-creating it through their own thoughts and understanding. Berger and Luckmann's view of marriage as an ongoing human production would be seen by some as woefully inadequate. Just as we need brains to think, social institutions cannot exist without members. The individual provides a necessary condition for the existence of society. That may not mean, however, that a proper understanding of society can be gained through studying individuals, even if we take into account the effects of their interaction with each other. Society may provide a distinct level of explanation.

One illustration of this is the family. Is that constituted by society or by the motives and wishes of individuals? An answer to this by some is linked to the understanding of social rules which we have encountered in Wittgenstein. It is holistic in emphasis, explaining the family in social terms. David Rubinstein puts it this way:

> The family is constituted by the rules that obtain in a given society. The biological uncle may be the social father if societal rules establish him to be. The social scientific definition of the father must therefore be tied to the rules of the society under study. . . . As there is no game of chess apart from its rules, there is no family, in the social sense, apart from the rules that constitute it.[19]

The rules are grounded in ways of life, and they may be imperfectly understood by some individuals. The existence of the institution with its public rules gives meaning to actions, whatever the inward thoughts of participants may be. The argument would be that it is the existence of institutions, like marriage, that gives individual actions their social significance. Indeed, they give actions the only significance they can have. Two people are not married just because they regard themselves as being. Saying 'I do' in accepting marriage vows means nothing outside the proper institutional setting. Even a wedding rehearsal is not a wedding. Abstracting such an institution from its social background is, in fact, to destroy it. The proponents of this position could argue that the casual arrangements often made whereby a couple live together with regard only to their own private wishes does not so much modify previous understandings of marriage; rather, it begins to undermine the social institution, and hence eventually the nature of our society itself.

This approach appears to break sharply with emphases on the role of individual consciousness, but both share an important feature. If the source of meaning is the individual, this reduces the significance of external contingencies. Human nature seems irrelevant. The same conclusion can be drawn when society is made the focus of meaning. No greater scope is given to human nature, and society seems as unconstrained as the individual. A constant danger for a phenomenological approach is that, in stressing the importance of the individual subject, it lapses into a position which makes all judgements valid for the person making them. It finds itself embroiled in a rampant subjectivism which could easily turn into solipsism, according to which I am trapped in my own world. It is difficult even to state such a position clearly, since it is almost impossible consistently to assume that other people exist only in so far as I believe that they do. If 'my world' and 'the world' are coextensive, I can never be mistaken, since there is nothing objective with which my judgements can be compared. Other people do not then really exist. It is all too easy to lapse into the position of the old lady who wrote to a famous philosopher saying that she was so convinced of the truth of solipsism that she could not understand why other people did not agree with her.

In view of this, the step from individual to society as the source of meaning might seem a natural one to take. Whether it solves the underlying problem is another matter. Many positions try to mediate between the apparently stark alternatives of individual or society. Some stress the importance of 'symbolic interaction' between minds and the meanings found in human societies. The individual consciousness is thus not completely isolated, but interacts with others to form society, while being itself a product of society. One account of this position says that 'society is to be understood in terms of the individuals making it up and individuals are to be understood in terms of the societies of which they are members'.[20] A drawback of this type of compromise is that it is very easy for it to favour one or other of the alternatives. Symbolic interactionism does try to avoid the dilemma that behaviour is caused either by forces internal to an individual, such as instincts, or by social forces impinging from outside. Yet we are told that it emphasizes 'the social origins of the self and human nature'. Thus in the end it appears to devalue the position of the individual and ignore the possible contribution of human nature.

Once this step has been taken, and due note made of the way in which society moulds us, it is easy to locate meaning in the rules of a society and to deny that an individual can be abstracted from the context. Everything that makes us what we are and gives sense to our lives, it will be said, comes from our society. A baby chimpanzee does not need to be initiated into a society in the way that a human baby does. It seems to follow that an individual even gains his or her own identity in the context of society. A strong emphasis on the social will suggest that the self is created by society, so that society cannot be made by individuals. Individuals are created by society. Even our concept of an individual, it will be emphasized, is created by our society, and may indeed have emerged in particular historical conditions. The same arguments apply to our concept of human nature. The very notion might seem to have been produced in society. Human nature cannot therefore have created society, because society would have formed our ideas of human nature.

Only if it is accepted that society is much more than a conglomeration of individuals can the category of the social be given prominence. Emile Durkheim certainly accepted this and says firmly: 'Social phenomena must be considered in themselves, detached from the conscious beings who form their own mental representations of them.'[21] He explicitly contradicts those who locate the origins of society in the consciousness of the individual, and stresses the priority of the social with an emphasis on 'social facts'. He says that they are 'like moulds into which we are forced to cast our actions'.[22] He talks of 'external coercion' and takes as an example what happens in a gathering when there is an outburst of collective emotion.[23] This is a well-known phenomenon. We may be gripped by the fervour of an election rally or of a football match. Representatives may be swayed by a feeling of common purpose when a difficult matter is discussed in a parliament or a synod. Many know that being caught up in a crowd can produce startling results, and individuals behave collectively as they would not if they were each on their own. Sometimes the mood can become ugly, and the crowd demands what the decent individuals composing it would not normally tolerate. At other times, a collective purpose can extort nobler behaviour than any of the individuals involved thought themselves capable of. Yet the problem remains the same, whatever the occasion. Durkheim maintains: 'The group thinks, feels and acts differently from the way its members would if they were isolated.'[24] This illustrates his belief that 'society is not the mere sum of individuals' but instead forms a specific reality.

Once this position is adopted, the consciousness of the individual becomes merely the reflection of society. Human nature cannot be considered of primary importance, since that could only operate in the first instance through individuals. Explanations in terms of human nature are invariably rivals to those which invoke society. Durkheim not surprisingly rejects the idea that psychical states can be the causes of social phenomena. In asserting the 'given' nature of society, he not only discards the idea of the priority of the individual consciousness but also criticizes all accounts rooting society in human nature.

Although the social epitomizes the human for many thinkers, the idea of human nature is often anathema to them. It seems fixed and unalterable and, as such, appears irrelevant as an explanation for the many different forms of human society. Faced with a wealth of human differences, appeals to one human nature seem irrelevant. Yet the differences may be more apparent than real, since we may too easily take for granted our similarities and become obsessed with our differences. However that may be, cultural differences are a fact, and any theory in the social sciences has to take account of them. Whether the differences can be explained is controversial, and the easy way out will be to accept them as ultimate, so that each society has to be seen in its own terms. Wittgenstein maintains that we ought not to look for explanations but ought merely to say that 'this language-game is played'.[25]

Durkheim is impressed by cultural differences and resists the temptation to explain them in terms of human nature. He may accept that human nature helps to set the scene for human social life, but it will not be relevant, he considers, in explaining even fairly constant phenomena in human social life. For example, religion seems well-nigh universal in human societies, or so it is claimed. Family relationships often seem of fundamental importance to human life. Is marriage really a mere product of particular societies and not related to basic pre-social needs? Questions concerning religion, marriage and the nature of the family constantly recur in accounts of what constitutes human social life. Durkheim explicitly rejects any suggestion that they are the product of innate tendencies in individuals:

> It has been held that a certain religiosity is innate in man, as is a certain minimum of sexual jealousy, filial piety, or fatherly affection etc., and it is in these that explanations have been sought for religion, marriage and the family. But history shows that these inclinations, so far from being inherent in human nature, are either completely absent under certain social conditions, or vary so much from one society to another that the residue left after eliminating all these differences . . . is reduced to something vague and schematic. Thus these sentiments result from the collective organization and are far from being at the basis of it.[26]

It may seem that Durkheim is at least partly making an empirical point. Perhaps some societies do not possess religious belief, and perhaps their family arrangements are so utterly different from ours as to be virtually non-existent. Yet at this juncture we must begin to wonder at what point a society is so different from ours that our concepts cannot apply. At some point cultural divergence must be so complete that talking of 'religion' or 'families' or 'fathers' as we understand these terms becomes totally inappropriate. Societies that are so utterly different from each other would not have enough in common to enable the beginnings of mutual understanding. Indeed, because of their differences from us, it would just be true by definition that they do not possess 'religion' or 'families' as we understand these terms. It seems that, once the concept of human nature is abandoned, the task of understanding other societies becomes enormous.

NOTES

1 Case quoted in Richard Passingham, *The Human Primate*, 1982, p. 181.
2 Ibid., p. 188.
3 Alfred Schutz, *Collected Papers*, Vol. I, *The Problem of Social Reality*, 1962, p. 56.
4 Max Weber, *Theory of Social and Economic Organization*, 1947, p. 80.
5 Schutz, *Collected Papers*, Vol. II, *Studies in Social Theory*, p. 85.
6 David Rubinstein, *Marx and Wittgenstein*, 1981, p. 70.
7 P. Berger and T. Luckmann, *The Social Construction of Reality*, 1967, p. 107.
8 Ibid., p. 146.
9 Ibid., p. 78.
10 Ibid., p. 73.
11 T. Luckmann, *Life-World and Social Realities*, 1983, p. 179.
12 Ibid., p. 162.
13 Weber, *Theory of Social and Economic Organization*, p. 92.
14 Ibid., p. 97.
15 Schutz, *Collected Papers*, Vol. I, p. 59.
16 Ibid., p. 53.
17 Berger and Luckmann, *The Social Construction of Reality*, p. 79.
18 Ibid., p. 91.
19 Rubinstein, *Marx and Wittgenstein*, p. 37.
20 See B. N. Meltzer, J. W. Petras, L. T. Reynolds, *Symbolic Interactionism, Genesis, Varieties, Criticism*, 1975, p. 2.
21 Emile Durkheim, *The Rules of Sociological Method*, 1982, p. 70.
22 Ibid., p. 70.
23 Ibid., p. 56.
24 Ibid., p. 129.
25 Wittgenstein, *Philosophical Investigations*, I, § 654.
26 Durkheim, *The Rules of Sociological Method*, p. 131.

4

Understanding Other Societies

Philosophical views which demand that we start with the products of the individual consciousness raise questions about how we can understand each other. A dualist view of mind and matter naturally gives rise to the so-called 'problem of other minds'. Holistic views starting with some idea of society as prior meet an analogous problem. How can we understand the members of societies which are very different from our own? Both positions stress the distinctiveness of the human, and in so doing are paradoxically quick to dismiss appeals to human nature. Those who stress the importance of consciousness do not wish it to be constrained by anything extraneous, while those who emphasize the priority of the social feel that appeals to human nature explain little. It seems as though consciousness is not to be explained further, whether it produces society or is produced by it. This is not surprising, since neither position would welcome any reductionist programme. Those wishing to stress the importance of the individual mind, and those who stress the significance of the society into which we are born, are both united in resisting explanations in naturalist terms. They do not want the social sciences to become a branch of physics or of biology; they agree that the social sciences are radically different from the physical sciences. Social reality is utterly distinct from physical reality, so that, whether it is constituted by the thoughts of individuals or has a life of its own, it is bound up with meanings and human consciousness. Man is thus more than an animal.

This comes out very clearly in the early writings of Karl Marx, which, it is sometimes alleged, are more 'humanistic' than his later work. He inveighs against workers becoming mere commodities. In talking about 'alienation' he protests against the way in which the products of labour can seem to confront the worker as a 'power independent of the producer'.[1] People can become slaves to what they have produced. We are told that 'the more the worker externalizes himself in his work, the more powerful becomes the alien, objective world that he creates opposite himself, the poorer he becomes himself in his inner life and the less he can call his own.' The workers' products exist outside them in a way that even becomes a threat. Man's work is alienated from man, and his free activity, which, Marx considers, is what distinguishes man from animals, is distorted so that 'man makes his vital activity and essence a mere means to his existence'. The significant feature is that Marx has a definite view of human consciousness as what makes the distinction between human beings and animals. He says that 'free conscious activity is the species-characteristic of man'. Alienation means that man can no longer express his true nature as a free and active producer.

This emphasis on the importance of consciousness perhaps reveals the influence of idealist theories of Marx. However that may be, he makes human consciousness the mark of the species. However much man is forced to live in a way that is not true to his 'species-being', the fact remains that man should be free. His work, Marx believes, should be his own free expression and not be torn from him as a mere means towards his physical existence. My work no longer belongs to me when I am forced into an alien activity. Only free production as an end in itself can confirm man as a 'conscious species-being'.

Nevertheless this Marxian emphasis on consciousness should not be interpreted as a covert emphasis on the individual. Marx tries to abolish the dichotomy between individual and society. He denies that society is a 'fixed abstraction opposed to the individual', because he believes that individuals are social beings.[2] He refers to a particular individual as 'the subjective existence of society as something thought and felt'.[3] Thus society and individuals cannot be separated from one another in any futile argument about which comes first: 'as society produces man as man, so it is produced by man'.[4] The outcome is that the dependence of society on man is stressed at the same time as it is recognized that man is his true self only in a social context. Even when we are not engaged in communal enterprises, all that we do is, as Marx put it, 'a manifestation and confirmation of social life'.[5]

Once it is accepted that man is a social being who cannot be understood apart from his social context, understanding individuals entails understanding the society of which they are a part. We have seen how Wittgenstein's view of rules involves an emphasis on the public and the social. Like Marx, he does not oppose the individual to society, arguing that one or the other is prior. He brings the two together by suggesting that an individual can only be understood in a social context. Despite their manifest differences, Marx and Wittgenstein have sometimes been compared in this respect. Both appear to stress that social practices provide the essential context for understanding ideas. One writer comments that for both 'the social level of explanation is irreducible'.[6] Such a remark highlights the fact that this kind of position is inevitably opposed to an atomistic understanding of the individual as source of meaning. Its stress on the social nature of the individual ensures that meaning can only be found at the level of social practice.

In the case of Wittgenstein, the comparison of the rules of society with those of games gives rise to the question of understanding. When we are embedded in the rules of one society, how can we hope to grasp those of another? Wittgenstein's coupling of meaning and use implies that if we are not able to use a word in a particular context ourselves we cannot hope to understand its meaning. Understanding seems to entail participation in a society. The great danger is that we encounter an unfamiliar society and assume it is just like our own. We then proceed to interpret its practices in our terms and assume they will fit exactly.

Marriage is a good example, since this is certainly something which anthropologists look for in strange societies. I have already remarked that marriage is a social institution, and that two people cannot be married just because they see themselves as married: the society has to recognize the fact. Nevertheless it is important that individuals have some idea of what is taking place. Social institutions do not normally exist when no one in the society is aware of them. Whatever room we may wish to leave for the phenomenon of false consciousness, it cannot be easily applied to something like marriage. Animals may mate and can stay together for life, but we should hesitate to call that marriage. They do not understand the significance of what they are doing, and in fact it has no social significance. Human marriage is embedded in society, but this does not mean that the marriage partners can be oblivious of the institution. The rules may be public rather than private but participants must understand *what* they are doing. Just as the players of a game do not do so blindly and accidentally but must have some grasp of the rules, the same applies to participants in a social practice.

Peter Winch has argued for the distinctiveness of social science from natural science by emphasizing these points. He contends that a historian or sociologist of religion 'must himself have some religious feeling if he is to make sense of the religious movement he is studying and understand the considerations which govern the lives of its participants'.[7] He refers to this as a 'common-sense consideration', but it is in fact highly controversial. It suggests that atheists and agnostics cannot study religion because they cannot make sense of it. However that may be, Winch insists that any reflective understanding of a society depends on an understanding of how participants understand what is occurring. The one is built on the other.

The argument that meaningful behaviour is rule-governed and that rules are rooted in social life leaves out the question whether the participants understand the rules. The temptation will be to say that, if they follow the rules, they understand them. Yet is there a difference between a couple marrying in accordance with the practice in their society and marrying because of an understanding of that practice? Behaviourist philosophers would say nothing more needs to be added. Dualists will distinguish between private understanding and public practice, even if the latter must ultimately be defined in terms of other people's private understanding.

These reflections are important when we examine what it means to understand another society. Even if this involves understanding that society's rules, the question arises whether this is achieved by observing behaviour or by understanding what the rules mean to the participants. Wittgenstein's strictures against private languages would make many hesitate to adapt Weber's notion of *Verstehen*, since that would seem to suggest that each individual's consciousness is private. Winch insists that 'the concepts in terms of which we understand our own mental processes and behaviour have to be learned, and must, therefore, be *socially* established'.[8] This means that 'private' understanding of social rules is, in fact, dependent on public criteria. Thus reference to the understanding of a participant does not undermine the emphasis on the social. Admitting that individuals differ from animals in having understanding need not entail a dualist approach. The public world still has priority, and 'private understanding' need not involve reference to private mental processes.

The dualist is unlikely to be satisfied by this. The emphasis on public criteria for understanding a rule forces us back to the position that consistently acting in accordance with the rule *is* understanding it. We would refuse to accept that those who went against the rule understood it, or, at least, their breaking of the rule would have to be *prima facie* evidence that they did not understand it. Yet it seems plausible that rule-breakers know whether they are acting intentionally or not.

To return to the example of marriage, the mere fact that a couple marries in accordance with the rules of their society leaves some questions unanswered. Do they themselves make sense of the rule, or just blindly act in accordance with it because of the coercion of society? No doubt in a very settled society there would be one institution of marriage and one understanding of it. In a very complex society, like those comprising modern industrial nations, there may be many different understandings of the one institution. Some will have a Christian view of marriage, as vows for life made in the sight of God. Others will regard it as a purely legal contract to be terminated if either of the partners wishes. Some will have little reflective understanding of what they are doing, and merely do what is conventional. Those who are more reflective may well disagree. Some will see marriage as particularly designed for the protection of women, while others will regard it as a method, designed by men, for enslaving women. It seems implausible to suggest that there are different institutions for each of these groups. Indeed, one of the troubles is that a single institution is being given different, and incompatible, functions. There may be different views of marriage, but there are not different marriage practices in Western society.

Some may question this and wonder whether those who enter into a series of marriages, divorcing their partners at regular intervals, are not changing the nature of marriage. If enough members of a society begin to treat marriage as a temporary legal arrangement rather than a solemn undertaking broken only by death, it may well be that the institution of marriage will change. Saying this, though, suggests that institutions do depend on the understanding of their participants to such an extent that, if the latter changes, then eventually so will the former. The rules will be changed to take account of the changed understanding and thus cannot be thought logically prior to that understanding.

PUBLIC PRACTICE AND PRIVATE UNDERSTANDING

Discussion of institutions such as marriage may be complicated by the suggestion that, despite appearances, there is more than one society in a country such as England. The mere existence of one set of legal rules may cloak the fact that there are many different forms of life coexisting. Each may have its own rules for, and its own understanding of, the institution of marriage. In other words, there may be several different institutions of marriage within the same nation. This only serves to raise the question how different ways of life, or cultures, with different social practices, can be identified. For an anthropologist visiting a geographically isolated tribe, it may be reasonable to see the tribe as a unit. A modern state which comprises citizens of many different backgrounds and beliefs provides more of a problem. Is it one society or many? Sometimes reference is made to a pluralist society. According to some definitions of a society, that is bound to be a contradiction in terms. One society cannot encompass practitioners of many different religions and of none. In Wittgenstein's sense of the term, they would belong to different forms of life, basing their lives on different sets of agreed judgements and possessing different concepts. Yet they all live together under one legal system and, perhaps not surprisingly, experience tensions.

The problem confronting us, however, is a strictly conceptual one. What counts as a society? Tension between black and white, Muslim and Hindu, or Protestant and Catholic may be a symptom of different societies clashing. It may equally be an example of groups of like-minded individuals clashing with other groups in the same society. What criteria can we appeal to in order to settle this? The concept of a society is complex, but Wittgenstein's emphasis on agreement in judgements would mean that basic disagreements are an indication of clashes between societies. The scientist will belong to one society with one set of assumptions; the believer in oracles to another. The Christian has one society, the atheist another. Once we begin to identify societies in this way, it is obvious that many overlap. Some scientists will be Christian and others atheist. Every time a new basic disagreement appears, we can go on multiplying societies, assuming that we can identify 'basic' disagreements, which presumably involve a clash of conceptual schemes. Some atheist scientists will believe in marriage as a lifelong bond, and others will not. Some Christians may countenance divorce, and others will not. It is difficult to know where to stop once this process is started. Every issue on which different groups cannot reach agreement seems to raise the question whether we are encountering a fresh form of life.

Is a disagreement a matter of two groups sharing the same concepts but contradicting each other, or does something occur analogous to the incommensurability of scientific theories? In the latter case, different concepts are applied and the parties to the dispute do not so much disagree as talk past each other, because they are members of different societies, each of which has its own standards of truth and falsity. In fact, if we accept that apparently insoluble disagreement is a criterion of different forms of life, we shall eventually arrive at a situation where forms of life contain only one person. Everyone disagrees with everyone else on something. The class of Christian, conservative scientists who are against divorce can no doubt be distinguished from atheist, radical non-scientists who see nothing wrong in it. Such classes can easily be further subdivided, with Christian non-scientists, and conservative atheists, not to mention new issues arising to complicate things still further.

If we refuse to start on this slippery slope down to subjectivism and even solipsism, we have to accept that one society can comprise individuals who disagree very firmly with others in the same society. The definition of a society will not, then, include the condition that there be agreement on basic issues. The sharing of concepts will not depend on a unanimity of view. Judgements about what is true will be separated from the social background against which they are made. Personal understanding of social institutions cannot then be identified with the way they work. People may even follow the rules while disagreeing with them. They can marry while not really believing in marriage as an institution. When this happens, however, a society is in trouble. If private understanding and belief begin to diverge from public practice, the practices themselves will eventually be changed.

Wittgenstein's emphasis on the public and the social is more plausible as a description of a settled society, and is not so well designed to explain how societies can develop and change. Like Kuhn's account of scientific theories, it runs into trouble at precisely the point at which one theory is superseded by another or a society is fundamentally changed. The stress on holism ensures that all fundamental change has to be revolutionary. There has to be a massive upheaval when one system is superseded by another, with gradual transactions ruled out. All such change must be catastrophic, one way of living being replaced by another. There may be a period in which an earlier way of life comes to mean less and less to its participants. For instance, strongly held religious beliefs become watered down, yet the form of the religion remains after the content has gone. In the same way Kuhn believes that anomalies in a theory will begin to pile up. In the end, however, the change is a revolutionary one and the previous system is destroyed. This is inevitable if all explanation is in terms of societies or systems of one kind or another, since the only way of changing a whole system is by putting another in its place.

Issues about the definition of a society or a community are not of mere academic importance, because there are times when that can have marked social consequences. It is no doubt implausible to pretend that scientists really form a homogeneous community in any sense, whatever some philosophers of science might say. Yet those concerned with race relations often talk of 'community relations' and run the risk of reifying communities which are in fact far from internally homogeneous. An example is provided by the position of Pakistanis in Britain, who are sometimes grouped together in the minds even of well-meaning promoters of good race relations. Pakistan is a young country and its population spans five main ethnic groups. One commentator suggests:

> Those who speak of a Pakistani ethnicity are misinterpreting their experi-
> ence of individual contexts and specific situations by stressing cultural dif-

ferences between the British and Pakistani populations. They ignore the internal differentiation of the Pakistani population.[9]

Pakistanis can, in fact, be classified together only on the basis of religion or of a nationality which many of them only acquired when they were already adults. To term them a community or to imagine them constituting an identifiable society is highly misleading. What is happening is that the resident English population fairly arbitrarily imagine a group of immigrants to form the 'Pakistani community', and even hope that they can deal with 'community leaders'. The classification is made more on the basis of their difference from English people than similarity among themselves. Saifullah Kahn writes that 'although Pakistanis in Britain do not perceive the population of their fellow nationals as a community (in the sense of a group of people with common identification, values and perspective, who interact with each other and have common associations and leaders) they become aware over time of how outsiders see them.' External pressures may eventually force them to see themselves as a distinct community, even though that was originally far from the truth. The way other people see us will affect the way we see ourselves, and our own self-understanding will govern our behaviour. The paradox is that, although sociological definitions may be inaccurate, they may none the less have real consequences in society through their influence on how individuals see themselves. If individuals are made to feel members of a separate community, they will act accordingly.

Once it is accepted that communities, institutions and social practices do not provide the sole context of social explanation, we see that individual understanding is also important. Changes will not come at the level of systems without operating through individuals. If enough people's understanding of an institution like marriage is changed, the institution itself will be changed. Conversely, the change of an institution will be pointless unless the attitudes of the individuals who participate in it also change. Even if the institution of marriage were abolished by political action, people might still want to commit themselves publicly to each other, if they continued to believe in it. Political revolutions often do not achieve all they are intended to for precisely this kind of reason. The system may have been apparently changed but the individuals involved in it may not have.

Winch tries to make several different distinctions simultaneously. One example he gives is the following:

A historian of art must have some aesthetic sense if he is to understand the problems confronting the artists of his period; and without this he will have left out of his account precisely what would have made it a history of *art*, as opposed to a rather puzzling external account of certain motions which certain people have been perceived to go through.[10]

He thus wishes to distinguish the understanding of human activity from 'the natural scientist's understanding of his scientific data'. This puts him squarely on the side of someone like Weber criticizing positivism. Human action cannot merely be observed in a detached, scientific way. To understand its significance we have to see the situation from the point of view of a participant. We cannot conflate the reasons a participant has for an action with the causes as seen by a scientist. The 'internal' and 'external' perspectives should not be confused, and genuine social explanations, according to Winch, lie with the internal one.

However, Winch also wishes to combine the *Verstehen* approach with a Wittgensteinian account of concepts. The 'internal' perspective turns out to be irreducibly social, rooted in modes of social life. It appears to follow that this kind of perspective does not so much involve seeing a situation from the point of view of an individual as participating in a society. The emphasis has swung from the individual to society, and *Verstehen* is turned into the need to participate in whatever society is being studied. Yet all Winch said about the need for an aesthetic sense seemed to demand not participation in social practices but the kind of empathy which a more individualist theory would demand.

Much of the attraction of Winch's theory lies in his insistence that knowledge of society is nothing like knowledge of physical regularities. The latter leaves out of account the meaning agents give to their activities. Yet once the emphasis drifts away from individuals to societies, and from the subjective to the publicly verifiable, a similar gap threatens to open again. The scientist may study observable behaviour and leave out of account what Winch himself refers to as 'the participant's unreflective understanding'.[11] The study of social rules in a form of life still leaves precisely this out of account. Despite his apparent endorsement of *Verstehen*, he seems to have removed its very possibility.

Winch would reply that this is to ignore the importance of Wittgenstein's argument concerning a private language, according to which private meanings have to be excluded. This is to rule out by definition the point of view of a participant in a practice, except in so far as it merely reflects the practice. Such a conclusion follows from the verificationist bias built into the position, favouring the publicly accessible over the private. The shadow of positivism lingers even in the work of the later Wittgenstein. The exclusion of the private, or at least its dismissal as irrelevant for the formation of concepts, is arbitrary, and fails to do justice to the basic features of human experience. The concept of pain, for example, which Wittgenstein uses as an example, may certainly depend on public criteria if it is to be properly taught.[12] We can learn that pain is the kind of reaction we normally feel in particular situations. Nevertheless what that feels like depends on personal experience, and the phenomenal quality of the private sensation of pain is fundamental for understanding the concept. We cannot apply the concept properly unless we recognize what the sensation is like. For this reason, those who are congenitally insensitive to pain and have never felt it are unable to grasp the meaning of the concept. It is no use their concluding from the fact that they are in the same circumstances as normal people that they must be feeling pain. They are not if they do not feel a definite kind of sensation, just as a colour-blind person does not see red.

Shared public concepts may need public criteria for their application, but we should not ignore the reality and importance of private mental events. The association of concepts and language has been particularly pernicious. Private mental experiences seem otiose if concepts are identified with the use of words. Yet this involves the identification of thought and language which even suggests that animals and infants can have no determinate experience merely because they lack linguistic competence.[13] It assumes that they cannot recognize what they cannot talk about. This leaves unexplained how language is learnt in the first place, since, without some prior ability to perceive objects as the same again, we would not be able to learn when the use of words is appropriate and when it is not. Being taught the use of words by means of public criteria itself presupposes an ability to recognize things in the world in the same way as our teachers. Learning language becomes very problematic without this. Because people totally blind from birth cannot see colours, for example, their group of colour terms is bound to be somewhat tenuous. They may understand that green is the colour of grass, but will not be able to grasp *what* colour that is or even understand the nature of colour. Private experience cannot be ignored in the teaching of language, since language presupposes it.

Winch's attack on the view that the scientific observation of behaviour can give a proper understanding of human action is a distinct issue from the argument about public and private languages. It deals with a problem which remains even if we are reluctant to treat social explanation as irreducible to the explanation of individual behaviour. The dichotomy between public and private, and the associated distinction between social and individual, must not be confused with that between a scientific view

of a society and the viewpoint of its participants. The problem of interpretation still arises, whether one is trying to understand an alien society
as a whole or its individual members. Doctrines of forms of life set up
self-contained societies with their own conceptual schemes which are
distinct from those of the outsider. They thus preach conceptual
relativism, and such schemes are apparently made unintelligible to non-
participants by definition. Yet a problem remains if we see our task as
one of understanding individuals with strange beliefs. How do we avoid
the charge of ethnocentricity or parochialism, of judging others in terms
of our own concepts? It is always a great temptation to do so. Some
would say that we can do nothing else. The snag is that there is a suspicion that in doing so we must actually falsify what we are studying.

UNDERSTANDING ALIEN PRACTICES

An anthropologist may wish to study different forms of marriage in
human societies. It should be obvious that there are different forms of
association between men and women in different places. Lifelong
monogamy is not the only pattern. One may take a series of husbands or
wives, and in some non-Western societies one husband can take several
wives. In some circumstances, a woman could have more than one husband. The question is whether it is right to talk of 'marriage' or even of
'husbands' and 'wives' in contexts which may be so radically different
from our own. Can our concepts be used to refer to other societies
without taking into account the participants' understanding of what they
are doing? We may seem to be restricting the term 'marriage' unduly, if
we apply it only to monogamous relationships. Why cannot a man be
married to more than one woman? If we deny that is genuine marriage,
we may be presupposing one particular understanding of marriage which
may not be universally shared. Yet all bonds between men and women
may not count as marriage even if they are sanctioned by a group or
society. Some societies make distinctions between wives and official con-
cubines. An alternative danger is that an anthropologist may decide that
marriage is universal before examining particular societies, and may
assume that in each society it is merely a question of deciding which relations between the sexes are to be termed 'marriage'. It is hardly surprising if the consequence is that anthropological investigation appears to
establish that marriage occurs in every society.

   If we concentrate on the beliefs of the participants in a society, we may
find, assuming that we are able to interpret them, that the participants
have a concept for a bond between a man and a woman blessed by the

ancestral spirits. How would we settle whether that is equivalent to marriage or not? Let us assume they call this bond 'gamage'. Is 'gamage' to
be translated 'marriage'? One obvious difficulty is the question of the
ancestral spirits. The anthropological report of 'gamage' cannot involve
any ontological claims about spirits, and saying that a ceremony of
'gamage' took place cannot mean that the ancestral spirits did bless a
particular union. The participants may believe that, but the anthropologist presumably does not. Yet, if 'gamage' does mean to participants
that spirits blessed the union, are we to conclude that 'gamage' never
actually takes place in the society, even though the participants thought it
did? At this point the attraction should be obvious of a form of conceptual relativism, which relates concepts to their social background and
refuses to allow external standards of truth and falsity. Anthropologists
are reluctant to march into a society, quickly expose the ignorance and
superstition supposedly to be found there, and march out again, their job
done. There seems a lack of any real understanding of what is actually
going on, and it looks as if all that has been shown is that the natives do
not think like the anthropologists. There is too, it must be admitted,
something of a post-imperialist reaction in all this. Anthropologists are
very reluctant to make adverse judgements about societies different from
our own, in the commendable belief that it shows a misplaced arrogance
and intolerance.

One example of this is the following:

> Religions re-state and then reveal to people the 'true' nature of Nature. By
> 'true' here is meant 'culturally true'. Thus religion may tell a person that a
> certain kind of animal is sacred and must not be killed or eaten; or in parts
> of South America, it may insist that good crops occur only when the spirits
> of the ancestors so wish it, and the spirits have to be approached with
> reverence and ritual before planting seeds.[14]

By restricting the notion of truth to a culture in this way, we are not
involved in making embarrassing judgements about the value of some
beliefs. Yet it is clear that by 'culturally true' is meant nothing more than
that the members of that particular culture believe certain things to be
true. The concept of truth is again being reduced to what is held true.
This can only be done by repudiating a realist notion of truth, since the
question of objective truth cannot be brushed aside if things are either
the case or they are not, whatever people happen to believe. It is not surprising that anthropologists can easily start talking of how the members
of different cultures inhabit different worlds. A relativist view of truth
inevitably leads to a view of reality being created by people's conception

of it. Different systems of belief then inevitably entail different realities.

We might well wonder how social anthropologists can do their work if there are so many different realities. The reality of professional anthropologists would clearly be different from the realities of the various cultures they wish to study. This is another instance of the problem which arose in connection with the sociology of knowledge, namely that of reflexivity. If all societies create their own realities, this applies to anthropologists too, or to the wider society to which they belong. In any case, the scientific character of their discipline is in jeopardy, since it becomes merely the reflection of their own construction of reality. It certainly becomes impossible to compare societies. One may compare beliefs, but if these are all trapped in different realities, with different 'cultural truths', access to them and all cross-cultural comparison must be ruled out. Perhaps there is one inclusive reality encompassing the others. This suggestion, though, gives the game away because it allows that there is after all an extra-cultural background against which cultures can be examined and even judged. There has to be, or we could not talk of 'different realities' in the first place. If talking like that was merely a result of the culture of anthropologists and is not meant to tell us about what is actually the case, there is no point in listening to what anthropologists say if we are not already one. Their beliefs are irrelevant and can tell us nothing about 'the world' because *ex hypothesi* there is no such thing.

Real issues are connected with such questions. For example, in nineteenth-century India there was a deliberate practice of killing female babies. This was connected with the Hindu caste system, whereby parents endeavoured to arrange marriages for their daughters which would improve their social position. Unfortunately, though, high-born women could not easily be married to men of lower castes, while Hindu society has little room for unmarried women. As a result many women found themselves in difficulties, needing to marry but not being able to acquire a husband of a suitable social background. Parents, therefore, would prefer sons, and some villages produced twice as many as girls, who were killed at birth.

Reynolds and Tanner, writing from the standpoint of anthropology, say the following about the situation:

> The British administration waged a long campaign against these practices based on the Christian premise that they were no less than murder, without really understanding the Hindu preference for sons, let alone the over-population problem.[15]

The implication of this is that the campaign was a Christian one against Hindus, undertaken without due regard for the way an alien society worked and viewed things. Indirectly the British were attacking the caste system, and even the Hindu religion, without probably having any clear perception of what they were doing. They simply saw what was wrong in Christian terms and tried to stop it, with some success. The problem is whether they had the right, as opposed to the power, to interfere with another culture in this way. It is easy to produce cases like this from the history of the British Empire. It is perhaps no coincidence that its passing has coincided with a growth in the feeling that such interference is misplaced. The confidence of imperialism is replaced by something tantamount to loss of nerve. This is far from being a philosophical point and is precisely the kind of issue likely to be raised by sociologists of knowledge. It may certainly help to explain why philosophical arguments for relativism are readily accepted.

Was the Hindu practice murder, and should it have been stopped? The morality of infanticide from a contemporary standpoint is a separate issue which I shall not discuss. The question is whether, given the belief of the British that infanticide was murder, they were justified in classifying the Hindu practice in that way. Were they justified in treating the killing of an infant girl in a village in Mysore in the same way as an apparently similar killing in a Glasgow slum? Can an action be torn out of its cultural context and treated as if it is in fact very different from the way the agent conceived it? Few would consider it an adequate defence against a charge of infanticide in Western society that the person killing the infant did not see it as murder. There are sad cases of mercy-killing where our sympathies may be aroused, but even there the relevant considerations would be the facts of the case and not just how the agent saw the situation. Why should the fact that it takes place in a different cultural context make a significant difference? This is a genuine question, but suggesting that the social context does matter elevates the notion of a society or a culture to an important position in social explanation. Viewing one culture through the assumptions, or concepts, of another will seem to create major problems of understanding. Reynolds and Tanner imply just this, that the British did not understand, and perhaps because of their Christian background could not. The awkward fact, though, is that Reynolds and Tanner themselves are British and do claim to understand. They are able to give a plausible account of the working of Hindu society. Their reference to the problem of overpopulation in giving reasons for infanticide show that they are willing to give explanations for what occurred which may not have been the ones given by Hindus. It is not clear how far a Hindu would have realized that a preference for sons arose from the working of the caste system. Quite possibly he just did not want daughters without ever fully understanding why.

Anthropological accounts have themselves to depend on an understanding of alien societies, and very often give accounts of the working of those societies in terms which would be unintelligible to the participants. The discipline of anthropology depends on the falsity of cultural relativism. The post-imperialist squeamishness of anthropologists is just that. The problem of how far it is right to interfere with other societies is a moral and not a conceptual question. If, indeed, we are all locked up in our separate societies, unable to see the world in terms other than our own, anthropologists are the very last people to warn us of this. If they do so, they admit that their discipline is engaged in a hopeless enterprise.

Understanding other societies depends on the simple assumption that there are not different realities. Each society confronts the same reality, but may try to deal with it in different ways. The British in India went to considerable pains to work through native rulers and forms of society. They intervened when basic questions about the worth of human life were at stake. Another famous example is that of suttee, a practice in which widows sacrificed themselves on their husband's funeral pyre. Wifely devotion was, and is, venerated by Hindus, and there was no provision, at least in higher castes, for the remarriage of widows. The British attempted to stop the custom by an Act in 1829. The question is whether they were importing the concepts and standards of the England of George IV to an alien and inappropriate context. The fact that it is impossible to translate 'suttee' into English might suggest this. Yet there is something odd about a position which would hold that 'to us it is a suicide which is barely voluntary because forced by social pressure, but to them it is a noble and admirable sacrifice'. There is some truth in that, because of the difference in background belief, but it is impossible to leave it at that. Who sees correctly what is happening? Once anyone starts saying that to us it is the murder of a child but to them it is a religious sacrifice, or to us it is despicable cannibalism but to them a sacred meal, they are treading a dangerous path.

Such people opt out of the need to make moral judgements about what is occurring, but they might consider that as gain. However, they also involve themselves in deep incoherence. They stress the radical nature of cultural differences by spelling them out in an intelligible way. However abhorrent female infanticide might seem, it is perfectly possible to understand why there should be a preference for sons. Even in Western society a wish for a son to carry on a family business is not unknown. Hindus were not acting without an intelligible reason. Similarly the emphasis on wifely devotion might seem somewhat excessive, particularly to modern 'liberated' women, but the idea that a wife should be devoted to her husband is also one that has been found in Western society.

THE BASIS OF UNDERSTANDING OTHER SOCIETIES

Understanding the practice of other societies does very often come down to realizing that there is a common base which they share with us. Humans have similar wants and needs, and strange behaviour can become intelligible when we realize that people like ourselves are reacting to a very different environment. There is also the complication that they may have different beliefs from us about that environment. The key question is whether we are in fact dealing with people like ourselves, or whether society shapes people in such radically different ways that we cannot assume a common human nature.[16] Without any chance of using human nature as a basis for interpreting an alien society, the possibility of understanding and comparing the activities of the members of different societies seems remote. They would be as difficult to understand as those of the alien life forms beloved of modern science fiction. In fact, it is significant that the latter often turn out to be very human after all, even to the extent of mysteriously being able to speak English. Otherwise they would be so far beyond our understanding that it would be impossible to include them in any intelligible story.

Winch recognizes this and takes up with approval Vico's idea of natural law as basis for understanding human history. He quotes Vico as saying that all nations 'keep these three human customs: all have some religion, all contract solemn marriages, all bury their dead'.[17] Thus Winch takes birth, death and sexual relations as what he calls 'limiting notions'. He says:

> The specific forms which those concepts take, the particular institutions in which they are expressed, vary very considerably from one society to another; but their central position within a society's institutions is and must be a constant factor. In trying to understand the life of an alien society, then, it will be of the utmost importance to be clear about the way in which these notions enter into it. The actual practice of social anthropologists bears this out.[18]

Certain typical human desires and tendencies are taken as basic, and we are then entitled to look for points of contact between alien societies and our own. Undoubtedly Winch is right in saying that this is how many anthropologists proceed. Yet my earlier point that those intent on finding forms of marriage in every human society will be certain to find them remains. How can we be sure that in our eagerness to establish points of contact we do not arbitrarily treat as similar institutions that are very different? Must the assumption that humans always 'marry' be a necessary presupposition for the understanding of relations between the sexes in different societies? Winch was perhaps wise to talk of sex rather than marriage. The assumption that the members of another society are like ourselves need not involve the assumption that the institutions of their society correspond to those of our own. They may, but they may not. It is an empirical question whether what we call 'marriage' is to be found in all societies. Nevertheless there will always be some basic human needs and interests which will have to be expressed in one way or another. Men and women will have sexual relations, and these will be regulated in a society.

One distinction between a society and individuals randomly mating with each other is that there will be settled procedures governing contact between the sexes. This is particularly important because of the question of the status of children. Modern methods of birth control may have broken to some extent the correlation between sexual relations and the birth of children, and this has had profound repercussions in some societies. The fact remains that relations between the sexes and the rearing of children both provide a set of constraints which human societies cannot ignore. A society must provide a framework in which such basic needs are met, if it is to be distinguished from a set of individuals arbitrarily interacting with each other. The important point, however, is that because of the basic features of human life, all human societies have to possess a similar framework. Societies can respond to basic human needs in many different ways, but, if they fail to respond, they will not flourish and probably cannot even survive. A society banning sexual intercourse, or killing all its children, is unlikely to last long.

What constitutes a basic human need depends on our view of human nature. Whatever that may be, understanding other societies presupposes an assumption about the universality of human nature. Too much emphasis on the strangeness of alien societies and their inhabitants can result in an inability to interpret what is occurring in them. Kuhn's notion of the incommensurability of scientific theories is not a good model for societies. Saying that each society can only be judged by its own criteria removes the point of studying other societies. We may become dissatisfied with our own society and go to join another, but that should not be the position of an anthropologist doing fieldwork.

It is often used as an argument against conceptual relativism that it makes understanding other societies impossible unless we become participants. We are, either members of a society, seeing everything through the eyes of a participant, or we fail to find it intelligible. This is a telling criticism. Such relativism makes any scientific understanding of cultures impossible, since detached study and comparison of different cultures becomes impossible. Sometimes the stress on fieldwork might almost result in this position, so that absorption in an alien culture could become an end in itself. Yet this criticism may already concede too much, since it assumes that it is possible for a member of one culture to join another and acquire its concepts. Even if it is not thought possible to compare different conceptual schemes, it is taken for granted that one can acquire a fresh scheme. The problem is whether conceptual relativism explains how this is possible. Presumably the way in which we can learn the concepts of our own culture is a model. We are taught them, so why should we not also be taught another set later? We simply adopt a different form of life and learn how to use the appropriate words in an appropriate setting, just as children are taught how to speak their native language. Even this, however, stands in need of explanation. Children may latch on to what is said, but this is precisely because they see what their teacher sees. The child and teacher see the same world in the same way. When people enter an alien culture they must assume that they and the natives also see the same world in the same way. This requirement remains, even if they have abandoned any hope of translating from the native language of their own. Even while consciously trying to learn as a child might who does not already possess a language, they must assume that they are able in some pre-linguistic manner to grasp what the natives are talking about. For example, the visitor can see a cat, without knowing what the natives call it. Thus conceptual relativists may try to undermine all possibility of translation, but they are still forced to rely on the fact that they and the natives share common human reactions to a common, objective world. Otherwise teaching and learning become impossible. Paradoxically, however, this then means that translation is possible after all, since different languages must after all refer to the same world.

A thoroughgoing relativist may wish to resist this argument by denying any basic similarity with the members of another society, whose culture may have conditioned them to see things differently, to act differently, and to divide up the world differently. People within a culture would be similar enough to communicate, but there would be a great divergence between cultures. This is a possibility, but such radical differences would surely not just undermine the possibility of translation between the language of one society and that of the other; it would prohibit participation by anyone in a society that was not their own. If I have been moulded by my society to live in a world constricted by that society, I cannot unmake myself. I am what my society has made me. Although it might appear as if another society could then mould me in another pattern, I could never truly free myself of the influence of my own society. The only conclusion could be that if indeed the conceptual relativists are correct (and that notion of correctness is not a relativist one) we are locked in the culture into which we are born. If it *is* possible to leave one society and to join another, then membership of a society is not the most important fact about people. Their conceptual schemes are not totally conditioned by a society but depend at least in part on their membership of the human race and on the same objective world in which they all find themselves.

SAMOA: AN EXAMPLE

In 1925–6 Margaret Mead spent some months in Samoa, and as a result of researches there into the life of adolescent girls she published *Coming of Age in Samoa*.[19] This proved to be a work of enormous influence within social anthropology and beyond the confines of the discipline, and is still widely read. It purports to be an account of a society in which the stresses of adolescence are avoided. Because these have occurred in Western societies, but not, it is alleged, in the very different environment of the South Pacific, they appear to be induced by culture rather than by biology. This is not only significant for those confronting the specific problem of how to educate young people, but seems to add further support to those who are convinced that culture or 'civilization' rather than biology determines how people behave.

The book was explicitly used to disprove the arguments of those who were at that time emphasizing the importance of biological inheritance in moulding human character. Much attention was then being devoted to the study of 'eugenics', a discipline finally discredited by its association with the racist theories of Nazi Germany. Franz Boas was bitterly opposed to eugenics and set about showing with the resources of cultural anthropology how misguided such views were. He was the major figure in American cultural anthropology when Margaret Mead began her career, and he exercised considerable influence on her. He wrote a foreword to *Coming of Age in Samoa*, concluding with the resounding sentence:

> The results of her painstaking investigation confirm the suspicion long held by anthropologists, that much of what we ascribe to human nature is no more than a reaction of the restraints put upon us by our civilization.[20]

In fact, Margaret Mead went to Samoa in order to demonstrate this as a fact, although we may wonder how she hoped fully to understand a culture she regarded as utterly different from her own, without assuming that she and the natives had something in common. The more different she assumed the teenage girls she met were from herself in their emotional reactions and their view of the world, the more impenetrable their life would be likely to be. She manages to give a confident account of life in American Samoa, while showing it to be radically different from anything experienced in America. There is little doubt that she wanted Samoan life to be different because of philosophical preconceptions about the importance of culture. It is ironic that an ability to understand native girls sufficiently to show how different they were could only depend on an actual underlying similarity. Otherwise understanding and interpretation would have to be ruled out from the beginning. In fact, Margaret Mead appears to have been thoroughly misled about the nature of Samoan life in general and adolescent life in particular. Her account of it certainly paints a picture of an exotic society, as she intended, but at crucial points it seems highly implausible.

Derek Freeman, whose experience in Samoa as an anthropologist far exceeds the few months spent there by Margaret Mead, has presented a devastating attack revealing the deep misconceptions which she acquired about Samoan society.[21] Mead wrote of carefree South Sea Islanders who indulged in promiscuous sexual activity without incurring any harm. Her account seems to owe more to Western fantasies about tropical islands than to actual conditions in Samoa. For instance, she implies that Samoans avoid stress by not becoming too committed to any individual. The life she portrays is one of careless ease, where the anxieties and tensions of civilized society do not arise: 'From the first months of its life, when the child is handed carelessly from one woman's hands to another, the lesson is learned of not caring for one person greatly, not setting high hopes on any relationship.'[22] Freeman, on the other hand, presents evidence which enables him to conclude: 'The primary bond between mother and child is very much a part of the biology of Samoans, as it is of all humans.'[23]

Mead's account of promiscuity among teenagers runs into trouble when it is contrasted with the Samoan cult of virginity. She says that adolescent ambition is 'to live as a girl with many lovers as long as possible and then to marry in one's own village'.[24] Yet virginity was highly prized in pagan Samoa, and the acquiring of a virgin wife was especially desired. This was reinforced by the conversion of Samoans to Christianity in the early nineteenth century. It seems that that the girls' alleged ambitions were likely to be mutually incompatible. No man would readily marry a girl with a reputation for promiscuity. The predominantly Congregationalist London Missionary Society was very active in Samoa. As had happened to Fiji and Tonga, where the missionaries had been Methodist, the conversion of the islanders had made a profound difference to their lives, in some cases making fierce warriors into men of peace. Cannibalism was eradicated. Mead, however, hardly mentions Christianity. Were she to admit its influence, the whole point of her fieldwork would be lost. She wanted to show the differences between a simple, primitive paradise and complicated, civilized society. Were she to admit, even to herself, the fact that Samoans were as strict and sincere in their application of Protestant Christianity to their lives as any American, the whole point of her researches would be lost. She preferred to imagine that pagan Samoa had been left virtually untouched by the missionaries.

Mead was far too sanguine about how easy it was to get to grips with an alien society. She claimed that 'a trained student can master the fundamental structure of a primitive society in a few months'.[25] She believed that it was possible in that time to learn the native language sufficiently to enable her to use it to extract the most intimate details of their private lives from teenage girls who were likely anyway to be shy with foreigners. She did not even live in a Samoan household. When these disadvantages were coupled with the fact that, as a methodological assumption, she was looking for differences from, and not similarities with, American girls, it is hardly surprising that her conclusions must be regarded as dubious. Freeman says: 'I have yet to meet a Samoan who agrees with Mead's assertion that adolescence in Samoan society is smooth, untroubled and unstressed.'[26] This itself is of great importance, since Mead is allegedly depicting the experience of individuals in Samoa. It is scarcely surprising that Freeman maintains that her main conclusions 'are, in reality the figments of an anthropological myth, which is deeply at variance with the facts of Samoan ethnography and history.'[27]

Mead's misreading of Samoan society was undoubtedly encouraged by her belief in what she termed 'the tremendous role played in an individual's life by the social environment'.[28] She placed little reliance on human nature as a basis for understanding, and her researches were used as empirical evidence to show the radical differences that are alleged to exist in humans placed in different cultures. Cultural anthropology was established as a discipline in its own right, freed of the need to be dependent on biology. Freeman explicitly links the final establishment of anthropology as an independent discipline with the results of Mead's researches. He suggests that her findings were a major influence in the exclusion of biology and the acceptance of the absolute priority of culture as a force in the moulding of society. Referring to such 'cultural determinism' as a myth, he says:

> On the basis of Mead's writings, Samoa came to be recognized in intellectual circles and in the social sciences as providing conclusive proof of the cultural determinism central to the Boasian paradigm. . . . So enthusiastically was Mead's vision of Samoa accepted that her conclusions, as they were elaborated by herself and others, gave rise to what has become the most widely promulgated myth of twentieth-century anthropology.[29]

The disproving of Mead's account of Samoan life does not disprove her views about the primacy of culture over nature. Nevertheless her conclusions cannot any longer be used as an example of the magnitude of cultural variations. Her refusal to assume the existence of any universal human nature not only led her into notable errors. It gave the discipline of anthropology an exceedingly precarious basis. Without the assumption of some similarities between humans, any account of their behaviour becomes speculative, and there is no standard by which it can be judged'whether people are likely to be telling the truth or not. It seems highly likely that the teenage girls to whom Margaret Mead spoke gave a highly coloured view of their life which was largely untrue. Mead's adherence to what Freeman calls 'cultural determinism' left her defenceless against this treatment. A believer in the universality of human nature might have been more aware that this is just how such girls might react to a stranger who asked about their sexual activities.

NOTES

1 Karl Marx, *Early Texts*, 1971, p. 135.
2 Ibid., p. 150.
3 Ibid., p. 151.

4 Ibid., p. 149.
5 Ibid., p. 150.
6 Rubinstein, *Marx and Wittgenstein,* p. 180.
7 Winch, *The Idea of a Social Science*, p. 88.
8 Ibid., p. 119.
9 V. Saifullah Kahn, 'Pakistanis in Britain: Perceptions of a Population', *New Community*, 5, 1976, p. 228.
10 Winch, *The Idea of a Social Science*, p. 88.
11 Ibid., p. 89.
12 See my *Pain and Emotion.*
13 See my 'Thought and Language', *Proceedings of the Aristotelian Society*, 79, 1978–9.
14 V. Reynolds and R. Tanner, *The Biology of Religion*, 1983, p. 5.
15 Ibid., p. 55.
16 See my *The Shaping of Man*, 1982.
17 Winch, 'Understanding a Primitive Society', reprinted in his *Ethics and Action*, 1972, p. 47.
18 Ibid., p. 43.
19 Margaret Mead, *Coming of Age in Samoa*, 1928, reprinted 1943.
20 Ibid., p. 6.
21 Derek Freeman, *Margaret Mead and Samoa*, 1983.
22 Mead, *Coming of Age in Samoa*, p. 160.
23 Freeman, *Margaret Mead and Samoa*, p. 201.
24 Mead, *Coming of Age in Samoa*, p. 129.
25 Ibid., p. 14.
26 Freeman, *Margaret Mead and Samoa*, p. 259.
27 Ibid., p. 107.
28 Mead, *Coming of Age in Samoa*, p. 11.
29 Freeman, *Margaret Mead and Samoa*, p. 94.

5

Rationality

The prestige of the physical sciences has not only ensured that the social sciences have tried to adopt their methods. It has also resulted in scientific standards of rationality being assumed to be the only ones. It appears rational to believe whatever science can establish and to dismiss as unscientific and hence irrational belief in anything beyond its scope. This raised problems in the study of 'primitive' societies which are motivated by beliefs that seem thoroughly unscientific. The African Azande are often quoted in this connection. They believe in witches and try to protect themselves against witchcraft. They consult oracles and use magic medicines. Apparently primitive beliefs can live on in more sophisticated Africans. One British Foreign Secretary thought Kwame Nkrumah, first President of Ghana, was fond of birds since he saw cages full of doves at his home. Nkrumah, however, only wished to consult their entrails, particularly before travelling in an aircraft.

This example indicates that any view of such practices which merely embeds them in a particular culture is too simple. Cultures intermingle. 'Superstition' and advanced technology can live side by side. No doubt some may consult birds' entrails before flying by Concorde. Such practices stem from a different background from that of technologically based society and perhaps can best be understood in their original context. In the end, however, we cannot ignore the question whether it is rational for anyone to hold such beliefs. Is a commitment to magic, or a belief in the power of witchcraft, mere superstition? Can we simply dismiss such views as primitive?

Winch is quick to point out that our criteria of rationality derive from the culture to which we belong. When we make the beliefs and practices of another society intelligible to ourselves, we try to make them satisfy our criteria of rationality. He remarks that our culture's conception of rationality 'is deeply affected by the achievements and methods of the sciences'. He goes on to say that it treats 'such things as a belief in magic or the practice of consulting oracles as almost a paradigm of the irrational.'[1] The question seems to be whether we are right to apply the standards of one culture to another. Yet this just raises the spectre of relativism again, since it assumes that cultures are monolithic, and indeed makes a large assumption about the standards of rationality in our 'culture'. It is false, as a matter of sociological observation, that our culture rigorously upholds the austere standards of scientific rationality, at least as understood by the empiricist. The popularity of astrology is hard to explain otherwise. It is even doubtful if science provides the unchallenged standard among those who aspire to rationality. In the heady days of positivism many championed scientific method as capturing the essence of human rationality. Once, however, empiricism is challenged, rationality can no longer remain the monopoly of scientists. The great danger, then, must be that the very possibility of rationality is denied. Many have tried to jettison the idea of rationality, as we have seen, instead of admitting that the methods of the physical sciences might provide too restrictive a model. The fact remains that humans may reason differently from each other, but some merely reason better than others.

The question of rationality challenges the social scientist at two levels. There is the problem of how rational are the people being studied, but there is also the question of the social scientists' own rationality. If scientific rationality is taken as the model, social scientists can both criticize those who fall short of the idea, even if they are quite oblivious of it, and attempt themselves to apply the rationality of science in their explanation of why some societies are so ridden with superstition. Once it is accepted that science merely forms one set of practices alongside others, social scientists are left without any standards for judging a society. This might appear a gain, but the corollary is that their own discipline can no longer claim to embody the application of any kind of rational principle. The aftermath of positivism can produce a paralysing nihilism. Understanding, instead of causal explanation, may seem to be the new goal of science, but mere understanding is of questionable value.

This is brought out particularly in some manifestations of what is called 'ethnomethodology', which studies everyday activities. When scientific pretensions are removed, all that seems to be left for a social scientist is to describe how participants in a society view their activities. The repudiation of causal accounts of how societies gain their character and the consequent distrust of any notion of rational standards allow little but the description of the varying viewpoints to be found and the recognition that the viewpoint of the social scientist provides one such example. Ethnomethodologists uphold a policy of what they term 'ethnomethodological indifference', and when they study what they term the 'formal structures' of everyday activities they restrict themselves to the task of describing members' accounts.[2] The point of their 'indifference' is that they wish to abstain in their study of such phenomena 'from all judgements of their adequacy, value, importance, necessity, practicality, success or consequentiality'. In other words, ethnomethodologists do not want to import any of their own assumptions about rationality into their descriptions.

Other writers on ethnomethodology say firmly that it 'treats social science as one more reality among the many'.[3] They criticize social science on the grounds that it 'distorts other realities because it views them only through the lenses of its own system'. Once again we must note the incoherence involved in talking of 'many realities'. Presumably if there *are* many realities we are forced to envisage one reality including them all. Just as crucial is the question what is the function of social science if it is prohibited from viewing other 'realities' through the lenses of its own system. The point is certainly being made that the assumptions of science should not be arbitrarily imposed on alien systems of belief. The authors complain that 'the scientific reality is used as *the* standard against which all other realities are compared'. For example, they say, native sorcery can be made to appear merely a bizarre example of aberrant drug use.

We may agree with the familiar objection that practices should not be torn out of context, but repudiating science can involve us in great difficulties. Many go much further than simply holding that science cannot give us all the answers and that human knowledge is obtainable from other sources. The reaction against science can produce the feeling that there are no answers. Mehan and Wood say that 'every reality is equally real', and further claim that 'no single reality contains more of the truth than any other'.[4] This introduces an odd notion of truth in addition to their curious idea of reality. They obviously wish to purge any belief-system of aspirations to superiority. They even attack Schutz for treating the reality of everyday life as the *one* paramount reality. Yet the way they put the matter suggests that truth is obtainable, whereas they clearly mean that there is no such thing. It is not that each system of belief has its own window on the same truth. What counts as true is different in different systems, so that no one can claim the others are mistaken. They go on, in fact, to quote Wittgenstein with approval, and equate 'forms of life' with 'realities'.

Ethnomethodology certainly takes the problem of reflexivity seriously, and encounters similar problems to the sociology of knowledge. Social science merely becomes one system of belief among many, at the same level as the Azande's predilection for oracles. Yet, however much we need to be wary of distorting other people's beliefs by imposing our assumptions on them, it is dangerous to argue that that is all that can happen. Mehan and Wood say: 'There is no way to look from the window of one reality at others without seeing yourself.'[5] Once this is taken to heart, an infinite regress seems inevitable. Ethnomethodologists must realize that any empirical findings they make are as much the outcome of their 'reality' as of the one they are investigating. Yet they cannot investigate their own reality without already bringing their assumptions to bear on it. It is hardly surprising that Mehan and Wood maintain that ethnomethodology 'is not a method of pursuing the truth about the world'.[6] Instead, they say, its task is to examine the many versions, including its own, of the way the world is assembled.

Why, then, should anyone practise ethnomethodology if it is understood in this way? Mehan and Wood admit that the problem of reflexivity has worried many, so that some have suggested that all 'empirical rhetoric' should be abandoned. The problem is how far any discipline which emphasizes that it is merely one form of life among many can get a grip on the world. Once experience of the world is explicitly relativized to a particular conceptual framework, empirical research is seen as merely the outworking of a particular system of belief. It cannot justify it, and it is difficult to find any answer when someone wonders why they should adopt or hold to such a system or what the point of any empirical research might be. Instead of being the paradigm of rationality, the methods of empirical science are reduced to the status of seemingly pointless ritual. Mehan and Wood admit that ethnomethodologists who become worried about the status of empirical ethnomethodology 'typically quit ethnomethodology and the academy in search of some other way of life'.[7] Nothing could demonstrate more strikingly the paralysing effect of relativism in the social sciences. It is one thing to assert that the physical sciences have no monopoly on truth but it is another to jettison the concepts of truth, reality and knowledge. It is one thing to resist a narrowly scientific paradigm for rationality, but it is another to widen the latter so that the most rigorous social scientist can be no more rational than the most superstitious tribesman. The only consequence of such a position is to cast complete doubt on the value or purpose of social science, or indeed of any intellectual activity.

RATIONALITY AS A SOCIAL PRACTICE

The social sciences aim at more than a simple understanding of other cultures. Anyone can adopt the outlook of another society if they go to live in it and attempt to forget their own. It is possible to 'go native', and there are examples of Westerners even joining cannibal tribes and living like them. It would be ludicrous to suggest that the more cannibalistic someone became, the more successful he or she was as an anthropologist. Total absorption in a tribe cannot be the aim of social science, although demands for participation through fieldwork may have been an effective antidote to armchair anthropologists. One will find out more about New Guinea tribesmen in New Guinea than in Oxford. Yet the fundamental problem remains of how one treats the knowledge gained about the life of a tribe. Anthropology is a useless discipline if the assumptions of social science are dismissed at the outset as the product of a particular society. Some people may just happen to enjoy visiting exotic parts of the world and seeing strange customs, while others prefer to stay at home.

Something more is needed, and social scientists need to examine a culture with a certain detachment. The immediate response will be that they will not be detached about their own culture. The very notion of scientific detachment is itself a particular cultural assumption. Yet that contention is analogous to the response in a fierce argument that 'that is only *your* opinion'. Every opinion is the opinion of someone and the important question is whether good reasons can be produced for the belief. The point of any argument or discussion is lost if you are told that an apparent reason can only be what *you* think is a good reason. Without the ability to discuss what *are* good reasons, what *is* true or what *is* real, all talk becomes the expression of non-rational attitudes, or even tastes. Some may be culturally conditioned, others may be an individual matter, but all hold in common the fact that argument will not and cannot touch them. The treatment of the ideal of rationality as a cultural construction by Western man, and only that, means that apparently rational discussion is the mere exhibition of culturally conditioned prejudices. Western man has been brought up to prefer that kind of intellectual game. While conditions in some societies may have favoured the development of rational thought, the question is whether such thought can claim any validity. Is the intellectual pursuit of 'truth' just an expression of the workings of one culture among many, or can it set standards to which all should aspire?

This question is of particular relevance to the study of other societies, but it does raise a very deep issue. The American philosopher, Richard Rorty, asks it in the context of a discussion about the purpose of philosophy itself. The repudiation of an empiricist epistemology with its sure foundations in experience leaves open the possibility that there may not be one overall framework in which rational discourse can take place. There could be many different kinds of discourse. Rorty uses the terms 'epistemology' and 'hermeneutics' to describe two different strategies. He writes about whether there can be common ground between various discourses or whether there cannot in fact be presupposed any 'disciplinary matrix which unites the speakers'. Is there a common rationality? He says:

> For hermeneutics, to be rational is to be willing to refrain from epistem-ology – from thinking that there is a special set of terms in which all contri-butions to the conversation should be put – and to be willing to pick up the jargon of the interlocutor rather than translating it into one's own. For epistemology, to be rational is to find the proper set of terms into which all the contributions should be translated if agreement is to become possible. For epistemology, conversation is implicit inquiry. For hermeneutics, inquiry is routine conversation.[8]

Thus he wishes to hold that conversation is 'the ultimate context within which knowledge is to be understood'.[9] Truth is not an objective matter arrived at through the correspondence of our ideas with reality. It is a matter of negotiation and of mutual understanding and compromise, if indeed it is possible to continue talking of truth at all. Rorty sees alter-native social practices of justification, each presumably having to 'con-verse' with the other. Without any notion of objective truth, he still feels it important 'to keep the conversation going'.[10] Why, though, should philosophy have to keep on with what appears a pointless and trivial task? Even allowing for the metaphorical nature of the phrase 'the con-versation of mankind', philosophy seems reduced to the level of the idle chatter of a cocktail party. What, indeed, is the status of Rorty's own philosophical arguments? If he is not attempting to provide rational arguments, it is difficult to see what he is writing for. If he is, he must himself be presupposing some framework of rationality.

The influence of Kuhn and the later Wittgenstein on Rorty is explicit. Yet whether we deal with the possibility of rationality at the most general level of all, that of philosophy and epistemology, at the level of scientific practice or at the anthropological level, the issue remains the same. Is rationality a social practice, historically conditioned, or is it possible to appeal to standards of rationality which transcend what may be accepted at a particular place and time? It is perhaps significant that questions about rationality are so often linked with questions about objective truth. The assumption of a reality independent of what we think itself provides a constraint on what it is reasonable to believe. Our standards of what it is reasonable to believe are adequate if reality is created or constructed by our beliefs, as an idealist might hold. If, on the other hand, what we believe in no way affects the nature of reality, as 'common sense' might assume and the realist maintains, it is completely possible that our assumptions about what it is reasonable to believe lead us far astray. Our beliefs may be totally false.

Rorty arrived at his position through repudiating empiricist views of knowledge. Yet philosophy seems cut adrift without the security of a foundationalist epistemology. Part of the trouble is that empiricism relied heavily on the notion of experience of the world to the detriment of any emphasis on the world as such. Consequently, once the theoretical or even cultural influences on what seemed 'raw' experience are exposed, it is difficult to recover any conception of the world or reality which does not itself seem to be merely a theoretical or cultural construct. Yet without such a conception the hopelessness which leads some ethnomethodologists to give up ethnomethodology can soon set in. What is needed is a concept of objective reality which is divorced from the presuppositions of empiricism and which, as a consequence, is not tied too closely to the methods and findings of empirical science. The latter may be a source of knowledge, but its claim to be the *only* source has undoubtedly led many to intemperate opposition to the idea of knowledge or of objective truth.

How far does this illuminate questions concerning alleged superstition and possible irrationality in 'primitive' societies? Someone with Rorty's views will not invoke rational standards and criticize a society for not abiding by them. Their standards are different from ours and we must, it seems, endeavour to enter a conversation with them without any comforting rational framework with which to assess their views. Yet is this position adequate when we are faced with, say, magic and witchcraft? Wittgenstein would have accepted that it was and was particularly critical of the anthropological work of Sir James Frazer: 'Frazer's account of the magical and religious notions of men is unsatisfactory: it makes those notions appear as *mistakes*.'[11]

Wittgenstein's own interpretation of such notions, however, rests on a refusal to accept that anything true is being claimed in religion. He refuses to accept that Augustine was mistaken in calling upon God, but this is not because he thinks Augustine was correct. He would not allow that a Buddhist or an adherent to some other religion was mistaken either. The concept of a mistake would be inappropriate in this area. He claims: 'A religious symbol does not rest on any opinion. And error belongs only with opinion.'[12]

This type of move is, in fact, extremely popular with modern social anthropologists. It is encouraged by a desire not to treat magical and religious practices as if they are just bad science. Frazer certainly seemed to be doing just that. Wittgenstein takes exception to his view that ceremonies to make the wind blow or the rain fall will persist because such occurrences will normally take place at some time. Frazer maintains that 'primitive man may be excused for regarding the occurrence as a direct result of the ceremony, and the best possible proof of its efficiency.'[13] Wittgenstein's rejoinder is that 'it is queer that people do not notice that it does rain sooner or later anyway'.[14] From a scientific point of view the conclusion has to be that the people concerned are irrational. Yet refusing to make this step must involve a refusal to impose our scientific standards on a 'pre-scientific' society.

The relativist reference to different realities will only lock different cultures in self-contained compartments, and it is perhaps not surprising if many social anthropologists prefer to stress the non-scientific character of much 'primitive' belief. We are told, for example, that 'magic is a symbolic activity not a scientific one'.[15] Thus, to save tribesmen from the accusation of being irrational, their activities are interpreted not as ways of making things happen but as ways of showing how they feel about events. The expressive and symbolic character of what is being done is emphasized. A rain-dance is, then, to be viewed not as an ineffective way of producing rain but as a ritual expressing a belief in the importance of rain and a desire that it should fall. In a drought-ridden society, any apparent rain-making rituals will embody these attitudes, and be potent symbols of something held very important. The problem is whether they are just that and whether the members of that society may not just be wrong in their beliefs about how rain can be produced. Even in Western societies, there may be prayers for rain when there is a severe drought. Sophisticated believers may feel that prayers of that sort are not means of altering the world but just express our deepest concerns. More likely, they will be reluctant to use them at all. Unsophisticated believers will certainly feel that such prayers may be answered. It is easy to assume that the latter are wrong, but it is inconsistent to think that of members of one's own society, while shrinking from judging apparently similar beliefs in other societies in the same way.

Why is it so easy to consider that prayers can make no difference to the world? The answer must surely be found in the prestige of science and in the prejudice that what cannot be explained by science cannot occur.[16] This is mere prejudice, since even scientists must admit that contemporary science has its limitations. If the belief is that science can *in principle* explain everything, even though some things will be for ever out of reach of flesh-and-blood scientists, this becomes vacuous. Whatever is real is scientifically explicable, it seems, but the snag is that *we* may never be able to explain it. We will not be so ready to equate science and rationality if we take the limitations of human science seriously. When science cannot at the moment, or in the foreseeable future, explain everything, it is not necessarily irrational to hold beliefs which are not provable scientifically. This does not thereby mean that it is automatically rational, but good and bad reasons for belief need not be restricted to what contemporary scientists would accept as such. It may be irrational to go against the findings of science, but it does not seem rational to be restricted by its limitations. We may not reasonably say that the earth is flat, but nor can we refuse to face all issues which have not been conclusively settled by science. Doing so would be merely to continue allegiance to a narrow positivism.

How does this affect our judgement of non-scientific beliefs? They cannot be judged irrational merely because they are non-scientific. The practical rejection of all religion, and indeed all metaphysics, embodied a commitment to the standards of science which could not itself be rationally justified. A persistent criticism of those who stressed that the meaning of a statement was to be understood by the way it could be scientifically verified was that this belief could not itself be scientifically verified. It was merely laid down from the beginning as an axiom, which others were accordingly free to reject. The determination to view metaphysics as nonsense, in the manner of the Vienna Circle, was simply a determination to count science as the source of rationality. It made scientific rationality synonymous with rationality. This defined certain positions as rational and others not, but its dogmatism left untouched the basic issue of whether all non-scientific beliefs about the world could be dismissed as irrational.

'EXPRESSIVE' AND 'SYMBOLIC' PRACTICES

The eagerness of many social anthropologists to emphasize the expressive character of many rituals and to stress the role of symbols in thought reflects both the influence of positivism and an unhappiness about its consequences. The same tendency is present in the way that some philosophers of religion try to interpret religion in Western societies. The first assumption made is that truth is the province of science, and that religious beliefs cannot claim 'literal' truth, whether they are about spirits in the trees or the Trinity. Then some hesitate to dismiss so completely the basic beliefs of so many. Saying that they are false, if not nonsensical, implies that those believing them are irrational. The next stage is to attempt to rescue the beliefs by showing that they have a definite function in the societies concerned and that the believers are in fact doing something perfectly sensible. Since questions of truth and falsity have already been handed over to science, explanations have to be given which show that the beliefs in question have nothing to do with beliefs about what is true. Rituals which are apparently designed to produce rain should not be understood in that way. Tribesmen do not have false beliefs about the weather but are, despite appearances, doing something perfectly sensible.

The same type of analysis can be, and is, given to religious beliefs in Western societies. The tacit assumption is often made that science cannot explain miracles or have any dealing with the transcendent or the supernatural. Therefore it seems that talk about God and divine intervention in the world cannot be literally true or false, and that if religious believers are not irrational they must be understood as doing something other than believing facts about the world. One of the most famous examples of this type of response to empiricism is that of R. B. Braithwaite, who said: 'The primary use of religious assertion is to announce allegiance to a set of moral principles.'[17] Religion is thus reduced to a determination to live a particular kind of life. Its apparent claims to truth are merely pictures, used as psychological aids. More recently, a radical theologian, Don Cupitt, has responded to what he sees as the challenge of science: 'Our highly refined and elegant scientific world-picture carries the clear implication that our moralities, art and religions are purely human constructions that are in no way endorsed by the universe at large.'[18] He recognizes that it is possible to refuse science the status of arbiter and truth, and to treat it as 'one human cultural activity among others'. Yet on either interpretation of science – the positivist one or the reaction against it – religion cannot claim objective truth. If positivism is correct, religion is strictly meaningless, since only science provides knowledge. If the reaction against positivism prevails, religion may be understood as part of forms of life, or as a distinctive one itself. The concept of objective truth has itself been banished.

Cupitt tries to save a place for religion by claiming that 'we have to come to see religious language as being not descriptive but expressive, action-guiding and symbolic'.[19] He says that 'the development of critical thinking and of the scientific outlook has now demythologized or demystified all the things that people have traditionally lived by.' Thus we can no longer think of God as a transcendent reality, let alone the ultimate explanation for everything. He offers the view that we have 'to make do with the use of the word "God" as an incorporating or unifying symbol connoting the whole of what we are up against in the spiritual life.'[20] It seems that believers in God cannot possess a putative fact about the world if facts are the province of science. Unless they are professing gibberish or holding irrationally to a belief which they should recognize as false, the belief must have some other function. It regulates their lives, and perhaps the life of their society, in some significant way, and without it they, or their society, would be different.

The significant feature of this type of analysis is that it is the same as that given by social anthropologists about 'primitive' religion. The same pressures to dismiss its beliefs as unscientific and hence false are exerted. The desire to compartmentalize areas of human experience, so that science is kept in its place, results in talk of different ways of life, and of symbolic and expressive speech. Social anthropology can insulate other societies from science by stressing the difference between those societies and its own. Some apologists of religion in Western society insulate religion by holding that science and religion, even within the one society, entail different practices or ways of life. In the end, however, the problem is the same. Armed with the insights of modern science, how are we to treat the persistence of practices which cannot be justified scientifically? The issues encountered by social anthropologists are no different in kind from those we encounter in Western societies. How is it that some people are able to hold beliefs which cannot be judged rational according to a strictly scientific understanding?

Two philosophers, MacDonald and Pettit, writing about the problem of cross-cultural understanding, suggest that, 'in fastening on the religious/scientific contrast, anthropologists have been led to over-emphasize the differences between our culture and more traditional ones.'[21] They consider that in the latter there would be no tradition of reflecting on the rationality of particular beliefs. The occurrence of contradictory beliefs might perhaps be less surprising in these circumstances. They conclude that 'it may be that the anthropologist, or at least the atheist anthropologist, will find the sharpest challenge to the assumption of human rationality not in researches among the alien, but in investigations among her own.' This is fair comment in so far as it points out that the same type of problem recurs when religion and science confront each other in Western society as when science meets primitive religion and magic. If what is at issue is the repudiation of all beliefs which are not scientifically supported, it is a clear error to assume that all Western society functions according to the presuppositions of positivist scientific method. Indeed, as we have seen, few now believe that even science does.

Many of the problems of interpreting 'primitive' cultures have arisen because they have been judged according to narrowly scientific standards, as understood by positivists. Challenges to assumptions about human rationality appear more acute because scientific procedure is taken as the paradigm of rationality. The cultural relativist would limit the criteria of science to Western societies, but that does not remove the problem, since non-scientific beliefs occur there too. The view that all religious beliefs, wherever they occur, are merely symbolic accepts the positivist claim that only science can provide a path to truth. It is similar to relativist views in that it provides religion with its own set of standards so that 'symbolic truth' or 'religious truth' can still be talked about in a way that science cannot touch. There is, though, the strong implication that 'real' or 'literal' truth has been passed over to science.

What is needed is a conception of reality, and hence of truth, which is not restricted to the present findings of science. Modern science has proved a powerful technique for making important discoveries about the world, but the view that it is the only path to knowledge can result in grave distortions in the interpretation of non-scientific belief. 'Scientific realists' may still be inclined to restrict the concept of reality to what science can discover, but this is prejudice. We dare not assume that all non-scientific beliefs must be false or that their holders are thereby shown to be irrational.

Charles Taylor points out that modern science has been able to develop only because we have disciplined ourselves to 'register the way things are without regard to the meanings they might have for us'. A chasm has appeared between the detached view of reality exemplified by science and a richly meaningful world as delineated by symbols: 'This kind of contrast is one that has developed out of our form of life. But exactly for this reason, it is probably going to be unhelpful in understanding people who are very different from us.'[22]

Thus the very idea of a symbol, as opposed to what is literally, or scientifically, true itself arises from a scientifically based society. It is obvious that it must do, since otherwise the contrast could not be made. Rightly or wrongly, we have learnt to make such a dichotomy, while other cultures will not have done so. Yet it may be suggested that this is beside the point, unless we are conceptual relativists, restricting the application of concepts to the societies in which they originated. A valid distinction should be applied even to those who would not apply it to themselves. Other cultures may not recognize the symbolic nature of their beliefs. This is one of the major problems in interpreting other cultures. Are we entitled to describe or explain practices in terms that would not be accepted by the people we are investigating? Can we say that prayers for rain are purely symbolic or expressive, even if those using them do not accept that interpretation? They may not accept it because they do not possess our concept of symbol, but many who do share the concept would still reject it as inapplicable to their prayers. Alternatively they might stop praying for rain precisely because they come to see that it does correctly describe them. In either case, categorizing the prayers in this way involves more than a neutral description. It does not allow that anyone could intelligibly try to use prayer to alter the world by super- natural means.

By definition science cannot cope with the supernatural, so that kind of prayer is not in accord with a scientific view of the world. What is at issue is whether humans may in fact use prayer for this purpose. They may also use magic or witchcraft to attempt to alter the world. The automatic assumption that all of these practices must be irrational and are therefore unlikely to occur is a mere application of a prejudice in favour of science. In fact some of the practices may be surprisingly rational, given a fairly profound ignorance about the physical forces at work in the world. Even the objection that magic often does not work derives from a scientific training in which predictive success is recognized to be of primary importance.

BELIEF AND RATIONALITY

Rationality is a relative concept. What it is rational to believe depends on what you know already. Scientists can easily dismiss primitive belief in the power of magic as irrational because they possess greater knowledge about the world. From their point of view such beliefs are mere super- sition, and perhaps the scientists are right. Sometimes, however, scientists have been tempted to claim knowledge they do not possess. A scientist may find it impossible to explain the apparent efficacy of prayer on some occasion, and be unhappy that the alleged effects of prayer cannot be reproduced under laboratory conditions. Yet this might just as well point to the limits of science as to the shortcomings of prayer. This is an exceedingly controversial matter, but this very fact suggests that it cannot be solved by treating certain beliefs as unscientific and therefore not really about the world. The controversy arises precisely because science cannot take account of forms of explanation which are at variance with a scientific outlook. Interpreting them in such a way that they do not conflict is a subtle way of re-asserting the supremacy of science in an alarmingly positivist manner. Accepting the conflict as real need not make us lose our bearings about what it is rational to believe. The scientists could be right, and those disagreeing with them wrong. The symbolist approach makes it impossible to expose false belief and ignorance, since all beliefs are made to express sensible attitudes.

John Beattie argues that 'Magic is the acting out of a situation, the expression of a desire in symbolic terms; it is not the application of empirically acquired knowledge about the properties of natural substances.'[23] He is right to suppose that native magic is not just a silly scientific theory, since this imports our ideas of Western science to an inappropriate situation. What he fails to realize is that, when he concludes that it must therefore be totally different, he is still applying the distinction between science and non-science. Yet the point is not that native magic occurs in a society which does not have scientific beliefs, but that the very distinction between science and non-science does not apply there. It certainly would follow that if only scientists can have access to the nature of reality, native practices cannot be understood as involving conceptions of reality. This is, though, a travesty of the situation.

Once it is accepted that science is just a particularly efficient method of obtaining knowledge, we may reasonably expect to find knowledge in other cultures. The corollary of this is that we shall also find ignorance. Nevertheless, when our beliefs conflict with theirs, the view that reality is as independent of our views as it is of theirs has salutary consequences. We cannot be certain that our methods of obtaining knowledge are always superior to theirs. We may be able to learn from them. Traditional remedies in tribal medicine, for instance, may actually sometimes *be* remedies. Too great a reliance on the impressive technology of modern surgery might blind us to important facts that simpler societies may long have known.

The assertion that 'pre-scientific' societies somehow could not have any knowledge about the world, but are involved in practices that make sense only in their society, itself involves the application of positivist distinctions. Yet although a culture's grasp on reality may be slight, and although it proves unable to control powerful natural forces, there may often be the glimmerings of deep insight. It is a gross error to say that either a belief is scientific or it cannot be concerned with reality. When we see a tribal society relying on magic, it is inappropriate to impose our theoretical categories on it, even if we merely intend to exonerate it of the charge of irrationality. An analogous situation arises when we study the early days of philosophy and of science in Ionia in the fifth century BC. It is difficult to determine whether some beliefs were scientific or metaphysical. Science, with its empirical methods, had not been explicitly distinguished from the simple exercise of human reason. Saying that the early atomic theory of Democritus, not to mention Thales' theory of water as the underlying reality, was scientific merely imposes categories not recognized at the time. From our point of view there may be scientific elements involved, but the imposition of anachronistic categories does little to assist our understanding.

The basic question should be the truth of beliefs rather than their rationality. Given a deep enough ignorance about the world, many practices which seem obviously irrational to us are, in fact, perfectly rational. If I do not know how to cope with the contingencies of my life, and am totally at their mercy, I might indulge in what seem weird practices in an attempt to gain some control. Winch suggests that the magical rites of the Azande 'express an attitude to contingencies'.[24] He describes the attitude as one involving recognition that one's life is subject to contingencies rather than an attempt to control these. Yet the tribesmen used sarawa leaves in the apparent belief that they made things flourish. Evans-Pritchard quotes how the Azande address a leaf of sarawa: 'Medicine, you protect my ground-nuts from witches, you make my ground-nuts flourish.'[25] Only someone in the grip of a philosophical theory could think that this does not result from a genuine fear of witches and a belief that sarawa leaves would make the ground-nuts grow well. Similarly, only someone who was already in the grip of the assumptions of modern science could think of a prayer for rain as anything other than a request to a supernatural power to produce rain. The view that the people concerned would surely see that these methods did not 'work' merely imports a rigorously scientific view into the situation. If they had possessed that sophisticated a view of cause and effect, they would probably not have had the beliefs they did have in the first place. Anyway, often the ground-nuts would flourish.

The very fact that missionaries in the nineteenth century and scientists in the twentieth have been able to convince many people that some of their beliefs are primitive and should be discarded bears witness to the rationality of their holders. It is surprising how rapidly the beliefs can be discarded when irrefutable evidence is provided that the witch-doctor does not have the power everyone believed he had, or that rituals can be discarded without ill effects. South Sea Islanders discovered after the arrival of missionaries that the taboos and rituals connected with sailing and fishing could be given up without anything terrible happening. Once one seaman had the courage to omit the practice and still did well, everyone else would follow. Their reasons for participating in the traditional rituals were shown to be grounded in false beliefs.

Symbolist interpretations of traditional beliefs may be intended to protect the holders of such beliefs from the charge of irrationality, but what they do is to ignore the fact that people hold beliefs for reasons, good or bad. The explanation given by many social anthropologists for the persistence of practices in a society often ignores the individual understanding of the participants. Just as the later Wittgenstein thought that beliefs gain their significance from their social role rather than from what they purport to be about, a symbolist understanding of belief ignores its actual content and looks for the truths expressed about that particular society. Individual belief when seen from a holist standpoint may well have a certain role in society, but the ordinary believer may not be aware of it, and certainly does not hold a belief for that reason.

THE EXPLANATION OF RITUAL

D. Z. Phillips gives a Wittgensteinian account of ritual when he says:

> Where rituals express a wish, to know in what sense the ritual acts out the wish, we would have to take account of the role played by the ritual in the details of the lives of the people who celebrate it.[26]

From the standpoint of an anthropologist, the social context may be illuminating, but unless the ritual is a *mere* ritual the viewpoint of the individual participants must be different. Phillips, however, refers to an example, also used by Winch, of mountain-dwellers 'who, before specifically religious expressions develop in their language, contemplate the mountains, prostrate themselves before them, celebrate rites in relation to them, in such ways that we call them primitive religious responses.' Phillips continues:

> Later, they come to speak of gods in the mountains. Rituals and stories develop which can be said to be *about* these gods. Must we then say that talk of the gods expresses the existential presuppositions of the primitive reactions?

Phillips's conclusion is that it is wrong to *explain* their looking to the mountains in terms of their reverence to the gods. There is in fact a 'conceptual connection' between their ritual and what they understand by their gods, so that the two cannot be separated. The conclusion is that 'a decline in the religious practices would be an aspect of loss of belief in the gods, not a consequence of it'.[27] The practice embodies the belief, and is not justified by it as if the latter was something separate. Yet this account is at variance with what Phillips posits as the account given by the mountain-dwellers themselves. When they speak of gods in the mountains, they presumably believe that there are gods in the mountains. The fact that this belief was expressed in religious practices before it was properly articulated does not mean that, when it is articulated, it should be rejected. Phillips would doubtless claim that what is meant by 'there are gods in the mountains' can only be understood by locating the ritual in the life of the people. Yet what the belief *says* is very different, and the ritual would not be the same without that belief. In fact, identifying religious practices in some respect with belief in gods makes it difficult to see how a ritual could live on without the belief. What, though, is to prevent a sophisticated tribesman participating in the ritual and even encouraging it, even though he knows full well there are no gods in the mountains? His reason may well be that he has read the works of modern anthropologists and he realizes the wider social significance of the rituals. Perhaps the ritual becomes something different for him and he may find it difficult to be gripped by it in the same way. It becomes a *mere* ritual. The difference, though, is that an existential belief has been removed.

Once a practice is consciously recognized as a ritual, or a symbolic activity, it is very difficult for it to play the same part in the life of a society. Religious rituals that presuppose a belief in gods or a god are different from rituals that do not. It becomes very difficult to participate in them in the same way once it is recognized that they do not. No doubt Sunday worship in a Christian church plays a particular role in society and the lives of those participating in it. Once, however, a 'sophisticated' philosopher of religion accounts for it as a purely expressive or symbolic activity, with no presupposition that God is being worshipped, it becomes much more difficult to participate on the same terms as before. It is an intriguing point that again and again the same issues confront social anthropology and modern philosophy of religion. Phillips himself remarks that where philosophers stand on issues concerning anthropological understanding 'determines the treatment of some of the deepest issues in contemporary philosophy of religion'.[28] In other words, what provides difficulty in the understanding of the religious practices of other cultures is not that they are embedded in other cultures, but that they are *religious*. The positivist assumption persists that no religious belief, when taken at face value, can be rational, whether it is about gods in the mountains or the Christian God.

Some rituals *are* mere rituals. When the British Parliament is opened in state by the monarch, she summons the House of Commons by sending Black Rod to fetch them. When he arrives at the door of the Chamber, it is ceremoniously and defiantly slammed in his face. This expresses the independence of the Commons from interference by the Crown. The Queen's messenger can only enter when invited. Memories of Charles I linger on. Yet, while this ritual expresses a constitutional fact and has a social role, it is performed self-consciously as part of the picturesque traditions of Parliament. No one is really trying to keep Black Rod out or wishes to refuse to go to the Queen's presence in the House of Lords. No one believes that Elizabeth II is a menace to the power of Parliament. Members of Parliament are in fact eagerly waiting in their best suits to process in front of the waiting television cameras. The ritual is viewed as such. When religious practices come to be seen in the same light, as picturesque traditions expressing truths about our society, religion will be in an advanced state of decay. Its whole basis, namely a belief, whether true or false, in an independently existing God, will have been eroded. After that, nothing can be the same. The role played by a ritual in people's lives is the result of their beliefs about what is true.

The social role of belief should not be confused with the reasons why a belief is embraced. Its content is distinct from its consequences. Here, as so often, there can be a subtle slide from what is believed to the fact that a certain belief is held. The social sciences may legitimately have ambitions to explain the latter. Social anthropologists will probably throw light on why primitive beliefs and practices could persist even though they were poor ways of manipulating the real world. A symbolist interpretation of, say, the casting of a spell on crops helps to explain why members of a society go on doing it. The spell is an expression of the dependence of their society on the crops, and collective rituals always help to enhance loyalty to the group. Other plausible explanations may locate the practice firmly in its social context. The society would be a very different one without such rituals, and might eventually fall apart. Yet, however persuasive such explanations may be, they only explain why beliefs *of that sort* may be held and rituals *like that* performed. Many other similar types of belief would do just as well. Any religious ritual would probably be equally successful in reinforcing group loyalty. Indeed, the conversion of tribes to Christianity and the replacement of one set of rituals with another need be of little importance to the symbolist anthropologist. One set of symbols is replaced by another, but it might appear that much the same thing is being symbolized.

Sometimes not enough weight is put on the intrinsic nature of the symbol. The fact that participants in a ritual may not be conscious of what is being symbolized (the unity of the tribe, for instance) suggests that, whatever the social context of their actions, further explanation is needed. Why do they choose this ritual rather than another? Why is a particular incantation used? Unless we treat the participants as automata, the perspective of the individual cannot be ignored, and the content of his or her belief becomes relevant. What do the participants think they are doing? Treating individuals as merely agents caught up in a social process of which they understand little, takes too little account of their own rationality. If a religious believer becomes convinced that prayer cannot be understood as a definite request for supernatural help which may be successful, he or she will probably stop using such a prayer. One has to be a very sophisticated theologian to be able to go on using language to make requests in prayer, while knowing that is not really what one is doing at all. No doubt many prayers could be interpreted by such a theologian as simply expressing our dependence on God, or, more radically, showing our attitude to the contingencies of life. That, however, is not what the prayers say. It is hard not to conclude that the reluctance of many to use such petitionary prayer stems from the fact that they no longer believe what they would be saying. Whatever the social context and however much an individual's rational processes are influenced by it, the beliefs of individual participants in a society cannot be ignored. What they believe and their own reasons for believing it are not unimportant. The identification of a particular belief cannot be made by simply appealing to its social role. The slot it fills in a society does not explain why *it* rather than another belief fills it.

The social sciences in general and social anthropology in particular face limits to what they can explain. Explaining the social context of a belief is not the same as assessing the rationality of the belief itself. The latter is outside the professional competence of social scientists. In the end, we cannot sidestep questions about individual rationality. The temptation in the past has been to deal with questions of such rationality by either bluntly applying contemporary scientific standards or by refusing to accept that our standards apply at all. Either way, the problem has been seen as a clash of systems of belief. It has then seemed inevitable that social scientists produce explanations for the existence of such systems. If, instead, we assume that humans are everywhere much the same and face the same reality that we do, we can conclude that varying practices exhibit varying beliefs about the nature of that reality. Without the benefit of sophisticated ways of gathering knowledge and of controlling the world, many humans quite rationally react to the world in what seem to us to be futile ways. They hold their beliefs not because they live in a different world from ours, but because they inhabit the same one but do not possess our knowledge of it. Sometimes they may know things which we wrongly reject.

The assumption that, although anyone can be stupid or foolish, by and large all humans share the same ability to reason and adopt the same basic standards of rationality is a crucial one in understanding alien societies. We shall never find them intelligible unless we can build a bridge between them and us. One such point of contact might be that they and we agree in most of our beliefs, particularly everyday ones about the world as we perceive it. This assumption is embodied in Donald Davidson's 'principle of charity' according to which, if we want to understand others, we must count them right in most matters. This seems implausible, since we may in fact be able to find others intelligible precisely in the cases where we do disagree with them. In place of the principle of charity, Richard Grandy has proposed a 'principle of humanity'.[29] This is 'the condition that imputed patterns of relations among beliefs, desires and the world be as similar to our own as possible', Rationality has to be presupposed before translation can begin. We must think what we would do if we had the relevant beliefs and desires. Obviously it is of great assistance if the people we are trying to understand share our beliefs and desires. Too great a divergence will prove troublesome. Yet, if the world we each confront is the same and we share the same kind of desires, it should prove possible to find alien beliefs intelligible without pretending that they are something other than they are. Moreover, we find them intelligible precisely because we assume the rationality of the person holding them. Irrational beliefs are much more difficult to find intelligible and translate.

As has been pointed out by MacDonald and Pettit, the principle of humanity rests on a 'belief in the unity of human nature' – 'a belief that people in different cultures are essentially similar'.[30] They elucidate this by saying that 'any differences there are across cultures, or at least any differences central to the attitudes and actions of people, should be explicable by reference to different circumstances.' In other words, if we were in the same situation as, say, tribesmen, without our technology, we might very well have adopted a similar way of life. They are not different kinds of creatures from us. This assumption of a common human nature is an important one, needing further justification. One retort could be that, as there is no such thing, we must expect to find major difficulties in understanding other cultures. Questions about human nature cannot be ignored by the social sciences. If the assumption of a universal human nature is necessary, it could be argued that, even when the social sciences are demonstrating the supposed radical differences between cultures, they are, through their understanding of those cultures, bearing witness to the fact of human nature.

NOTES

1 Winch, 'Understanding a Primitive Society', p. 9.
2 H. Garfinkel and H. Sachs, 'On Formal Structures of Practical Actions', in J. C. McKinney and E. A. Tiryakin (eds), *Theoretical Sociology*, 1970.
3 H. Mehan and H. Wood, *The Reality of Ethnomethodology*, 1975, p. 37.
4 Ibid., p. 37.
5 Ibid., p. 31.
6 Ibid., p. 114.
7 Ibid., p. 167.
8 Rorty, *Philosophy and the Mirror of Nature*, p. 318.
9 Ibid., p. 389.
10 Ibid., p. 379.
11 Wittgenstein, *Remarks on Frazer's Golden Bough*, 1979, p. 1.
12 Ibid., p. 3.
13 James Frazer, *The Golden Bough*, 1922, p. 59.
14 Wittgenstein, *Remarks on Frazer's Golden Bough*, p. 2.
15 J. Beattie, *Other Cultures*, 1964, p. 209.
16 See my 'The Limits of Science' in H. P. Duerr (ed.), *Science and the Irrational*, 1984.
17 R. B. Braithwaite, 'An Empiricist's View of the Nature of Religious Belief', in I. T. Ramsey (ed.), *Christian Ethics and Contemporary Philosophy*, 1966, p. 63.
18 Don Cupitt, *The World to Come*, 1982, p. viii.
19 Ibid., p. xiv.
20 Cupitt, *Taking Leave of God*, 1980, p. 97.
21 G. MacDonald and P. Pettit, *Semantics and Social Science*, 1981, p. 54.
22 Charles Taylor, 'Rationality', in M. Hollis and S. Lukes (eds), *Rationality and Relativism*, 1982, p. 97.
23 Beattie, *Other Cultures*, p. 207.
24 Winch, 'Understanding a Primitive Society', p. 40.
25 E. Evans-Pritchard, *Witchcraft, Oracles and Magic among the Azande*, 1937, p. 452.
26 D. Z. Phillips, 'Primitive Reactions and the Reactions of Primitives', Marett Lecture, Oxford, 1983, p. 18.
27 Ibid., p. 22.

28 Ibid., p. 4.
29 Richard Grandy, 'Reference, Meaning and Belief', *Journal of Philosophy*, 70, 1973, p. 443.
30 MacDonald and Pettit, *Semantics and Social Science*, p. 31.

6

Facts and Values

When the beliefs of apparently primitive societies are judged by the standards of scientific rationality, they can seem singularly foolish. If they are treated as scientific hypotheses, we might well wonder why they continued to be held in the face of what seem to us to be so many counter-instances. We have seen how the influence of positivism has resulted in the restricting of rationality to the procedures and techniques of modern science. Forcing primitive belief into the mould of hypotheses to be tested by experience only assumes that scientific method is the unique path to truth and the only proper expression of human rationality.

The categories of empiricism and positivism are also applied in another way which has a fundamental effect on the social sciences. It is a dogma, often repeated unthinkingly, that facts and values are logically distinct. Science seems to deal with facts, but the values placed on them cannot be logically deduced. The argument continues that we must have, as a result, much greater freedom to choose our values than to decide what the facts are. The latter is an objective matter, susceptible to scientific verification and falsification. Scientific method can provide an agreed procedure in case of factual disagreement, but there is no such procedure to settle differences about the values to be ascribed to the facts. Hume's injunction that what *ought* to be the case must not be confounded with what *is* the case epitomizes the empiricist approach. Whether we talk of 'ought' and 'is', or emphasize that values can never be deduced from facts, or stress the distinction between description and evaluation, the message is the same. Science can tell us what the facts are, but people's reactions to them are subjective matters, perhaps emotional reactions or feelings.

It is real enough that people make evaluations, but it appears that they can equally well view the same thing as good or bad. Some will see it one way and some another, and there is no way a scientist could suggest any procedure for setting the issue. Therefore there is no real issue, and it is not a factual matter, or so the positivist would say. Just as, if I hate bananas and you like them, there is no way it can be shown that I am right and you are wrong, the most basic human judgements about what is worth pursuing or to be avoided are reduced to mere matters of taste. How they arose may be explicable scientifically, but they cannot be justified. The sociologist may be able to explain why they have been produced. Hume himself tended to assume that basic desires were shared by all humans, so that we all naturally approve and disapprove of the same things.

This picture of the different status of what is factual and of what happens to be valued by humans comes from a particular view of science, which assumes that 'values' have no part in the operation of science. It has always seemed harder to exclude values from the social sciences because they deal with human concerns. The quest, though, of a 'value-free' social science has seemed indispensable if the social sciences were to acquire parity of esteem with the physical sciences. Yet just as a social anthropologist's approach to a culture is bound to be coloured by how far he or she considers it to be relying on false beliefs, so an estimate of how worthwhile some of its practices are must enter into attempts to explain them. For a start, it will influence what the anthropologist selects as in need of explanation. Time spent on growing crops for food hardly needs to be explained, since the activity is necessary. The very fact, though, that an anthropologist might be bewildered at a neglect of crops in favour of an involved religious ritual means that he or she will search for an explanation of the ritual. Yet the search is a reflection of what that anthropologist considers important. In other words, it is a reflection of values.

The desire to purify the social sciences of all values stems entirely from the assumption that the physical sciences have achieved the total separation of fact from value. Science appears to embody the dispassionate search for truth, abstracted from the partiality of particular points of view. If that is not so, the social sciences may themselves be aiming for something impossible by wishing to be 'value-free'.

The major shifts in the philosophy of science away from empiricism are relevant to this issue. The question of the place of values in science particularly arises when we ask what constraints there are on the adoption of new theories. A consequence of the new philosophy of science is that theories, and not passively received experience, are given priority. Yet, because of the underdetermination of theories by data, there must be a gap between a theory and the empirical evidence for it, even if the latter is not already 'theory-laden'. Theories cannot be deduced from the evidence, and so a gap is opened up between evidence and theory which is in some respects similar to the one allegedly existing between facts and values. It therefore does not seem very extraordinary to hold that values are needed to close the gap between the evidence and an underdetermined theory. Indeed, the very way we perceive the world is itself impregnated with values if our language is already theory-laden and our observations theory-dependent. The risk is that the notion of empirical evidence can get completely lost, so that it is impossible to talk of a theory being underdetermined by anything outside itself. There are just different conceptual schemes positing different worlds. The distinction between facts and values breaks down because no sense can any longer be given to the notion of 'fact'.

The challenge to empiricism remains, even if the depths of conceptual relativism are not plumbed. It seems that choice between theories is influenced by values, rather than determined by rules. This distinction is one that Kuhn invokes in an article which goes some way to making room for the rational assessment of theories. He wants nothing to do with positivist conceptions, but is happy to allow that characteristics such as accuracy, consistency, scope, simplicity and fruitfulness can all be relevant for evaluating the adequacy of a theory. This still will not serve to reduce disputes between scientists, but the different weight given by different people to the various criteria may well explain why the disagreement has arisen. Kuhn writes:

> I am suggesting that the criteria of choice . . . function not as rules which determine choice but as values which influence it. Two men deeply committed to the same values may nevertheless in particular situations make different claims, as, in fact, they do.[1]

Mary Hesse concludes that, 'if we take the thesis of underdetermination of theories seriously, relativism is a consequence that is inescapable in some form.'[2] This may partly stem from a view that what cannot be deduced from empirical evidence must be consigned to the realm of value. She refers to comprehensive theories in the human sciences as 'ideological' on the grounds that they incorporate evaluations of their subject-matter. She then says: 'Evaluations may be constrained by facts, but cannot be determined by them.'[3] Values are apparently guides to our choice to theories when the facts do not settle the matter. Perhaps they could be defined as such. Mary Hesse also maintains that, 'as in the natural sciences, social theories are constrained but not determined by facts'.[4] She assumes that the theories involve evaluations, but this means that what she terms our 'criteria of acceptability' for theories in social science are pluralist. She says that they are as pluralist as our choices of value goals and continues: 'If we wish to talk of *choice* of values, it also follows that we presuppose a certain area of freedom in the activity of theorizing.'[5]

The view that emerges is that both the natural and social sciences are impregnated with values, and might even be termed 'ideological'. Empirical facts do not suffice to explain the adoption of theories. We are apparently free to choose our values, and this entails that different people may make different choices. Yet it appears that these are left with no rational basis and cry out themselves for the kind of sociological explanations beloved of the sociologist of knowledge. Although Mary Hesse believes that a strongly determinist view is self-defeating, incurring all the problems of reflexivity, she concedes that theories may be shown to be 'partially determined' by the social environment.

SCIENTIFIC VALUES

Many contemporary philosophers no longer make any clear distinction between what is factual and what is not. This is not just because they find it hard to draw the line between the categories of fact and value. They cannot give any clear sense to the notion of anything being factual, and 'values' cannot any more be compared unfavourably with 'facts'. The one is not subjective and the other objective. What people choose to regard as real and what they view as important, valuable or worth pursuing cannot be regarded as belonging to two different types of discourse, the descriptive and the evaluative. Even the suggestion that scientific theories are value-impregnated from the beginning itself relies on a distinction that cannot be made, since values cannot in principle be separated from other ways of selecting what we are to believe. It seems likely that reference to values only makes real sense as a contrast to the scientifically established world of facts. It is difficult to destroy conceptions of the latter merely by talking of 'value impregnation', since values seem by definition to be non-factual. Without facts there is a sense in which there can be no values either. The concept of value is itself imbued with positivist assumptions.

People judge some things worth pursuing and others not, and they adopt some beliefs while rejecting others. We are all faced with choices at different levels which are not wholly determined. Our choices are very often governed by what we judge important or 'value'. Once the contrast with facts is discarded, though, there is no reason why what we value may not be as rationally based as any existential belief. Our valuings are no longer understood as taking place in some epistemological vacuum beyond the reach of respectable science. They need no longer seem merely subjective, and the possibility of rational justification for our valuings has to be looked at again. This is crucial for the question of the rationality of science itself, since, if the adoption of different scientific theories depends on what we judge important, any arbitrariness about the latter will infect science itself. If, on the other hand, choices between theories are made on the basis of rationally adopted criteria, science will remain the outworking of human rationality. It may, though, be only one expression of that rationality, instead of providing its standard.

The most obvious 'value' at the root of science is truth itself. The whole purpose of any science must be the pursuit of truth, and any understanding of science which ignores it runs the risk of undermining the whole edifice which scientists have constructed. This is the reason why the sociology of science can have a corrosive influence. Truth, of course, can itself be understood in various ways, and the great temptation is to identify it with one of the proven routes to it. In the end, however, the nature of reality becomes irrelevant to science if truth is not understood as some form of correspondence with reality. What, then, are the proven routes to truth in science? Western science has through the centuries tried to filter out prejudices and assumptions which have proved bad guides. Scientists have realized, for instance, that religious and political beliefs may incline them to one theory rather than another in ways which can be unhelpful to the basic aim of acquiring knowledge.

A desire for predictive accuracy has proved a good guide, although it is *only* a guide. A new theory may yield predictions which are not borne out. A strict falsificationist, like Karl Popper, would hold that the theory must be discarded. It may nevertheless be the case that there is more right than wrong with the theory, and a scientist who perseveres in the face of adverse results may still be more likely to acquire knowledge than one who gives up at the first setback. The theory might be better modified rather than totally rejected. The ability to give correct predictions is one test of truth but it should not become a substitute for truth. Similarly the internal coherence of a theory is important and is rightly valued by scientists. Unless reality is fundamentally chaotic, coherence within a theory and between theories will be a precondition for understanding the world. If a theory actually contradicts itself, it may not actually be stating anything. Yet the popularity of the coherence theory of truth bears witness to the readiness of many to substitute a test of truth for truth itself. Such tests always seem inadequate to those who want rigorous definitions and strict rules for the adoption of theories.

Scientists also value other features of scientific theories. The ability of a theory to bring together aspects of knowledge which were previously separate is important, as is its ability to generate new theories and research programmes. Many have valued simplicity, though this sometimes seems more like an aesthetic criterion than a method of searching for truth. It is a criterion which can result in the ruthless dismissal of superfluous entities in a crude reductionist manner. In our quest for the nature of reality, it can be disastrous to assume that it is less complicated than it is. Nevertheless, this example itself shows how scientists may legitimately disagree about which criteria of choices between theories are more likely to lead to knowledge or have led to knowledge in the past. There is no clear way of resolving such disagreement or differences in emphasis. From the viewpoint of anyone influenced by positivism, these criteria can only be seen as values influencing our choice of theories. It is no simpler to resolve a dispute between scientists about the importance of predictive accuracy in a particular case than is to resolve an overtly moral dispute. Whereas the positivist must hold that all such disputes are beyond the scope of rational resolution, we are under no such constraint. Once we realize that scientific method is the product of human rationality, rather than what defines it, disputes about scientific method and its application can themselves be regarded as part of our attempt to understand the world better.

The idea that scientific method demands the filtering out of 'extraneous' values, irrelevant to the pursuit of truth, is itself controversial. Once positivism is discarded, it is difficult to maintain a clear distinction between 'internal' and 'external' reasons for adopting theories. Some philosophers lump all 'values' together as playing a part in conditioning choices, without recognizing that some are more relevant to the pursuit of truth than others. When truth disappears as a goal, as in some sociology of knowledge, it becomes impossible to distinguish between values on that basis. Yet, if we maintain a realist perspective, it should be obvious that some reasons for preferring one theory over another may not be very good ones. The world is not always as we want it to be.

To a convinced feminist, the fact that a modern scientific theory, such as sociobiology, contains certain assertions about the nature of women is a conclusive reason for rejecting it. She is so convinced of the truth of her belief about the female predicament that she is unwilling to accept anything conflicting with it. Similarly a fundamentalist Christian will wish to reject the theories of modern evolutionary biology because he is so sure that God made the world in a different way. This is not an arbitrary, or even necessarily irrational, thing to do. He is convinced of what is the truth of the matter, and will not listen to modern scientists who disagree. The problem is not that he is basing his views on 'values' rather than 'facts' but that he disagrees with scientists about the facts, just as scientists disagree with each other. They each put weight on different criteria of truth, and the argument should be about which criteria have proved to be the best guides to truth.

Scientific theories about the origin of the universe are themselves sometimes influenced by theological or anti-theological criteria. Some scientists may oppose, say, the theory of the universe beginning with a 'big bang' because they feel that such a theory might give comfort to theists. Others might put it forward partly because it coincides with their belief in a God who created the universe. Both positions may appear unscientific and therefore wrong, but this must be too hasty a conclusion. It is not irrational for those who consider they have grounds for certain metaphysical beliefs to allow them to influence their scientific work. It is not a matter of shame that they are governed by factors external to science. What would be irrational is if they carried on their scientific work in a manner which detached it completely from all their other beliefs. If people know what is true in some area, they must let that knowledge impinge on their scientific work when relevant. Otherwise the latter cannot itself hope to produce truth. The catch is whether someone really possesses knowledge in the first place. Science has proved a successful way of challenging prejudice and bigotry, even though it can itself also generate bigotry. Those who allow their scientific outlook to be governed by other beliefs have to be very certain that they do have good grounds for them and must be prepared to justify them in open, rational argument.

OBJECTIVITY IN SOCIAL SCIENCE

Anyone who subordinates the proper methods of science to the demands of certain preconceptions must have good grounds for thinking that the preconceptions help rather than hinder in the search for truth. Otherwise the rational person will abandon them. Some may wish to suggest that science is itself imbued with non-rational values and that any attempt to prove otherwise is merely to indulge yet again in a rational reconstruction of science that pays scant attention to the way science has actually developed. Yet this position not only removes science as the paradigm of rational activity but is liable to undermine the very idea of rationality. It suggests that scientists see what they want to see because of their values and cannot change them rationally.

Why must it be assumed that such values cannot be changed? They may be so much part of the fabric of one's conceptual scheme that it could be impossible to know one has them. Even the interests governing one's quest for knowledge may not be made explicit. However, the ambition of many sociologists of knowledge is to perform precisely this task and unmask the ideology at work in different cases. It seems arbitrary to rule out this possibility at the outset. Much more likely an explanation for assuming that values are beyond the scope of reason is the lingering shadow of positivism, according to which one cannot use reason to change values because only value-free science is genuinely rational. If positivism is repudiated, but reason is still excluded, some deterministic thesis is being put forward, according to which the values people have are totally the product of, say, their economic background. The drawback of such global claims is their reflexivity. The person making the claim is also the prisoner of his or her own economic background, and so the claim itself will be infected with values.

One writer, Loren Graham, on the connection between science and values contrasts two approaches to the problem which he dubs 'expansionist' and 'restrictionist'. Expansionists 'cite evidence within the body of scientific theories and findings which can supposedly be used, either directly or indirectly, to support conclusions about sociopolitical values.'[6] Graham cites sociobiology as an example of science encroaching on territory which previously belonged to values, because it attempts to provide scientific explanations of sociopolitical values. On the other side is 'restrictionism', 'an approach that confines science to a particular realm or a particular methodology and leaves values outside its boundaries.' One example he gives is the view that science and religion cannot conflict because they are concerned with entirely different things. Scientists found that they were better able to continue their work unmolested, by keeping away from religious and social controversy. Similarly defenders of existing social values benefited by a clear demarcation between science and values. Graham remarks: 'If you insist that science and values do not mix, then the antecedent values of society are protected.'[7] This perhaps suggests that the idea of science as 'value-free' is itself the result of a human decision about values.

While trying to move away from what he terms the 'polarities' of 'value-free science' and 'science-free values', Graham is apparently still in the grip of positivist prejudices about science. He assumes that science is the source of knowledge and that the problem must be basically how far it encroaches on other areas. When he talks of values he means 'social values',[8] so that, if science is seen as a spectrum, fields such as astronomy and physics will be at what he terms 'the far "value-free" end'. Yet, if we take values to encompass the strategies adopted in the pursuit of truth, physics is far from value-free. The whole idea of values being mixed with science to a greater or lesser extent itself trades on the assumption that facts and values are in principle separable. The concessions made by writers like Graham amount to little more than a demonstration that this is very difficult to achieve in practice. In fact he begins his book by accepting that 'the intellectual prohibition against confusion of "is" and "ought" still reigns.'[9] Modern philosophy of science has to question this distinction, since 'facts' are established by processes of human reasoning identical to those which establish 'values'. One possible response to this is to conclude that science rests on the same shaky subjectivist foundations as morality. That appears to be the position of Feyerabend.

A more obvious conclusion must surely be that questions of values need no longer be compared unfavourably with scientific questions, so that it appears that only the latter are capable of rational resolution. Disagreement between scientists is not only healthy but may itself be an indispensable part of scientific method. There are, however, no set procedures for resolving such differences, despite what traditional philosophy of science has maintained. When one scientist rates accuracy of prediction more highly than another, it may be impossible at that stage to say who is wrong. Similarly, when conflict arises in areas beyond science, the mere fact that immediate resolution of the difficulty seems unlikely does not mean that it is all a matter of subjective taste and that human reason must be impotent.

Some wish to preserve the distinction between scientific and non-scientific method, by accepting that science depends on values, but asserting that some are internal to its method – as when scientists value truth – and others, such as political values, are external. 'Value-freedom' for science would then involve the removal not so much of all values as of those that are considered inappropriate. That involves accepting that values as such are integral to science and govern what we accept as a fact. Once the argument is seen to be not about purifying science of the taint of 'values' but about which values are essential to its purposes and which bias us away from them, any distinction between fact and value becomes irrelevant.

Graham remarks that in the social sciences 'some concepts are irre-trievably value-laden'.[10] This phrase itself reflects positivist prejudice. If no part of the quest for human knowledge can fail to be value-laden, it seems pointless to regret the fact. Each quest for knowledge involves the selection of some features as relevant and the dismissal of others. Sometimes, as in the physical sciences, the criteria for this can be made explicit, but in other cases this may be harder. The social issues are concerned with human activities, and it is inevitable that social scientists are influenced by their own views about man's place in the world. Religious and political issues can never be far away. To many imbued with positivist principles this will seem dangerous and unscientific. What is more dangerous, however, is that methods developed by the physical sciences for predicting and controlling the physical environment are assumed to be the only ones available for gaining knowledge in other areas.

The quest for a 'value-free' social science has permeated all the social sciences. The scientific outlook appeared to dictate that personal view-points and all contents of consciousness were subjective and to be ignored in a properly scientific account. What people valued, and indeed the value to be put on people, seemed to be part of this. True scientists, it seemed, should not be concerned with mere feelings, whether their own or other people's. As Habermas remarks in connection with the whole issue of value-freedom, 'positivism has permeated the self understanding of the social sciences.'[11]

One consequence has been the unfortunate use of the concepts of objectivity and subjectivity. Science is concerned with what is objective, and therefore true. Questions of value are to be consigned to the category of the subjective, and therefore unconnected with any claim to knowledge. Yet there can be a marked slide from one meaning of 'objec-tive' to another. Malinowski, writing about culture, flatly says: 'Nothing can be objective which is not accessible to observation.'[12] This links objectivity with detachment from any particular point of view, so that what is objective has to be public. Yet this is a different idea of objec-tivity from that invoked in a claim to objective truth. The latter is what is true, whatever people may happen to think. The dispassionate, detached objectivity of a scientist at work in the laboratory does not confer a monopoly on objective truth. If I have a pain, it is real enough, even though it may not be examined in a laboratory. What is objectively there may not always be divorced from all particular points of view.

The physical sciences may have good reason for seeking the kind of objectivity which ruthlessly ignores the perspective of the individual.

When scientists investigate the properties of matter, their own experience of the relevant stuff is irrelevant, since that will tell us about the scientists and not about matter. When social scientists investigate the functioning of some aspect of human society, it is much more difficult to maintain that human experience and the perspective of individuals must be ruled out of account. Such a view may have seemed scientific, and it is obvious that, in so far as social scientists are investigating other societies, their own perspective should be excluded as far as possible. Yet there is a danger in treating human beings and human societies in the way physicists deal with physical objects. Behaviourist and reductionist methods have at times seemed the only ones which social science could use if it were to be recognized as genuine science. The measurement of publicly verifiable behaviour seemed the hallmark of an objective approach. The task of the social sciences appeared to be the discovery of laws governing human behaviour.

A genuinely objective and scientific approach to the study of human society will not copy the tactics of the physical sciences, but is constrained by the nature of what is being studied. If the social sciences are governed by the reality they are investigating, they must recognize the differences as well as the similarities between social and physical reality. The desire of natural scientists to predict and control their environment need not automatically be shared by social scientists. In some areas general regularities in human behaviour may be discovered and some predictions may be successful. Mary Hesse remarks about this: 'Where these things are the case, we may speak of "objectivity" in the social realm, in whatever sense we wish to speak of it in the natural realm, and we *may* (not *must*) make the same choice of value goals for the social as for the natural sciences.'[13] This perhaps suggests that the term 'objectivity' should only be used when the social sciences ape the natural sciences. In fact, if the natural sciences are being truly objective, they are paying attention to the nature of what they are studying. If the social sciences adopt the same policy, they will be emulating the method of the physical sciences by reflecting the nature of social reality, even though this may mean treating it as very different from physical reality. Genuine objectivity involves being true to the reality under investigation.

THE VALUES OF SOCIAL SCIENCE

Our choice of theory will be guided by values which themselves are linked with our understanding of the reality we are studying. The criteria adopted by physical scientists for what constitutes a good theory are shaped by the desire to gain knowledge; the criteria for the choice of a theory by social scientists must be similarly shaped. Views about the adequacy of a theory will inevitably be influencd by assumptions about the nature of human beings and their relationship with society. There may seem an element of circularity about this. Surely the social sciences are going to discover for us some of the answers to this kind of question? Yet the physical sciences have progressed through a continuous winnowing of good theories from bad, and our understanding of physical reality is increased as our initial assumptions are modified. The way we evaluate a theory is itself the product of scientific progress. Only slowly has it been realized that theological preconceptions about the way the world was created may hinder rather than help our understanding of physical processes.

In the same way, the assumptions of the social sciences and our ideas of what makes a good social theory may have to be modified in the light of increased knowledge. This does not alter the fact that philosophical assumptions about human nature are built into any understanding about the way society works. Behaviourist views, like any others, coupled with an eagerness to quantify results in social research, undoubtedly carry with them basic conceptions about human nature.[14] All private and individual perspectives are ignored unless they can be expressed in behavioural terms. The result seems to many to be profoundly dehumanizing, in that anything distinctively human is ignored in the name of science.

Richard Rorty refers to the controversy in the social sciences between what he terms 'objectivity' and 'hermeneutics', the quarrel between those who wish to model the social sciences on the physical ones and those who emphasize the importance of achieving 'understanding':

> Foucault is doubtless right that the social sciences have coarsened the moral fiber of our rulers. Something happens to politicians who are exposed to endless tabulations of income levels, rates of recidivism, cost-effectiveness of artillery fire, and the like – something like what happens to concentration camp guards. . . . The rulers of the liberal democracies come to think that nothing matters but what shows up in the expert's predictions. They cease to think of their fellow citizens as fellow citizens.[15]

These are harsh words, and Rorty himself recognizes that it is important to 'take hold of social forces and use them to alleviate human suffering'. Mere hermeneutics is not enough. Nevertheless a scientific emphasis on prediction and control can lead to a desire to manipulate people as if they were mere physical objects. The attitude is justified if that is all people are, but it is significant that policy-makers cannot in all consistency apply that analysis to themselves. They have to see themselves as rational and responsible agents, deciding, perhaps in good faith, what is best for others.

Treating people in a scientific and detached manner can result in not treating them as persons at all. How, though, are they to be viewed by social scientists and those they advise? Social scientists cannot avoid facing the most basic questions about human nature, any more than they can avoid making choices between different sets of values. The pretence that social science can be 'value-free' itself results in a definite set of values and a distinctive way of regarding human beings. The scientific detachment of the social engineer, bleakly manipulating the lives of others, is even more horrifying when it is honestly considered that this represents some ideal of scientific neutrality.

The urge in social science to aim for successful prediction and control as basic values may not be linked just to explicit beliefs about human nature but also to a desire for some kind of professional expertise. The physical scientist knows how to manipulate the physical environment, and it might seem to follow that if social science is to be a source of knowledge it has to aim for similar control of social reality. High hopes vested in subjects such as sociology, or even economics, and later leading to disillusionment have very often depended on this simplistic view. The search for laws of human behaviour has seemed an integral part of the pursuit of knowledge, and the future of, say, sociology has appeared to depend on deterministic assumptions about human beings. Moreover, sociology had to prove that the most important causes of human behaviour were social if it was to be respected as a discipline. Perhaps, however, human beings are able to direct themselves on occasions in a rational manner and are not wholly determined by causes outside their control. If scientific knowledge is not the only kind of knowledge, the scarcity of laws on human social behaviour need not involve the collapse of social science.

The values of social science have to be rooted in its subject-matter, to enable it to see more clearly the nature of society. Anything distorting its vision must be bad, while anything helping it to discover truth must be good. The possibility of scientific neutrality is an illusion, if only because no scientist can be neutral in respect of truth and falsity. What, then, is the truth about society? As in physical science, we shall expect considerable disagreement to arise as different theories are adopted or rejected. In one respect, the social sciences have a harder job than the natural sciences. It can be argued that the latter must assume the existence of an independent physical reality.[16] The social sciences, however, cannot just assume the existence of 'social reality' as an independent entity. One of the major arguments in the social sciences is how much content can be given to this notion. It is possible to be a realist without accepting it. Even though it might appear that, if the physical sciences are concerned with physical reality, the social ones are concerned with social reality, this immediately weights the question in favour of holist views as opposed to individualist ones. The respective attention to be given to the individual and the society itself involves a major decision about values. The ontological priority given to one of them will undoubtedly be reflected in policital views. There is a major divide between those tracing the ills, and goods, of society back to the activity of individuals and those locating them in the structures of society. This is not a mere choice between 'values', but is also a factual matter about the working of society.

IDEOLOGY

Are we to say that all social theories are irredeemably ideological? Much depends on the meaning given to the term. In one sense, the term means no more than 'conceptual scheme'. People with an ideology think they know while others with different ideologies will not see things from their point of view. An ideology on this understanding could never be shown to be mistaken, and there could be no such thing as false consciousness. We could not talk of minds so distorted that they falsify everything they come across. Ideas of distortion and falsity could have no application.

Karl Mannheim tried to avoid the use of the word 'ideology' in his sociology of knowledge. He preferred to speak of the perspective of a thinker, meaning by that 'the subject's whole mode of conceiving things as determined by his historical and social setting'.[17] As a result, his approach was different from that of Marx. Mannheim comments:

> The sociology of knowledge actually emerged with Marx. . . . However in his work the sociology of knowledge is still indistinguishable from the unmasking of ideologies since for him social strata and classes were the bearers of ideologies.[18]

Marx thought ideology involved false belief, and this implied he had a standpoint from which to distinguish truth and falsity. Mannheim was more concerned with relating beliefs to their overall perspective. He thus invites the rejoinder that nothing can be claimed to be true if everything is perspectival. His 'relationism' can easily collapse into relativism. Whatever is claimed cannot 'be formulated absolutely but only in terms of the perspective of a given situation'.[19] He gives as an example of what he means the case of a peasant who moves to a city after growing up in the narrow confines of his village. Gradually he becomes more detached from rural ways of thinking and perhaps quite consciously distinguishes between 'rural' and 'urban' ideas. He can no longer take for granted what he previously believed. He has seen an alternative set of ideas, and the mere knowledge of their existence helps to undermine the absolute character of what he was brought up to accept without question. Mannheim comments that the distinction between 'rural' and 'urban' demonstrates the beginnings of the approach that the sociology of knowledge wishes to develop. He continues: 'That which within a given group is accepted as absolute appears to the outsider conditioned by the group situation and recognized as partial.'[20]

We have already seen how the sociology of knowledge has been used in an attempt to explain science as a social activity. This example shows how it can easily explain all human activity by relating it to its social background. Mannheim insists that all assertions have to be related to 'the perspective of a given situation'. Yet, if this is so, the familiar problem of reflexivity reappears, since we can say that his own claims about the sociology of knowledge are the expression of *his* perspective. Mannheim himself hankers after the possibility of a position 'from which a total perspective would be possible'.[21] He thinks of 'unattached intellectuals' as a group which might be able to transcend the narrow vision of particular classes and interest groups. He says hopefully: 'Thus they might play the part of watchmen in what otherwise would be a pitch-black night.' Yet intellectuals themselves form a class that can develop very definite interests which are economic as well as academic. The danger is that their viewpoint is as partial as that of anyone.

The more beliefs and ideas are related to their background instead of being examined on their own merits, the more truth becomes inaccessible. Our attention is directed at the social pressures on people rather than on the validity or otherwise of ideas. If we are convinced that we have no choice, since the possibility of independently assessing truth is an illusion, we are still being governed by an idea which claims some kind of validity. In fact, the view that everything is ideological is a very corrosive belief, striking at the very basis of our reasons for believing or doing anything. Once I realize that my beliefs are *only* the product of my background, I can have no grounds for continuing to believe them. Even Mannheim's peasant who goes to the city does not go this far, because he presumably thinks that city ideas are better. He is impressed by them and perhaps feels rather contemptuous of his simple origins, using words like 'unsophisticated' to criticize them. Only, perhaps, if he becomes a sociologist, will he relate the ideas of the city to urban styles of living just as rural ones are related to the simplistics of country life. Then a certain contempt of *all* ideas could set in, as he concludes that even the perspective of sociology is conditioned by its background.

Social scientists face a difficult task, since they are supposed to be detached and see how many viewpoints are partial and socially conditioned. They must be able to compare different cultures. Yet their insights must somehow be liberating rather than paralysing. Berger and Kellner insist that 'sociology is a science, not a set of doctrines',[22] but realize that this view stands in tension with what they term 'the "debunking" or negative threat of the sociological perspective'.[23] The trouble is that sociology seems to expose the way in which the world is 'made' by different cultures. It apparently demonstrates that absolute standards which we take as self-evidently valid, whether in religion, morality or science itself, are merely the result of the way a particular society has developed. What is good or true or rational seems to be merely what we have been trained to accept without question as such. There may too be forces at work in society sustaining these beliefs of which we may be totally unaware. Social reality may be only the visible part of a building with a complicated structure of interests and causal mechanisms. The apparent reality may not be the genuine one. Berger and Kellner sum up the way in which sociology can even play a subversive role, undermining our own confidence in our beliefs and even hankering after a total change. They say that sociology can show us that 'not only is the world not what it appears to be, but it could be different from what it is'.[24]

This approach, however, is not necessarily the same as that of Mannheim. The 'relationist' gambit relating everything to its social context certainly shows the arbitrariness of any social system. When everything is ideological, ideology ceases to matter. There is no way that it can be 'unmasked', and all that will happen is that one ideology may be replaced by another. The concept of ideology is only useful if it means more than a definition of reality. Ideology must be contrasted with a correct understanding of reality. The definition given by Berger and Kellner is that 'an ideology is a set of definitions of reality legitimizing specific vested interests in society'.[25] They hope to avoid vexed questions in sociology about who is right about reality, while still being able to say whether a particular standpoint is ideological. They regard a belief-system as an ideology if it explains and justifies the vested interests of a group. They continue by referring to a claim that a system is ideological.

Such a proposition, assuming that it is empirically grounded in evidence, is an objective and 'value-free' statement, despite the fact that the proposition brackets the question as to whether the belief system is finally valid or not.[26]

The relationship of a particular belief to vested interests can be shown, independently of whether it happens to be true or not. Whether a belief is ideological thus appears to be an ordinary matter of fact. Even a true belief could be ideological. Such an interpretation steers a middle course between the view that everything is ideological and the position that ideology is false belief. It seems to preserve the cherished neutrality of science while not undermining all notions of reality. In particular, it treats social reality as a reality about which discoveries can be made.

However attractive such a position may be, the argument of this chapter must raise questions about it. The association of what is empirically grounded with what is objective and value-free is itself unwarranted. The values of positivist science are conveyed only too clearly by it. No statement can be value-free in the sense required. We need to discover the appropriate values for the pursuit of truth in sociology. The desire for 'value-freedom' may often be an expression of fear that the wrong values will be adopted. Which are the right ones is itself controversial. If physical scientists cannot agree on the criteria for a good theory, we are unlikely to find agreement in the more recently established social sciences. There is broad agreement in the physical sciences on the kind of criteria to be used, but the social sciences may not even have reached that stage. A Marxist social scientist might make faithfulness to Marxist doctrine a criterion of a good social theory, while the liberal will feel that this is to allow political values to enter social science in an illegitimate way. Yet the liberal's desire for political neutrality can equally be seen as a 'value'.

Disputes about the distinction between facts and values are themselves usually disputes about which values are important for social science. They in turn depend on questions about the nature of the reality being investigated by social science. Whatever else it is, it must be social, and this means that the social sciences need not be called upon to adjudicate the truth of every belief in society. The social characteristics of a religion, for example, will be a fit object of study for sociology or social anthropology, and they exist because the religion is believed by its practitioners to be true. Whether it is actually true is a separate issue which cannot be settled by social sciences. Yet this very admission can be the source of trouble. 'Bracketing off' questions of truth may be a legitimate method in social science, since it ensures that social science deals only with social reality. Otherwise every sociological investigation of religious practices will become a debate about the existence of God. Yet 'bracketing off' may be the result, whether intended or not, of making the real nature of religion to appear a social matter, explicable by the sociologist. Because questions of the truth of a particular belief have been put on one side as being beyond the professional competence of the sociologist, it may seem as if it does not matter whether the belief is true or not. Theology seems irrelevant, and religious studies all-important. Social influences become central, and it is somehow forgotten that the belief is held because it is thought to be true.

Unless sociology embraces relativism, it must remember that the rational pursuit of truth may be a prime characteristic of those it studies. The scope for sociological explanation of particular phenomena may thereby be lessened, but sociology itself can claim truth for itself without blushing. In social science the 'values' or criteria for the choice of theories that are adopted must be subordinated to the quest for truth. They can then genuinely claim to be sciences in as full a sense as the physical sciences. This is not because they have the same methods. That would be inappropriate, because their objects of investigation are different. It is because both in a systematic manner tailor their methods and their 'values' to the nature of their subject-matter.

NOTES

1 Kuhn, 'Objectivity, Value Judgments and Theory Choice' in his *The Essential Tension*, 1977, p. 331.
2 Mary Hesse, *Revolutions and Reconstructions in the Philosophy of Science* 1980, p. xiv.
3 Ibid., p. xxiii.
4 Ibid., p. 201.
5 Ibid., p. 202.
6 Loren Graham, *Between Science and Values*, 1981, p. 6.
7 Ibid., p. 29.
8 Ibid., p. 356.
9 Ibid., p. 1.
10 Ibid., p. 9.
11 J. Habermas, *Knowledge and Human Interests*, 1972, p. 303.

12 B. Malinowski, *A Scientific Theory of Culture*, 1944, p. 69.
13 Hesse, *Revolutions and Reconstructions* p. 200.
14 See my *The Shaping of Man*, ch. 2, for a discussion of the views of B. F. Skinner.
15 Rorty, 'Method and Morality', in N. Haan et al. (eds), *Social Science as a Moral Inquiry*, 1983, p. 164.
16 See my *Reality at Risk*.
17 Karl Mannheim, *Ideology and Utopia*, 1936, p. 239.
18 Ibid., p. 278.
19 Ibid., p. 254.
20 Ibid., p. 253.
21 Ibid., p. 143.
22 Berger and Kellner, *Sociology Reinterpreted*, p. 17.
23 Ibid., p. 13.
24 Ibid.
25 Ibid., p. 70.
26 Ibid., p. 71.

7

Economics and Society

RATIONALITY AND DESIRES

The question of value-freedom is intimately connected with views about the nature of human society. Empirical disciplines which proudly eschew all values inevitably run a risk of applying inappropriate values to the task in hand. This is particularly so in the social sciences, where the methods, and hence the values, appropriate to the study of inanimate objects are sometimes adopted without question. Max Weber has been influential in the advocacy of value-freedom for the social sciences, considering that the choice of values must be left to the individual. He concluded that 'value-freedom' was a requirement in empirical matters, and that any debate about values could only have the purpose of understanding what each of the parties to a dispute really means. This presupposes, he says, an 'appreciation, quite simply, of the possibility that ultimate values might diverge, in principle, and irreconcilably'.[1]

According to this view, questions about the ends to be pursued in any empirical discipline can never be squarely faced. The empiricist, following Hume, can only be concerned with the means to given ends; the true scientist, *qua* scientist, must never consider what ought to be done but only show how people may obtain the objects of whatever desires they happen to have. The scientist's role is seen as similar to that of a senior British civil servant, who is supposed to devise means to whatever ends are chosen by the government of the day, and not play any part in the formulation of policy. The same civil servants can survive changes of government and advise on the undoing of the very policy they previously helped to implement. Whether this admirable neutrality is in principle possible is a further issue.

Weber had no doubts of the possibility of separating value judgements from empirical disciplines. He says:

> It seems to be possible to establish without a shadow of doubt that in the
> area of practical political value-judgements (especially in the fields of

economics and social policy), as soon as guidance for a valued course of action is to be sought, all that an empirical discipline with the means at its disposal can show is (i) the unavoidable means; (ii) the unavoidable side-effects; (iii) the resulting conflict of several possible value-judgements with each other in their practical consequences.[2]

Economists who allow themselves to be influenced by political judgements may be pursuing a dangerous course. This is not because economics can somehow be separated from values and put on a strictly 'factual' basis, but because political considerations, particularly those connected with short-term party interest, are irrelevant to the practice of economics. What a particular political party would like to be true, in order to facilitate the implementation of its policy, may not be the same as what is true. The economist should not get trapped into telling politicians only what they want to hear. If economics is truly a science, it must be geared to what actually happens in society, rather than to particular political interests. Of course there is bound to be disagreement about what does actually happen, and there will probably be connections between disagreements among economists and wider political arguments. This will at least partly be because of the underdetermination of economic theory by the facts. To put it another way, economists do not possess the requisite knowledge of the phenomena they are studying. Sometimes this will be because of the complex nature of the interactions involved, and it could also be that human beings are in the last resort unpredictable. Like all social sciences, economics often tries to discount the fact of human freedom of choice, because its desire to be a precise science seems threatened by a recognition of this. Yet, by the way it chooses to view humans, 'values' can be built into the nature of the discipline from the start. That may be unavoidable, but it is essential that the values aid the acquisition of knowledge and do not hinder it.

Weber advocated 'value-freedom' because of the empiricist assumption that agreement is possible about facts but may in principle never be reached about 'values'. The breakdown of the distinction between facts and values has had the result in some modern philosophy of science that agreement about what was considered a 'factual' matter seems impossible at times. It is, however, equally possible to see that obstacles to reaching agreement about values have been removed. They are expected to live up to an impossible standard. The existence of apparently irresolvable disagreement does not mean that there is no truth to be discovered in the area. Without any values to begin with, we have no guidance about where to start looking.

The assumption that ends cannot be rationally chosen and that we are restricted to discovering means to set goals is contentious. Philosophers have for long argued about whether human reason can establish what is worth pursuing or whether human desire provides the necessary and unalterable framework for the exercise of reason. Some desires themselves seem irrational, or even evil, and these are open to criticism. Must reason only show us how to obtain what we desire most efficiently, and how to eradicate conflicts between different desires? It is hard to avoid the conclusion that the subordination of reason to desire in empiricist philosophy often stems from the difficulty of resolving disagreements. Again and again we come back to the alleged fact that there are settled procedures in science for coming to agreement. Where agreement cannot be reached, the matter seems outside the scope of science, and hence neither factual nor a matter of reason. We are just left with the fact that different people want different things. We cannot go on to talk of what they should want, since that will merely reopen the disagreement. Science can deal with the fact that people do have varying desires, and may explain why they do, but it seemingly cannot cope with the question of what they ought to desire.

The dichotomy between fact and value, and reason and desire, goes very deep. It not only explicitly governs the way social scientists view their own activities but also influences the way they study human behaviour. If desire is logically prior to reason, it appears to follow that we act as we do because we want to, rather than because, at least on occasion, we rationally believe we ought to. What we want determines what we try to get, and our reason merely provides us with the means of getting it. If, though, we each act because of what we want, does not that inevitably show we are all ultimately selfish? It seems that we are each trying to get as much as possible of what we want. This is almost a travesty of an argument. Just as we can only think about what we think, and jibes about being imprisoned within our own conceptual scheme are misplaced, we can only do what we do. The rejoinder that we must have done what we wanted because that is what we chose to do reduces the idea of doing what one wants to utter triviality. The man who throws himself on a grenade to save his comrades is in a sense doing what he wants. He was not pushed. Saying that he is motivated by desire, and therefore by implication is selfish, is ludicrous. Wanting to save others at the expense of oneself is altruistic, not selfish.

Most people may indeed be selfish, but they do not have to be. If it becomes true by definition that everyone is selfish, the point is not worth making. It is important to distinguish the claim about how people happen to behave from a methodological assumption about how they behave.

Governments may well be called on to cope with the ingrained selfishness of their citizens, and perhaps exploit it by means of incentives to work harder. This is a distinct question from the way the social sciences should approach the matter. In trying to understand or to explain human behaviour, they have to make assumptions about the nature of human rationality and its effect on human action. They have to face the issue whether the rational policy for anyone is to maximize one's own personal advantage. In other words, is getting as much as possible of what one wants, even at the expense of others, not just a widespread human trait but a normal feature of human action? Such an assumpton is a very large one to make about human nature, but it appears to be made by much modern economics. Amartya Sen writes:

> While consistency is taken in economic theory to be a necessary condition of rationality, it is usual to supplement that requirement by some substantive view as to what the individual would maximize. The regularity of consistent pursuit of self-interest is a frequently used assumption of rational behaviour. . . . It is implicitly present in much of traditional economic theory.[3]

The possibility of prediction seems much greater if humans do indeed act in this way, since, if you know what they want, you know what they will try to obtain. On the other hand, what they try to get is by definition what they want. Desire is revealed in behaviour, and economists can keep well away from the difficulty of trying to grasp the contents of other people's minds. Their beliefs about priorities and their reasoning processes can seem irrelevant except in so far as they are exhibited in behaviour. The methodological demand for scientific objectivity excludes them, since they are inaccessible to the scientist.

ECONOMICS AND EGOISM

Economists are not just cynical about the prevalence of human selfishness but often make it a condition of rationality. The rational person becomes the one who seeks to satisfy his or her desires regardless of the impact this will have on others. Two economists feel able to refer to the 'archetypal economic man'. He seeks 'to maximize his own welfare without concern for how this compares with the welfare of others.'[4] They are themselves critical of this notion and point out the difficulty of providing 'public goods' if each person is assumed to be concerned only with personal advantage. No one will be willing to pay taxes merely to provide services for others. They also remark: 'Elemental personal values of honesty, truthfulness, trust, restraint and obligation are all necessary inputs to an efficient (as well as pleasant) contractual society, but all are without significant direct pay-off to the individuals providing them'[5]

There may be an indirect pay-off. Theories about self-interest usually have to acknowledge that enlightened self-interest demands a different policy from the ruthless pursuit of what is immediately in my interest. Co-operation with others is sometimes necessary for the achievement of long-term desires. It may be a disadvantage for me now to help you, but you may help me later if I do. Similarly, I may make more money now by being dishonest, but lose it all when others find that they cannot trust me. The maxim 'honesty is the best policy' could be fervently held by a very selfish person.

However this may be, economists make predictions on the assumption that all individuals are 'maximizing utility' for themselves. In other words, we each pursue a policy which we hope will obtain the most possible of what we want and the least of what we do not want. This can be put in mathematical terms, with weight given to different probabilities. Sometimes it is thought that the aim is to maximize overall utility, so that one's own interests are not counted as more important than those of anyone else. I can thus weigh costs to a society against total benefits, or I can restrict my vision to what will or will not benefit *me*. In both cases it may seem as if I merely reveal my own preferences. In the one instance I exhibit a preference for my own welfare, while in the other I show a preference for the welfare of others as well. Indulging the latter might seem selfish because it is my preference, whereas it is precisely the opposite. It may be for this reason that talk of behaviour revealing preferences seems so easily and so explicitly to lead to the assumption of egoism.

Sen suggests that the concept of preference is made to carry too much. It can be defined merely in terms of choice in such a way that I show that I prefer whatever I happen to choose. Saying that preference can be understood in a mathematical operation as the binary representation of individual choice, he comments: 'The difficulty arises in interpreting preference thus defined as preference in the usual sense with the property that if a person prefers x to y then he must regard himself to be better off with x than with y.' Sen himself points out that the separation of the concepts of choice, preference and welfare may make things less simple but produce an important conclusion. Economic incentives may not be the only means of affecting human behaviour. I may be open to influences other than appeals to my own material self-interest. References to the general good may not be as irrelevant as is assumed by 'traditional economic theory'.

Apart from the assumption that everyone acts in accordance with what they most want (and that is equated with the most powerful desire), much economics is firmly committed to explanation in terms of atomic individuals with fixed desires. Features of society are explained in terms of the desires, and are not allowed to explain them. Rationality involves working out the means to given ends as set by desire. In this respect, economics treads firmly in the empiricist tradition set by Hume. Like him, it can assume that desires remain constant, and there is thus a suitable basis for economic explanation and prediction. If tastes and desires were subject to change, the scope available for economics would be correspondingly reduced. Its prediction could only be valid given a particular set of human desires. What held in one society might not hold in another.

Given an assumption about the stability of human nature, the economist can be much more confident. Stigler and Becker explicitly propose the hypothesis that 'widespread and/or persistent human behaviour can be explained by a generalized calculus of utility-maximizing behaviour, without introducing the qualification "tastes remaining the same".'[7] By positing stable preferences, and assuming people act in accordance with them, the economist can remain on firm ground. Stigler and Becker were afraid that admitting a difference in tastes meant economists would have to hand explanations of behaviour over, as they put it, to 'whoever studies and explains tastes (psychologists? anthropologists? phrenologists? sociobiologists?)'.[8] They claim that on their preferred interpretation the economist never reaches this impasse, but goes on looking for differences in prices or incomes to explain differences in behaviour. They are against abandoning 'opaque and complicated problems with the easy suggestion that the further explanation will perhaps someday be produced by one of our sister behavioural sciences'.[9]

Any social science can quite reasonably take as part of its methodology the policy that it should not give up too easily. Saying that a particular matter is inexplicable by economists stops them looking for further explanations. As a result, they could be handing over to other social sciences issues which may after all be within the scope of economics. Nevertheless, refusing to admit the relevance of other social sciences can be equally dangerous. Stigler and Becker appear to be saying that economics has no need to take any notice of, say, sociology. Because they believe that human preferences remain stable even in different ages and times, they leave no room for a sociological understanding of the way desires can be created by society. It is often held, for instance, that in a consumer society advertising can create wants that were not there before. Stigler and Baker explicitly reject this.

One writer on the philosophic assumptions of economics notes that the methodological roots of the subject are highly individualistic. He says flatly that 'the tendency in economics is to explain society as the product of individual choice'. He continues: 'But in accounting for wants, the fact that they are in major part a reflection of cultural and social phenomena that precede the individual cannot be overlooked.'[10]

This is the edge of the large controversy about the forces at work shaping human nature.[11] The crucial point is that the assumptions made about the issue determine the character of any social science. Indeed, it sometimes seems as if the assumptions determine which social science one turns to. It is only a slight exaggeration to suggest that someone who believes that humans are rational agents, and that society is the result of their interactions, will be drawn to economics, while anyone convinced that humans are primarily moulded by their social background will be likely to be more sympathetic to sociology. Yet the social sciences should not provide alternative, conflicting viewpoints of man and society. There is something basically at fault with any methodology which invites confrontation with the other social sciences. Even ignoring the findings of other disciplines is an error. Economics cannot be right to view society in an individualist manner, if sociology is right to look at it from a holist point of view. Sociology cannot be right to talk to the social creation of wants, if economics is right to see everyone as having the same wants.

These disputes can break out within disciplines as well as between them, but it is important that the social sciences aim for a unified theory of society and man's place in it. Economics can be tempted to claim a monopoly of knowledge. Like, say, the sociology of knowledge, it produces all-embracing explanations which ignore the role of other branches of social science. For example, it cannot allow for alternative views of rationality, because of its equation of human rationality with a certain form of egoism. Either other subjects conform to the economist's idea of 'rational man', or they are dismissed as merely dealing with irrational aspects of human behaviour. McPherson comments:

> Extending the scope of rational explanations of conduct beyond the sphere of markets, as in the 'rational choice' theories of politics, has really meant pushing aside other modes of explanation in these areas and substituting economic methods. . . . When (as in the received view of economics)

sociology or psychology are seen as sciences of the irrational and economics as the science of the rational, prospects for meaningful communication between them seem pretty bleak.[12]

The economist's notion of 'rational man' is deficient, even according to its own criteria. The well-known example of the 'prisoners' dilemma' provides an illustration of this.[13] There are different versions but, put briefly, the situation is that two prisoners are known to be guilty of a serious crime, but there is not enough evidence to convict them of it, unless one gives evidence against the other. They are kept separately and told that they may confess and implicate the other. If neither does, they will each only be convicted for a minor crime and be given two years' imprisonment. If one does confess, he will go free and the evidence will send the other to prison for twenty years. If both confess, they will each be convicted but, because of their co-operation, the sentence will be reduced from twenty to ten years. As a result, each prisoner has a considerable incentive to confess so that he himself can go free. The situation is as follows.

If neither confesses:	2 years each
If A confesses, B does not:	A goes free, B gets 20 years
If B confesses, A does not:	B goes free, A gets 20 years
If both confess:	10 years each

If A is going to confess, it is in B's interest to do so as well. Otherwise he will go to prison for twenty years rather than ten. If A does not confess, it is still in B's interest to do so: he will go free, even though A will then go to prison for twenty years. A will reason in the same way about B and so they will both confess. It seems as if the rational strategy is to confess, whatever the other prisoner can be expected to do. Yet this produces a situation in which each will go to prison for ten years instead of two. The ruthless pursuit of egoism produces undesirable consequences even for the egoist.

It may not be sufficient for them to trust each other not to confess. Although mutual trust is of great importance in such situations, it will still be possible for one of the parties to trade on it. After all, if A can trust B not to confess, the rational course is then for A to confess and go free. His penalty for remaining silent would be two years' imprisonment. Yet B may well reason in a similar way. Mere confidence about the other's course of action will not necessarily help. Some feeling of an obligation which is binding, even if one is thereby worse off, appears to be essential. Moral standards of one kind or another are often invoked at this point.

The paradox seems to be that, if someone single-mindedly pursues his or her own interests, regardless of the cost to others, those interests will not in fact be served very well when everyone else is doing the same. Some form of co-operation becomes inevitable. The example of the prisoners' dilemma has suggested to many that society must provide the essential framework for the pursuit of one's own interests. The reasoning is similar to that of the seventeenth-century political philosopher, Thomas Hobbes, who tried to base the concept of political obligation on prudential considerations. He firmly believed in man's egoism, but saw that in a 'state of nature' disaster would follow. Life would be, in a famous phrase, 'nasty, brutish and short'. It is therefore in one's own longer-term interest to co-operate with sanctions, such as the punishments meted out by a state for those who do not. This would certainly alter the situation, and the egoist would have to take into account the likelihood of being found out and hence punished. As long, though, as one's only motive is one's own interest, there are going to be many situations, even in a social context, where egoism will only serve to undermine society, even if it is in no one's interest that this occurs. There will always be circumstances where I can uphold society only by deliberately forgoing my own immediate interest. The question must then be faced how far egoists can do this, particularly if they expect to gain from it. Indeed, they might even be called on to sacrifice their own long-term interests for the sake of society, perhaps even by laying down their own lives. Yet no egoist could consistently do this. It can never be guaranteed that the 'general good' and 'my good' will coincide.

Economists try to meet difficulties such as those illustrated by the prisoners' dilemma in various ways, but there seems to be a fundamental weakness in the whole notion of self-seeking rationality. It is certainly true that indirect consequences have to be taken into account as well as the direct ones, but even so the 'rational' course of action cannot be relied on to produce the best result. The insight that we do better through co-operating than by going it alone lies at the root of the formation of society. Nevertheless, if we are all only concerned for other people's interests as a means to furthering our own, we can easily produce a situation where everybody loses. Our commitment to the demands of society cannot be viewed according to the standards of rational egoism, of self-seeking 'economic man'. No doubt, if economists were right in their estimate of the motives of human behaviour, there would still have to be a certain measure of co-operation, but social arrangements would be in constant jeopardy, as each tried to gain an advantage over the rest.

Illustrations can be produced from many different contexts. In an arms race, two superpowers may aim for nuclear superiority at minimum cost. It is therefore in the interest of each to break any arms agreement fixing parity of weapons in order to get ahead of the other. It may be presumed that they will do so if they can without being detected. Unfortunately, however, this will not give them superiority if both reason in the same way. If each assumes that the other will break the agreement, they still have to continue the race, for fear of being left behind. Yet this will involve parity at great expense, whereas if they had both kept to the agreement they could have achieved the same result at a fraction of the cost. 'Rationality' apparently can produce a state of affairs which is not desired. Given a choice of superiority, parity at low cost, parity at great cost, and inferiority, it has only produced the third best possibility out of four options.

One practice at the heart of democratic society, that of voting in elections, itself often seems hard to explain if all the voters are self-seeking egoists. Not only does it become irrational for people to vote against their own interests and in what they conceive as the national interest, but it even seems hard to understand why many people vote at all. If the result of an election seems in doubt, most people will be anxious to cast a vote. Yet why should anyone suffer, say, the inconvenience of going out to vote on a wet night, when it is quite clear what the outcome is going to be? Predictions can sometimes be wildly inaccurate, but even so one vote is probably insignificant in a large election. Yet many still persist in voting. Suggesting that they are irrational seems to strike at the roots of theories about the working of democracy. The exercise of a political right like that would appear to many to need no further justification.

Amartya Sen is ready to consider the possibility of people making choices against their own interests, and suggests that we should not ignore what he terms 'commitment' in human behaviour. This notion appears to involve acting on principle, regardless of the consequences to the individual agent. The agent may thus act in a way expected to leave him or her worse off than available alternatives. Sen comments: 'The characteristic of commitment with which I am most concerned here is the fact that it drives a wedge between personal choice and personal welfare, and much of traditional economic theory relies on the identity of the two.'[14] He points out that, in the example of voting, people may be guided not so much by a choice to maximize expected utility but by a mere wish to record their preference. It must be a matter of some concern that such a normal and intelligible piece of human behaviour would be judged irrational in traditional economic theory.

PRIVATE INTEREST AND PUBLIC GOODS

Internal consistency is not enough to assure rationality. Some people may be completely consistent in the ordering of their preferences and the steps they take to achieve their goals. The preferences themselves, however, should not be regarded as necessarily fixed in human nature. Some may be, but others may themselves be the result of reason. Suggesting, as Hume did, that reason is the slave of the passions renders us powerless to modify our preferences or adopt new ones. His view was ameliorated by his belief that humans naturally felt sympathy for each other. If, though, it is assumed that our preferences are inevitably self-seeking, we seem to be left with a situation where rationality is construed as the most efficient and consistent way of destroying society through the ruthless pursuit of one's own short-term interests.

It has been suggested that one reason economists are reluctant to examine the origin of wants is that 'to do so would be to undermine a commitment to view the economic agent as an autonomous, free, chooser'.[15] Yet refusing to accept that human reason has any control over our desires strikes at the roots of all freedom. It merely locates the causes of our behaviour in whatever produces our desires. Transferring the causes from society to the individual organism does not make the position any less determinist. Denying the social determination of wants does not thereby increase the autonomy of the individual. Indeed, there are many who would feel that locating the origin of behaviour in society held out the possibility of change. They imagine that because societies can be modified there is the hope that, by changing society, they might eventually change the individual. By contrast, the ability to do what we want does not constitute freedom, if our wants are fixed and unalterable. We seem then to be mere puppets acting according to the dictates of something beyond our control – perhaps evolution through natural selection. In fact our autonomy seems undermined, whether our wants are created by biology or society. Impersonal forces seem to be moulding us, whether we are aware of it or not.

The economist's notion of rationality is a very widespread one, and it is often taken as self-evidently correct. John Rawls's theory of justice, for instance, explicitly makes use of a similar view. With the proviso that he believes a rational individual does not suffer from envy, he defines rationality as follows, saying it is 'the standard one familiar in social theory':

Thus in the usual way, a rational person is thought to have a coherent set of preferences between the options open to him. He ranks these options according to how well they further his purposes: he follows the plan which will satisfy more of his desires rather than less, and which has the greater chance of being successfully executed.[16]

There is nothing in this to suggest that preferences need be selfish. As I have suggested, I could have a preference for the welfare of others. Egoism is a further ingredient, although a tempting one to add once reference is made to 'preferences' and 'desires'. Rawls's version of liberalism leaves plenty of room for altruism. His focus of concern is not whether people should be altruists or egoists, but rather on the prior need that everyone should have equal liberty in which to make their choices. He wishes to achieve the kind of social co-operation in which each person is as free as possible to seek the satisfaction of his or her desires, whatever they may be. The only constraint is that others enjoy a similar liberty. The position is in many ways classically liberal, ensuring maximum freedom for individuals to implement their own choices. Since no conception of what is good is presupposed, everything depends on the preferences held by individuals. Some may very well seek to promote the welfare of others. Such a happy chance is not, however, enough to create a society. If any kind of community needs a willingness on the part of its members to sacrifice their own interests, there has to be a link between the existence of human society and the occurrence of altruism. The former is dependent on the latter, and so altruism must be more than a chance occurrence. It cannot be the result of randomly adopted choices. We need some theory which explains the connection between the claims of society and the wants of individuals.

This problem does not arise if individuals are considered abstractions from society, because society can then be assumed to create human desires. If we start with the individual, we need to close the gap between individual desires and the need for co-operation. This may be more than a theoretical matter, since individuals may have to be shown why they should care for the welfare of others at some expense to themselves. It is sometimes thought that laws and government exist for the precise purpose of plugging the gap. Hobbes believed, indeed, that rational egoists could remain true to their views and create such a government. Yet it remains problematic how viable a nation of rational egoists would be. Co-operation against one's immediate interest would always have to be enforced. Since it may be in the interest of each to obtain the fruits of co-operation without the cost, there will still be considerable incentive to break the law if it appears possible to escape detection. Much would depend on the efficiency of enforcement. It seems likely that a society would be very unstable if there was respect for the law only as a means to the furtherance of private interests, rather than as an end in itself. Law cannot be a substitute for morality, and no law can make people altruistic. It can serve as an important restraint, but there is no way it can make anyone act for the interests of others. Even if someone is compelled by law to make a contribution, he or she does not become an altruist. The effect of the action may be good, but because the person acted out of fear of legal sanctions, he or she is still pursuing a course of unremitting self-interest, and is likely to evade the law if possible.

The difficulties that arise when we envisage self-seeking 'economic man' in society can be shown by what has been called 'the free-rider problem'. Let us imagine a public good, such as the need for clean air. It is very often a characteristic of such goods that, while they are available to all, they can be produced by some without the participation of everyone. Yet there is often no way of preventing everyone from benefiting. The result is that individuals who refused to contribute to the production of the good may still share in the fruits of others' efforts. The problem arises why people should pay the undoubted cost of contributing if they can obtain the same benefits without doing so. Why should they not let others do the work? One smoking chimney may not make the air appreciably dirtier, and one outflow of sewage may not pollute the river unduly. One tax dodger will not bring the functioning of government to a halt. Why should one not use a hosepipe for one's garden in a drought, or use electricity in a power shortage? Why should one not seek a pay rise when general pay restraint is demanded? The problem is all too familiar. Each of us may find occasions when we are tempted to trade on the fact that others are contributing.

One stock retort to these questions is 'What if everyone did that?' A children's story once told of how a king wished the fountains of his capital city to flow with milk on a particular day of celebration. Everyone was to pour a contribution into the cisterns supplying the fountains. When they had done so, the fountains were turned on again, and flowed with water as clear as the previous day. Each person had reasoned that one pitcher of water, instead of milk, would make no difference. The 'free-rider problem', however, takes this type of possibility into account. Each member of a group is assumed to reason as follows. Either enough of the others will contribute to produce the desired results or they will not. If enough will, it is not necessary to contribute, as the good will be provided without cost to oneself. If enough will not, there is no point in contributing anyway. It seems, therefore, as if rational self-interest demands that one does not contribute.

The problem appears in a similar guise if we are concerned with maximum overall utility rather than just our own welfare. There still seems no point in contributing, because either enough others will contribute or they will not. It is often suggested that this is a question of rationality. One writer comments: 'The point is not that inaction is *compatible* with rationality. Rationality requires inaction.'[17] Something must have gone wrong with our conception of rationality for such a result to be produced. Any procedure which starts weighing costs to oneself against possible benefits may *seem* rational, but it is implicitly equating rationality with self-interest. The assumption is that those who prefer the interests of others to their own are irrational. Unless contribution to the public good can be immediately justified in terms of the pay-off to the individual, it is rational not to contribute. Individuals' it is assumed, can each exist in isolation from their community and decide how far they will contribute to it. Individualism can join forces with egoism in a manner which is supposed to be the epitome of rationality.

A rejoinder to this could be that, even if one is altruistic and genuinely seeks to further the interests of others, there seems little point if one's action is going to be ineffective. Unless my contribution is the one that tips the scales, I am incurring a cost without any corresponding benefit. Is it not right to conclude that such pointless behaviour is irrational? Wasted effort hardly seems rational even if rationality is not defined in terms of self-interest. Part of the trouble lies in the fact that we cannot often be certain our effort is wasted. The matter may seem to have been dealt with, in the initial calculation of costs and benefits, in terms of the probability of an outcome being achieved. Despite the apparent mathematical precision of this, it still remains true that we can often be wildly inaccurate in foreseeing the consequences of our actions, particularly when this involves predicting what others are going to do. The question of example, too, is often important. If we incur costs in cutting down pollution, others may be encouraged to do the same. Just because, on an individualist view, the community is nothing more than the combination of its members, what happens in it depends entirely on what each of its members does. Some may, quite unfairly, get a 'free-ride', and the resentment this causes is itself an important factor in society. The conclusion seems inevitable that an individualist understanding of society assumes a strict code of morality among its members, if public goods are to be provided. A sense of duty will ensure that everyone contributes.

The alternative would be a chaotic situation in which everyone is trying to benefit at the expense of others' efforts.

The demands of society are very often at odds with the consistent pursuit of self-interest. Moral principles may certainly be important in the commitment of an individual to his or her society, and there is a close relationship between the notion of a morality and that of a society. It even seems doubtful if there could be a society without some form of morality encouraging its members to be willing to sacrifice their own interests. Yet there are two problems which have been lurking in the background. The first is that questions about egoism and altruism will inevitably be linked with issues about human nature. Exhortations to consider the good of society are unlikely to be effective, if as a matter of fact human beings are basically selfish. Once more, a major problem about the functioning of human society appears to depend on considerations about human nature.

The second issue raises questions about the very basis of assumptions concerning the rationality of an individual contributing to society. Nowhere does the distinction between holist and individualist views of society become clearer than here. The problem has appeared to be one of inducing autonomous individuals to contribute to society, but, if society defines the nature of an individual, the latter's autonomy is a mere abstraction. The individual, it may be argued, has no existence outside his or her context in society. The very concept of an individual is perhaps the creation of particular circumstances in a particular type of society. The emphasis of both Marx and Wittgenstein on the priority of the social appears to undermine any view of atomic individuals coalescing to form a society. For Marx, the social context is specifically the socio-economic structures which have changed through history. They determine the way we think and will have to be changed if human life is to be improved. This means that Marxists should always be more concerned with changing the structures than changing the ideas that are produced by those structures. They will regard ideas as being more significant as symptoms of underlying social and economic relationships than as worthy of study in themselves.

One writer comments: 'Historical materialism is a substantive critique of ideologies which is premised on the denial of that ideological separation of ideas *as ideas* from the relation of ideas to their materiality as social praxis.'[18] Thus the more such ideas are examined in isolation, the more we allow our view of social reality to be distorted. Such a view trades on a strong distinction between appearance and reality. What appears to be the case to participants in a society may be far from what is actually going on. Marxism, as a science, is hence required to show the real nature of social relations. That view is controversial, even among the followers of Marx, since it is a strongly realist position, asserting that there is one reality underlying the various ideologies. Marxist theory, it is alleged, can claim to be scientific since it helps us to see this. Other views seek to modify this position by, for instance, attempting to overcome the distinction between the subject and object of knowledge. Marxists, however, face a dilemma, since they risk the threat of relativism if they give up their claim that their theory gives a unique insight into the nature of social reality, and stress the social origin of *all* ideas. On the other hand, claims to special knowledge can give rise to elites, who can become exceedingly ruthless in the pursuit of their aims because they are secure in the knowledge that they are right.

The shift of emphasis to structures in society empties the concept of an individual of any real content. All attention becomes focused on the social and historical preconditions for consciousness of different kinds. Marx was, particularly in his later work, opposed to any conception of fixed human needs or desires persisting through changed circumstances. He says, for instance, in *Capital* that, by acting on the external world and changing it, man 'at the same time changes his own nature'.[19] In an often quoted passage which serves as an inspiration for the sociology of knowledge, Marx says:

> The mode of production in material life determines the general character of the social, political and spiritual processes of life. It is not the consciousness of men that determines their existence, but, on the contrary, their social existence determines their consciousness.[20]

The stress on the priority of the social entails the repudiation of any conception of individuals exercising rationality in a vacuum beyond the reach of the influences of their time. Their reasoning will be the product of the society of which they are members, and Marx's materialism traces the form of society to the underlying economic factors moulding it. His thought is given many different interpretatons, but a common one is that he does not base the economic substructure on anything else, least of all human biology. If he had, the social character of some human needs and wants might thereby have been put in question: they might turn out to be grounded in something transcending the vagaries of history.

The abstract individual, as favoured by classical economists, was an explicit target for Marx. In fact in the *Grundrisse* he tries to trace the development of the idea of the abstract individual, showing how in the past the individual appeared inseparable from the social whole.[21] First society was just the family, then the family expanded into a clan, and then it was formed through communities arising from various combinations of clans. Individuation only arises, holds Marx, with the rise of bourgeois society, characterized by free competition. In such a society, he says, 'the individual appears detached from the natural bonds etc. which in earlier historical periods made him the accessory of a definite and limited human conglomerate'.[22] The point is, though, that this is an illusion created by the particular conditions of a particular economic structure. Belief in the abstract individual is itself the product of a definite kind of society.

This is a radical challenge to the individualist assumption of many economists. Far from the 'rational' individual being the origin of the economic facts of life, it is alleged that the conditions of Western capitalist society have given rise to the idea in the first place. This is not just a controversy in economics, since it matters enormously in society at large, whether we regard the individual or the structures of society as prior. Is society the creation of the interrelated effects of individuals, or are individuals only to be understood in their social setting, since they are themselves the creation of that setting? We have encountered this problem before, but in this instance it should be clear that the argument has political implications. If we wish to change society in some way, how is it to be done? Do we attempt to change individuals first, or do we change the economic structures of society? The latter is the Marxist way. The former is less catastrophic, but just because it is more gradual it may appear less effective.

If Marxists are right, the individual will only be changed by altering economic structures. If, however, they are wrong, and individuals are at least partly formed by other factors, whether their biology, or even their own rational choices, changing society will be somewhat irrelevant. If individuals are egoists, changing the system will leave their egoism untouched. It is a common criticism of Marxist theory that it is utopian because it assumes human perfectibility, in that it takes for granted that the achievement of a perfect society will of itself produce perfection in human beings. Yet it might be that people turn out as greedy and selfish under a new system as they were in the old. The cynic will observe that communist systems can apparently be exploited by party bosses for their advantage just as easily as a capitalist system may be manipulated by industrialists or bankers for theirs. Marxists will retort that existing communist systems are not necessarily good examples of Marxist theory put into practice. Nevertheless the difficulty of ever putting revolutionary ideals into practice may very well have something to do with basic facts about human nature. Too great an emphasis on socio-economic structures may ignore the brute fact of human selfishness.

Christian theologians express much this view of human nature when they refer to 'original sin'. They would certainly expect to find it reflected in the structures of human society, but would not expect to cure it by means of social change. What is needed is rather the kind of change expressed by the word 'redemption'. As a result, a theological understanding of mankind takes human selfishness seriously, but also assumes that it can be dealt with. Because of the latter, they are far from any notion of 'rational economic man' of the kind I have been discussing.

Christian theology, to the Marxist, is a prime example of ideology, an effect of social and economic conditions blinding us to their true nature because of the operation of vested interests. Because of this viewpoint, genuine dialogue between Marxists and non-Marxists would seem difficult. It would not involve a simple disagreement about what is true, which could be discussed reasonably. Marxists would trace their opponents' alleged distortions to their social background, while non-Marxists are, on their assumptions, still able to examine Marxist theory on its merits.

RATIONALITY AND REVOLUTION

The difference between a Marxist and non-Marxist view of the relationship between individual and society can be illustrated, for example, by the Christian idea of love. In particular, the love of neighbour exemplified by the parable of the Good Samaritan seems to be a matter of how individuals should treat each other, regardless of such factors as race or religion. It might even be plausible to suggest that the point of the parable is that individuals matter regardless of their socio-economic background, and regardless of what the power structures of society happen to be. Yet it is easy for those influenced by Marxism to insist that such love is pointless, and even illusory, if it allows socio-economic structures to continue which legitimize forms of oppression and exploitation. One writer, describing 'structures of domination', maintains:

> These structures are such that it can be only ideological to speak of loving within them. . . . Consequently, one side of Christianity – a sorely

understressed side of it – shares a parallel conviction with the Marxist, that it is in the business not of *loving*, but rather of securing the conditions of the possibility of loving.[23]

There is a major philosophical difference between a view stressing the significance of the individual, and the alternative position stressing the importance of having the right social structures. An emphasis on the individual need not involve ignoring the importance of wider social and economic considerations, but it may induce some scepticism about how much can be achieved by social and economic change alone. On the other hand, emphasizing the priority of society may involve absolving the individual of any responsibility for social evils. Whether the traditional Christian belief in the importance of the individual can easily be combined with a Marxist emphasis on the effects of the structure of society seems unlikely. Needless to say, this is a highly contentious issue.

There is another illustration of how individualist and collectivist perceptions can differ. It may seem puzzling sometimes why members of an exploited class should continue to support the very conditions which are responsible for their exploitation. Why, for instance, should members of the menial castes in India fervently uphold the caste system? Marvin Harris puts it this way:

Members of impoverished menial castes avidly uphold the rule of caste endogamy and insist that marriages be legitimized by expensive dowries. Abstractly, it would appear that the members of such impoverished castes would be materially better off if they practised exogamy and stopped insisting on big marriage payments. But the victims of the caste system cannot base their behaviour on long-term abstract calculations. Access to such menial jobs as construction worker, toddy-wine maker, coir maker and so forth depends on caste identity validated by obedience to caste rules.[24]

Anyone breaking ranks will be penalized by the system. Therefore, although it is oppressive, each individual has an interest in perpetuating it rather than lose all prospect of employment. Those at the bottom of the society have not the power to throw off all the privileges of the upper castes. Harris comments that, 'perverse as it may seem, those who benefit least from the system ardently support it in daily life'. This position is clearly intelligible from the standpoint of 'rational economic man'. No doubt the caste system could be broken if enough people refused to abide by it, but individuals would have to be willing to suffer to produce an eventual change, and they have not so far been prepared to do so.

At this point, a Marxist would speak of the necessity of revolution, but this is the nub of the matter. Are the members of the proletariat perhaps in an analogous position to the members of Indian lower castes? Those initiating a revolution may well have to suffer, and they might not be prepared to do so. The doubt arises if one assumes the kind of egoism already referred to. Altruists may be ready to die for the benefit of others, but those intent only on maximizing their own utility will not. The problem has been summed up as follows:

> Even if revolution is in the best interests of the proletariat and even if every member of the proletariat realizes that this is so, so far as its members act rationally, this class will *not* achieve concerted revolutionary action. This shocking conclusion rests on the premise that concerted revolutionary action is for the proletariat a public good in the technical sense.[25]

Thus, in addition to the question of altruism, all the paradoxes connected with 'the free-rider problem' come into play. Is it reasonable to expect anyone to attempt to establish new social structures regardless of what others do, particularly when death is a more than likely outcome? The 'rational man' might prefer survival under an unjust system to such a gamble. Yet this would suggest that it could be irrational to participate in a revolution, and such a conclusion would obviously be uncongenial to Marxism. However, assumptions have been made which Marxists would not accept. Apart from the picture of a society as a group of individuals, they would also reject the notion of rationality as maximizing utility. Rationality, in Marxism, is not a matter of finding the most suitable means for the satisfaction of personal desires. Since Marxists believe the latter are socially conditioned, their attention is directed at producing the best kind of society. That would, they think, be unlike a capitalist society in that apparent and real relations between people would coincide in it. There would be no room left for ideology, but we would be in conscious control of society, since our understanding of it would reveal the true state of affairs. This is the rational end sought by Marxists, and it thus defines rationality for them. As one writer puts it, 'From Marx's perspective the idea that rational action could lead to socially non-optimal – indeed disastrous – results is a *reductio ad absurdum* of the individual utility maximizing conception of rationality.'[26]

Marxists could also suggest that the very notion of rationality as maximization of utility, especially when combined with egoism, is itself produced by a particular set of socio-economic circumstances. It is, they would argue, a typical product of capitalist society, portraying people in terms which merely reflect the prevailing spirit of competition between individuals in a market economy. As such it is a good example, from the Marxist point of view, of ideology. It disguises what to a Marxist is the real situation in a manner which allegedly serves the interests of the existing power structure of that society. It sets as standards of human rationality what are apparently only the local conditions in a particular society, and seems to restrict the possibility of change. The argument that revolution is irrational further helps prevent any radical alteration of existing social relations.

Thus we are faced with two utterly different conceptions of human society and the nature of human rationality, the one based on the individual and the other on society. Yet although the views are in many respects polar opposites, rejecting one does not necessarily entail accepting the other. Not all positions emphasizing the priority of the individual are egoist. It is perfectly possible to hold that individuals need to use their reason concerning the ends to be pursued and to consider the interests of others as well as themselves. Similarly not all holist views need adopt a Marxist stance about socio-economic causation. It is possible, as Wittgenstein did, to root the notion of rationality in social practice, without accepting Marxist theory about the relation of ideas to the material substructure of society.

Both the economist's conception of 'rational man' and Marxist theories about society make assumptions about human nature. For the economist, human desires are fixed and unalterable, setting the stage for the living of human life, while for the Marxist they are the creation of a particular society. The assumptions about the nature of rationality made by each stem from their respective views about individuals. Can they be intelligibly viewed in isolation from society or not? The social theory we adopt, and even the economic system we prefer, depends on our answer to this question.

NOTES

1 Weber, *Selections*, 1978, p. 61.
2 Ibid., p. 85.
3 Amartya Sen, *Choice, Welfare and Measurement*, 1982, p. 5.
4 F. Hirsch and J. H. Goldthorpe, *Political Economy of Inflation*, 1978, p. 273.
5 Ibid., p. 274.
6 Sen, *Choice, Welfare and Measurement*, p. 67.
7 G. Stigler and G. Becker, 'De Gustibus non est Disputandum', *American Economics Review*, 67, 1977, p. 76.

8 Ibid.
9 Ibid., p. 89.
10 M. S. McPherson, 'Want Formation, Morality, and Some Interpretive Aspects of Economic Inquiry', in N. Haan et al. (eds), *Social Science as Moral Inquiry*, 1983, p. 107.
11 See my *The Shaping of Man*.
12 McPherson, 'Want Formation', p. 102.
13 e.g. as given by Sen, *Choice, Welfare and Measurement*, p. 62.
14 Sen, 'Rational Fools', *Philosophy and Public Affairs*, 6, 1977, p. 329.
15 McPherson, 'Want Formation', p. 98.
16 John Rawls, *A Theory of Justice*, 1972, p. 143.
17 A. Buchanan, 'Revolutionary Motivation and Rationality', *Philosophy and Public Affairs*, 9, 1979–80, p. 66.
18 Turner, *Marxism and Christianity*, p. 181.
19 Marx, *Capital*, 1967, Vol. I, p. 177.
20 Marx, *A Contribution to the Critique of Political Economy* (1859), 1970, p. 21.
21 Marx, *Grundrisse*, Harmondsworth, 1973, p. 84.
22 Ibid., p. 83.
23 Turner, *Marxism and Christianity*, p. 214.
24 Marvin Harris, *Cultural Materialism*, 1979, p. 62.
25 Buchanan, 'Revolutionary Motivation and Rationality', p. 63.
26 N. Holmstrom, 'Rationality and Revolution', Canadian Journal of Philosophy, 13, 1983, p. 324.

8

Culture: Function and Adaptation

SOCIAL FUNCTION

Whenever human nature is discussed, one fundamental feature is invariably mentioned. We are remarkable for the manifold ways in which we express ourselves in culture. Social scientists have to give some form of unifying account of this if they are to do more than catalogue the myriad ways in which human life is lived. One major issue is just how much of human behaviour is based on biology and how much on culture. Allowing that human genes, for instance, explain a fair proportion of human activity would suggest that the differences between cultures are more apparent than real: the same biological needs would underlie what are apparently different customs. On the other hand, insisting that human nature is socially produced would imply that biology is largely irrelevant to the understanding of social practices.

The argument is often presented as a choice between alternatives, so that one is governed either by biology or by one's cultural environment.[1] One is moulded either by one's genes or by one's society. For example, Marvin Harris puts forward a view called 'cultural materialism', and quarrels with sociobiologists who, he alleges, 'actively seek to expand the list of genetically determined traits whenever a plausible opportunity to do so presents itself.' He writes:

> Cultural materialists pursue a strategy that seeks to reduce the list of hypothetical drives, instincts and genetically determined response alternatives to the smallest number of items compatible with the construction of an effective corpus of sociocultural theory.[2]

As a result he looks primarily to non-biological factors in his aim 'to account for the origin, maintenance and change of the global inventory of sociocultural differences and similarities'. In particular, he examines the causal factors of culture in what he terms 'the infrastructure', which comprises 'patterns of production and reproduction'. Since this infra-structure is, as he admits, 'the principal interface between culture and nature', it remains problematic just how much influence human biology will have.[3] It transpires that Harris's disagreement with sociobiology is one of emphasis rather than of principle. He believes that most human culture is not under genetic control, and holds that '*Homo sapiens* has been selected for the capacity to acquire and modify cultural repertoires independently of genetic feedback.'[4] He points out the massive variety of cultures exhibited in the world, all of which can be acquired or wiped out within the space of a single generation. The language one speaks and the food one eats are matters of how one is brought up rather than of who one's parents are.

It is in fact exceedingly difficult to maintain either that human culture is totally unaffected by human biology or that it is totally determined by it. The fact of cultural variation seems sufficient to refute the latter. As to the former, it is only necessary to wonder what human life would be like if we were all ten feet tall, or if there were three sexes, to realize that biological factors do at the very least set the stage for human life. Partly, perhaps, because social scientists are not biologists, they have preferred to look at human culture in its own terms, taking the biological background for granted. Many suspect that treating cultural categories in biological terms will only squeeze out of them all that is most significant for humanity. There is the constant fear of reductionism, whereby reference to human concepts becomes transmuted into talk of genes and bio-chemistry. Since, too, the biologist will always speak of the individual organism, any switch from the social sciences to the biological ones apparently involves conceding that the individualist is right in his argu-ment with the holist. Moreover, if society cannot be reduced to its indi-vidual members, a scientific study of the biology of individuals is not going to help in understanding the functioning of society.

Any study of human society is almost bound to have to deal with two pervasive features. Most humans live in family groups and most human societies profess some sort of religion. Whether these two traits are universal, rather than merely widespread, is controversial. It is possible to define the terms so that they become universal. Is state atheism a type of religion? Is a commune a family? Whatever the answer, social scien-tists will wish to give explanations for these widespread social phenomena, and will tend to restrict themselves to social, rather than biological or physical, explanations.

One very popular form of explanation has been in terms of social func-tions. The point of culture has been taken to be the way it contributes to improving what Malinowski termed 'the individual and collective standard of living'.[5] He linked culture with human needs and concluded: 'Function cannot be defined in any other way than the satisfaction of a need by an activity in which human beings co-operate, use artefacts, and consume goods.'[6] Some needs, he thought, were biological and others were 'derived', that is, created by culture, as the theory could afford to be fairly neutral about the relevance of biology. He was convinced of the crucial importance of the family in society. Its function, he believed, was to supply citizens to the community:

> From the very outset of culture the family has been the institution in which most of the fundamental needs of human beings have been satisfied. It is the institution primarily based on the reproductive need, but also directly associated with the production, distribution and consumption of food. . . . Custom, order and authority are embodied in the family.[7]

With this kind of account, Malinowski explicitly attempts to fit all human cultures, with their manifold differences, into one universal scheme. A family may take many forms in different cultures, but Malinowski would assume, for instance, that its function of training children will always be performed. His search for the nature or 'cultural reality' of human marriage and the family will involve discounting the differences between societies, and attempting to find 'valid scientific generalizations' about the functioning of institutions. Like many other social scientists, he tried to copy the methods of the physical sciences without relating his work to them in any direct way. Yet the search for a common factor in what appeared to be great cultural variation explicitly leads to the search for the lowest common denominator in, say, different forms of family, or of religion. Malinowski wrote:

> When E. B. Tylor inquired at the beginning of his great work on 'Primitive Culture' into what religion was, in the widest sense of the term, or in his own words, when he attempted a 'minimum definition' of this subject, he was a genuine functionalist.[8]

This approach is illustrated further by Durkheim's treatment of religion. In attempting to show the function of religion, he inevitably considered the differences between religions as of little account. What was relevant was their similarity, and, since he approached the matter as a social scientist, he looked only at their social effects, which he felt were of the greatest importance: 'If religion has given birth to all that is essential in society, it is because the idea of society is the soul of religion.'[9] He believed that all societies have to reaffirm at regular intervals their collective sentiments and ideas. The unity of a society depends, he thought, on individuals assembling to participate in ceremonies which serve to draw it together:

> Hence come ceremonies which do not differ from regular religious ceremonies, either in their object, the results which they produce, or the processes employed to attain these results. What essential difference is there between an assembly of Christians celebrating the principal dates of the life of Christ or of Jews remembering the exodus from Egypt or the promulgation of the decalogue, and a reunion of citizens commemorating the promulgation of a new moral or legal system or some great event in the national life?

The answer may be: very little, in terms of social function. Religions, like other institutions, do have social functions, and not all of them are obvious to participants. A distinction has been made by Merton between 'manifest' and 'latent' function, between, as he puts it, 'conscious motivations for social behaviour and its objective consequences'.[11] There is a perpetual problem, particularly at a time of rapid social change, that social institutions will be deliberately altered without any awareness of their latent functions. The family provides one obvious example. Radical change can be made in patterns of family relationships without any conscious thought being given to the wider effects on society.

A social scientist can, and should, observe the social effects of social institutions, even when they are religious. Yet ignoring the major differences between religions with a view to stressing the basic similarity of their influence on society is a perilous undertaking. Identifying religion with its social role ignores the very different claims being made about the world in different religions. We have seen before that social scientists are very tempted to ignore the content of belief and concentrate on the fact of belief. Durkheim in fact deals with public ceremonies indiscriminately, whether they have a religious purpose or not. The function of an institution so overshadows it that it appears to cease to matter what kind of institution it is. The only significant question is whether the function is fulfilled.

Functionalism is sometimes alleged to have a conservative bias because it seems to approve of whatever institutions a society possesses on the grounds that they are meeting important needs. Yet the emphasis on social function can actually serve to weaken commitment to the institutions in question. The importance of religion in society might seem to be emphasized when its function is shown. Since, however, it does not matter which religion is invoked, it seems that any kind will do, and perhaps non-religious creeds may be able to fulfil the same function. Claims to truth by religion are put aside as irrelevant. The *real* explanation for religious commitment is, it appears, social, and no room is left for beliefs to be held on the grounds that they are true. Functionalism can have similar effects to those of the sociology of knowledge. In both cases, sociological explanation seems to replace explanation in terms of reasons. I cannot reasonably believe that God exists if I become convinced that the reason for belief is God has nothing to do with what is transcendent and everything to do with the needs of society. The great danger is that social scientists both dismiss questions of truth and falsity as being outside their professional competence and assume that they can still deal with the central issues of religion. There is bound to be an element of distortion in sociological accounts of religion if it is taken for granted that the social function of religion is its most important feature. Social science must also recognize that it is an important task to show why one religion, rather than another, has been adopted.

Even if it is accepted that any society needs religious institutions to remain in equilibrium, there remains the question why a particular society has one institution rather than another. As George C. Homans remarks in the course of criticizing functionalism: 'I take it that what sociology has to explain are the actual features of actual societies and not just the generalized features of a generalized society.'[12] He feels that in the end functional explanations have to rely on psychological explanations about what people are or are not likely to do. Discussion in terms of abstract social systems and the functions of institutions explains nothing beyond why a society is enabled to continue working. Causal explanations about the origin of institutions or indeed about social change seem to get short shrift from functional analysis. Religion may serve to integrate society, and the decline of religion may, as a result, have a disintegrating effect, but that does not wholly explain why people are religious. Given the existence of religion, the functionalist account can help to explain its persistence. Institutionalized forms of atheism can no doubt be devised to serve the same social function. Whether atheism satisfies other human needs is a further question. Because it may be outside the province of sociology does not mean it is not a real one.

THE ROLE OF CONSCIOUSNESS

The distinction between manifest and latent functions entails that participants in a social system may not always fully understand the significance of what they are doing. This involves a similar question to that of false consciousness. An institution could be different from the way it is perceived by its members. They may support it for one reason while in reality it may possess functions that are quite different. Social science may be able to reveal that this is so. One apposite comment on the situation was: 'Nowadays with sociologists busily ferreting out latent functions in every nook and cranny of society and their writings gaining general currency, latent functions are not likely to stay latent for long.'[13] The fact that such knowledge becomes widespread itself becomes an important factor in society, and some may consciously try to preserve institutions merely for the sake of such previously latent functions.

We have already seen how controversial this distinction can be between what is happening in a society and what its participants understand. Some sociologists would not accept that there is a difference. For instance, Peter and Brigitte Berger say flatly that 'our epistemological assumption is that society is not a functioning system, but a meaningful construction'.[14] They apply this particularly to consideration of the family: 'To the extent that people perceive the family as a major source of meaning, value and identity, *that* is what the family is – no matter what a systemic analysis might have to say about its functioning.'[15] This can be seen as a correction of the functionalist approach rather than a total repudiation of it. The institution of the family might have latent functions, but the central point remains. Just as a religion typically makes claim to truth, it can be argued that the central features of a family lie in the conscious relationship of its members with each other. In each case, social science can distort rather than clarify.

Peter and Brigitte Berger are particularly concerned that talk of the family as a system interacting with other systems itself encourages mechanistic imagery. As a result, social workers can approach the family with 'services' to fulfil its needs, without looking at 'the importance of meanings and values in human life'. The dehumanizing methods of bureaucrats can finally destroy what they were supposed to help. This is a good example of how philosophic positions about the foundations of the social sciences can affect social policy. Peter and Brigitte Berger take it as axiomatic that the understanding possessed by individuals determines the nature of the practices in which they engage: 'The situation cannot be understood except "from within", that is, by understanding what the situation means to those who are in it.'[16] This is a familiar point, often made by those influenced by phenomenology, but it becomes vital when an institution such as the family is being studied. It is apparent that ignoring the perspective of the individual can misrepresent the nature of the human family. Peter and Brigitte Berger deny that notions of 'systemic' functionality can be helpful if they ignore what individuals mean and intend. They comment that people are unlikely to see themselves as operating units in a social system, unless they have taken too many sociology courses.

Giving individual consciousness this kind of priority raises again the problem of the relation between social structures and consciousness. What is the role, for instance, of consciousness in initiating social change? Peter and Brigitte Berger see social change 'as the result of the interaction (or, if one prefers, of a dialectic) of institutions and consciousness'.[17] This contrasts with views which would regard consciousness as perhaps nothing more than a by-product (or epiphenomenon) of underlying structural changes in society. Even if the link between such changes and consciousness were weakened, there is still the question whether consciousness can itself be an agent of change. The rise of feminism provides a pertinent example. There has been a marked change in recent years in the way many women, particularly those with a higher education, perceive their role. Peter and Brigitte Berger acknowledge 'the difficulty of determining to what extent feminism *caused* changes in behaviour or merely legitimated changes that were happening anyway'. Their philosophical assumptions would leave open the possibility that consciousness can create social change.

Against such a position would be ranged many who, like Marvin Harris, stress the importance of infrastructure in determining consciousness. He himself also uses the example of the raised consciousness of women, and significantly traces it back to changes in the conditions in which contemporary life is lived, rather than to the inherent force of ideas. He points out that women's role has changed with increased urbanization. A society based on agriculture, particularly a frontier society, would emphasize the woman's role as mother and housekeeper. The conditions of living in cities, with greater opportunities in employment for women, combine with the increasing cost of having families when compared with the benefits received. Large families are not as important in the city as in a homestead. Harris looks to the vast changes in technology as part of the explanation for women's changed role, and is convinced of the asymmetrical nature of causal relationships between 'infrastructure' and 'superstructure'. In other words, the material conditions of life will influence the content of consciousness, rather than consciousness changing the conditions of life. To illustrate his case, he asks whether groups of males could succeed in reviving the sex roles of the nineteenth century.

Would a decisive factor be how far they were committed to their goal? Or, we might add, could ideas themselves be judged to have power, whatever the prevailing social conditions? Harris believes that the men would stand no chance 'as long as the present urban industrial infrastructure holds sway'.

This controversy is, in essence, the traditional argument between 'materialists' and 'idealists'. Can ideas, or the power of human reason, influence human life, or are they themselves under the control of material forces, which shape society in their image? The power of ideas can certainly be enhanced or checked by the general condition of the society in which they are presented. What is at issue, however, is not the truism that some societies will be more receptive than others to the force of particular views. The question is whether the way people think can itself initiate change in society. Thought may itself be only a symptom of currents already strongly flowing. Yet those who preach various brands of materialism hardly seem to believe this themselves: they certainly see fit to write and to argue in order to convince others. While such doctrines may be more acceptable in some types of societies than in others, most materialists bear witness to the effective power of thought by the very fact of their efforts to convince others. The fact that they themselves present rational arguments suggests that they are not content with what society may predispose us to believe.

Attempts to explain the contents of human consciousness will always be self-defeating since they are themselves the products of consciousness. As a result, social scientists may change the subject and talk of systems, structures and functions without doing justice to the nature of what they are investigating. Alternatively, they may feel that their task is not one of explanation at all, but of understanding the meanings of participants in society. The former course succeeds in examining society while apparently leaving the men and women who make it up out of consideration. Yet the second seems to offer little scope for the construction of any theory about human social behaviour. It is hardly surprising that there have been in recent years attempts to link the social sciences with the physical sciences, particularly biology. The disadvantages of merely aping the physical sciences and copying their methods in an appropriate context may disappear if social science is treated, at least to some extent, as a continuation of the rest of science. It would then be not so much a parallel enterprise trying to do for human society what physics does for the material world, but would actually use the insights of physical science in dealing with human behaviour.

Applying biology to social science may appear unpromising at first. How can the scientific study of biological organisms throw light on the complicated organization of human society? The approach needed for the study of insects or animals appears irrelevant once human consciousness and its products become objects of study. Admitting the relevance of biology seems to involve both reductionism and individualism. Reductionism is involved as all social categories have to be translated into something else if they are to be brought within the ambit of biological and hence physical explanation. Since, too, modern biology is concerned with the reproductive success of individuals, all its explanations will have to proceed through the behaviour of individuals.

The whole new discipline of sociobiology has grown up on the assumption that social behaviour does have a biological basis and that even complicated social arrangements may be illuminated by biological theory. The latter is, of course, essentially Darwinian, upholding evolution through natural selection. Unlike Darwin, modern biologists can refer to genes and even link differences in behaviour to genetic difference. Things are rarely so simple that one gene could be identified as the cause of a particular type of behaviour. Anyway, all genes interact in a complex way with their environment, so that even simple creatures under tight genetic control react to environmental stimuli and do not blindly act whatever the circumstances.

Sociobiology is devoted to the study of the biological basis of behaviour. Such a task is uncontroversial when insects, birds or animals are under scrutiny. It is easy in such cases to accept that natural selection influences the spread of some behaviour and impedes others. Birds with a taste for harmful food or without any desire to look after their young will normally leave few descendants. Even the cuckoo has to rely on other birds raising its young. If other birds had not been so gullible, cuckoos would have quickly died out. Similarly, if there were too many cuckoos, and the other birds only raised cuckoos at the expense of their own offspring, other species would quickly be at risk, so that there would soon not be enough to raise young cuckoos. In fact, a delicate compromise has been reached, which has been termed 'an evolutionary stable strategy'. There are sufficient cuckoos to perpetuate themselves, but not enough to put other species in danger.

Behaviour does have consequences. Some kinds of behaviour can further reproductive success and genes encouraging it will spread, but other kinds can have such deleterious effects that the agents or their off-spring fail to pass on their genes to further generations. The inevitable result is that genes encouraging harmful behaviour will die out. Natural selection will encourage some forms of behaviour and discourage others. With regard to non-human organisms, this appears to be the sensible application of Darwinian principles. It shows why animals naturally prefer their kin according to degree of relatedness, and look after their offspring. There has been a tremendous outcry, however, at the sugges-tion that sociobiology can also explain human behaviour.[18] Many believe that human beings cannot be simply classed as one kind of animal among many. Cultural variation seems difficult to explain solely in terms of genetic variation. Sociobiology, at least in its early stages, has certainly seemed to treat humanity as just another biological species. Yet the agility of the human mind, coupled with the fact of human culture, has ensured that human behaviour is much more flexible and variable than that of animals. It is easy to assume, with many social theorists, that humans are infinitely malleable, so that we are merely the product of a particular culture.

If, however, sociobiology is even only partially correct, our genetic inheritance gained over many thousands of years will predispose us to some patterns of behaviour and make us find others distasteful. This will both limit possible variation in culture and cause strains in a society when the prevailing culture begins to go 'against nature'. We would expect an underlying similarity between all human cultures, however great super-ficial differences may be. Different customs may be mere fronts for the same impulses governed by the same genes.

This is not to advocate a simple-minded genetic determinism in opposi-tion to an equally simplistic environmental determinism. Humans are educated within a culture. Nevertheless, the suggestion is that culture does not exist on its own, and cannot be understood except as an environ-ment in which human genetic impulses can be thwarted or find fulfil-ment. In other words, it has the function of serving the biological needs of individuals. Sometimes, however, it is allowed to stray a little. Lumsden and Wilson have referred to the 'leash principle', according to which 'genetic natural selection operates in such a way as to keep culture on a leash'.[19] This allows a certain independence to cultural development, and means that not everything in a human society can be explained from the standpoint of neo-Darwinian biological theory. It has been alleged, for instance, that the contemporary willingness to use contraceptives is not something that could be explained on sociobiological principles, despite its cultural importance. Is not the voluntary limitation of a family, or even the refusal to have one, inexplicable by a theory which preaches the importance of maximizing reproductive advantage? Sociobiology, however, has always recognized that maximum parental investment in a small number of children may be wiser than less care spread around a larger family. Even among animals, there is a difference between species, like rabbits, that find safety in producing large numbers of offspring, few of which are likely to survive, and a species such as an elephant which invests its care on few offspring, on the assumption that they will survive. It will not be surprising if humans consciously choose to adopt the latter strategy, if they are able.

A total refusal to have children raises a more difficult question, and it is here that the leash principle may be relevant. It is clear, according to neo-Darwinian theory, that an unwillingness to have children could not be encouraged genetically. Indeed, the reverse must be the case, since we should expect genes encouraging care for children to spread. Since children will be likely to possess half of a parent's genes, those who are cared for by parents, because the latter have genes prompting such behaviour, are likely to inherit the same genes. They are likely to survive to pass on their genes, while neglected children will be unlikely to do so. How then can people choose not to have children? A desire to have children is much more likely to be genetically based than indifference to children. Any genetic mutation encouraging parenthood would soon become established in the gene pool.

The leash principle acknowledges that culture is not totally dependent on genes. A simple model of genes causing behaviour is inappropriate for most aspects of human behaviour, particularly because of the influence of culture. Human consciousness has an active role to play, but that does not mean that culture is totally free of genetic constraint. It is not just a question of humans evolving to the point when they create culture and break free of genetic influences. Human genetic make-up does not just grant the ability to create culture and be influenced by it, but it must also be responsible for at least some of the content of human culture. The point of the leash principle is to assert both that culture can go against the promptings of the genes and that, if it does, it is eventually going to be pulled back. Whatever humans naturally desire, they can resist. Going 'against nature' will usually produce a cost. Individuals who rationally decide not to have a family may still find themselves sometimes yearning for one. Even if they do not, a culture encouraging childlessness is going to find itself in trouble. It will be possible for a small minority to choose not to have children, but, when a significant number do, the culture is signing its death warrant. It will be progressively debilitated, as it is passed on to fewer and fewer children. No culture can go against basic facts of human nature for long and hope to flourish.

E. O. Wilson, the 'founding father' of sociobiology, began by studying insect societies and then extrapolated his findings in a controversial manner to mankind. He has, however, modified his previous position to take into account the distinctive features of human consciousness. Writing with Charles Lumsden, he refers to the 'remarkable fact that sociobiology has not taken into proper account either the human mind or the diversity of cultures'.[20] This admission marks the introduction of human sociobiology as a distinct branch of sociobiology. Humans cannot be studied as if they are insects or birds, and attempts to explain human behaviour as if it is merely an example of animal behaviour are bound to fail. The existence of human consciousness and its products creates a new environment in which natural selection can operate for the most part only indirectly.

Indirect operation is still significant and will influence the content of culture. Any social science ignoring biological theory is bound to be grossly hampered. Treating culture and human society as phenomena to be studied in their own right will be bound to tell only half the story. Our understanding is going to be severely restricted if all explanation for the characteristics of society are to be sought only in social terms. The current orthodoxy in the social sciences, suggesting that biology is irrelevant, must be challenged. One does not need to be a reductionist, dissolving culture or consciousness into something quite different, to feel uneasy about dismissing biology. Lumsden and Wilson lay themselves open to criticism on this issue. While insisting on what they term 'gene–culture co-evolution' and giving culture an active role in human development, they appear, as we shall see in the next chapter, to want to reduce talk of culture to talk of individual human brains. They thus both reduce culture from the social to the individual level and reduce reference to the contents of the individual mind to talk of brains. Many will rightly repudiate this conversion of the study of culture into the study of the brain. Yet that does not mean Lumsden and Wilson are wrong in their general thesis. Culture and genes may not develop in total independence of each other. Cultures provide the environment in which genes can be passed on or in which they can die out.

Do genes predispose us to some forms of culture rather than others? The argument of Lumsden and Wilson is that, even if humanity had started in a *tabula rasa* state, completely malleable by the environment, genetic mutations would inevitably have begun to bias individuals towards some features of culture rather than others. They would have flourished if the features were beneficial and done significantly less well if they were deleterious. Some mutations would establish themselves in the gene pool and others would be quickly eliminated. Gradually cultural predispositions would be passed on genetically. A good example of a case where this kind of reasoning seems to work is incest.[21] Social scientists have often investigated incest taboos with the assumption that, because they are cultural, they can be explained only at the level of culture. Yet, once it is recognized that close inbreeding reduces biological fitness, it becomes obvious that a sociobiological account may itself help to explain this aspect of human culture. It seems fairly straightforward to explain avoidance of incest by means of genetic predisposition. Those indulging in incest have less fit offspring than those who do not, and their preference will not be passed on genetically for very long. There even seems to be evidence of positive aversion to incest.[22]

This type of sociobiological account seems very compelling, but it has its critics even in the case of incest. Marvin Harris asks: 'If incest avoidance is part of the human biogram, why are there, conservatively estimated, several hundred thousand cases of father–daughter incest in the United States each year?'[23] This point need not alarm sociobiologists. Unless they are putting forward a very simple version of genetic determinism, they must acknowledge that humans are perfectly capable of going against inherited tendencies. It is only necessary to insist that they will inevitably pay the price of doing so. Incest can have catastrophic biological effects. Harris's own explanation for incest taboos ignores the genetic costs and concentrates on the economic infrastructure. He suggests the following:

> Restrictions on brother–sister, father–daughter, and mother–son sexual intercourse within the nuclear family probably reflect selection against groups who failed to develop inter-band marital alliance and who therefore suffered from a lack of lability and mobility and who consequently had a constricted resource base and lacked trading partners and allies in the event of armed conflict.[24]

However valid these points may be, a sociobiologist will feel that they refer to secondary factors and do not mention the principal cause. Nevertheless the very fact that incest does occur suggests an answer to one important question. Why are cultural taboos necessary, if we are genetically 'programmed' to avoid incest? Human desires may be strong but they can always be overridden. A culture which reinforces natural aversion will do better than one which either ignores the question or positively encourages incest. The members of the former will be biologically fitter, while the cost paid in the latter is likely to be enormous. Van den Berghe says in his survey of inbreeding avoidance: 'Human nature and culture are inextricably interlinked to produce fitness-optimizing solutions.'[25] He believes that incest taboos are a product of puritanical societies and are a substitute for natural aversion. His view is 'that such taboos arise in societies that frown on nudity and sex play and segregate children by sex'. In other words, because familiarity breeds contempt, the lack of such familiarity particularly in this context prevents the conditions in which natural aversions develop in a subtle interplay of genes and environment. His conclusion is:

> Culture clearly has the potential of interfering with nature, and when it does, it often creates new problems down the road. Incest taboos are an example of a rather clumsy solution to the problems created by a puritanical way of raising children.[26]

Human flexibility ensures that we can resist natural tendencies, even if it is at a cost. In this case, however, there is no reason to link incest taboos with a puritan attitude in this manner, even if there were a general empiricist correlation. Puritanical societies may be more conscious of sexual 'dangers' and may be more ready to reinforce certain natural tendencies with explicit rules. Van den Berghe suggests, however, that somehow a natural tendency has been thwarted by puritanism. His argument is that such societies have to introduce taboos because of the arrested development of any ordinary natural aversion. Apart from the implausibility of a veiw which suggests that puritanism is accompanied by a greater natural readiness to indulge in incest, Van den Berghe makes the mistake of assuming that a natural tendency *removes* rather than *reinforces* the need for a cultural norm. Yet the very conditions which ensured that revulsion to incest would be under genetic control also serve to emphasize the importance of the problem for a culture. It need be hardly surprising if societies hedge their bets by forbidding what evolution has already decreed to be 'unnatural'. This is a mere consequence of the fact that simple genetic determinism is totally ruled out in the human context.

It may be suggested that, if a sociobiological account does not work in the case of incest, it will not work anywhere, because of the connection between incest and loss of biological fitness. Similar accounts, however, in terms of natural selection can explain many widespread human traits, particularly those important for self-protection. Fear of dangerous situations is an advantage from an evolutionary point of view. Fear of snakes, of running water, of heights or of thunder can all be explained in this way. Such fears seem to be inherited from our remote ancestors, and significantly we do not possess the same instinctive fear of contemporary situations which might be equally dangerous. Children will not, for instance, react initially to an electric socket as they would to a snake.

BIOLOGY AND ALTRUISM

Many might accept the power of sociobiological explanation for taboos and phobias, while feeling it must be irrelevant to the understanding of the complicated structures of modern society. Perhaps most important for the very existence of society is a willingness to co-operate with each other and perhaps subordinate one's interests to those of others. Can sociobiology explain that? The family is the most basic unit where co-operation occurs, and we have already noted that it is a source of perpetual interest to social scientists. Sociobiology may throw considerable light on family relationships, since the regulation of sexual liaisons and provision for the care of children must be central issues for any theory concerned with the transmission of human genes.

A general preference for kin may have a biological base. Our relatives are more likely to share our genes than our non-relatives, and an abstract love of mankind is difficult to pass on genetically. That would involve sacrificing our genes for those who are unlikely to share them. Concern for relatives, on the other hand, involves caring for those who may themselves possess a gene prompting such concern. Sociobiologists have introduced the notion of 'kin selection' to explain a natural preference for relatives, and they further differentiate between close and distant relatives. The basic question always asked is what is necessary for genes to spread. Sociobiology has to take into account the likelihood of a relative sharing our genes. If I sacrifice myself for someone unlikely to share the genes prompting such behaviour, the argument is that these genes are going to die out. Lumsden and Wilson refer to altruism towards relatives, meaning by it any action that increases their biological fitness at the expense of that of the altruist. Since a man's brother or sister will share half their genes with him through the fact of common descent, they say:

If a man makes a sacrifice on behalf of his brother or sister, and as a result of his act the sibling has more children, the man's altruistic act will cause an increase in the number of genes that are identical to his own. . . . The sacrifice of an altruist must result in at least a doubling of the number of the brother's offspring for the altruism carrying genes to spread. A first cousin has one eighth of genes identical: if the altruism is directed at first cousins alone, their offspring must be increased at least eightfold for the altruism genes to spread. And so on.[27]

Thus we would expect greater affection and concern for the welfare of brothers and sisters than for first cousins, and a much weaker concern still for more distant relatives. Nevertheless, the conclusion of sociobiology seems to be that love of one's family is natural, and an altruistic concern for those who are unrelated is not. This, however, fails to explain how societies can successfully work if they are composed of more than one family, however extended. Room is therefore made by sociobiologists for the strangely termed 'reciprocal altruism'. That enables them to explain co-operation in complex societies which are not tribally based. Indeed they accept that animals co-operate when it is to their mutual advantage, perhaps by grooming each other. Among humans there is a similar readiness to do favours as long as some are expected in return. Yet suggesting that I shall be altruistic to you only if you will be altruistic in return means that I am not being altruistic at all, but selfish. What is prompting me may be enlightened self-interest but it is still self-interest, and not the disinterested and even self-sacrificial concern for others which is the hallmark of genuine altruism. How far society can function if it is composed of rational egoists remains an acute question, and we have already seen how economic theory has found it difficult to account for 'public goods' using the assumptions made by sociobiologists in formulating their principle of reciprocal altruism.

Sociobiology thus raises in an acute form the question of what kind of society is possible. Is it going to be a purely competitive one, in which individuals try to get as much of what they want for themselves and their families, without caring for the interests of others as ends in themselves? Is co-operation itself merely a means to personal gain? The problem arises because contemporary biology tends to view selection as operating at the level of the individual organism, or even the gene, rather than at the level of the group or species. The notion of the individual being sacrificed for the good of the species is inexplicable from the standpoint of natural selection. The individual has probably benefited unrelated members of that species so that genes encouraging that behaviour will soon die out when they have to compete with mutants causing selfish behaviour. Similarly, 'group selection' is difficult to uphold, since sacrifice for unrelated members of a group seems self-defeating. Some groups may be sufficiently close-knit for every member to be related to every other, and group selection is then merely an example of kin selection. A group could flourish because it was in fact a large family.

Why, though, should not the unselfish behaviour of the members of one group enable it to succeed where competing groups fail? The group might enable its members to achieve greater biological fitness because of the self-sacrifice of some, even though the genes encouraging such altruism were not passed on. The group might have been able to seize more fertile land, even though some of its members were killed. Another group whose members were unwilling to take such risks might find its hold on natural resources weakened. In the end, even those who preserved their lives may find their future, and that of their children, at grave risk. A sociobiologist might still insist that this is all intelligible because of the way the biological interests of the *individual* are affected. The fact of a group flourishing or failing is still only important in so far as its members flourish or face difficulties. The group is nothing more than the individuals making it up. Even when we talk of one group succeeding and another failing, we only mean, it may be maintained, that the members of each are enabled or not to obtain biological advantage. The reason for this is quite simply that groups do not have children, but only individuals do.

Group selection may be normally unacceptable as a biological theory, but there may be good social grounds for the encouragement of altruism. It may be dangerous to reify societies, but nevertheless there is a sense in which societies teaching altruism may do better than those which do not. What is meant by that is that the members of an unselfish society will gain advantages which those in a selfish one will not. The sociobiologist may still be worried that an altruistic action which is not done for a relative or with the expectation of any favour to be returned cannot be explained genetically. Indeed it may not when there is competition between different kinds of genes, but there may be good reasons for the encouragement of such actions in a culture.

Sociobiologists are often tempted to conclude that what cannot be explained genetically must be of little account. As a result, they fail to take seriously the possibility of genuine altruism towards non-relatives. E. O. Wilson is even forced to say of Mother Teresa in Calcutta that she is motivated by basically selfish concerns.[28] She is committed to the supremacy of Christianity over its rivals, he thinks, and is no doubt striving for personal immortality. Altruism of this notable kind to people of a different race who can have no way of repaying the kindness done to them may seem puzzling from the standpoint of strict evolutionary theory. Yet the very fact that complicated beliefs, such as those of a religion, are invoked makes clear the relevance of cultural considerations. Human beings are not merely under the influence of genes. The very fact that Lumsden and Wilson now talk of 'gene–culture co-evolution' emphasizes that in the long run cultural considerations can have as great an effect on genetic development as the other way round.

A culture in which unselfishness is extolled as a virtue, and selfishness and nepotism frowned upon, will be radically different in its effects from one where selfishness is held to be the norm. Some sociobiologists have proved so enamoured of a simple form of their theory that they have dared to suggest that everyone is really selfish, even if we have been programmed by our genes not to realize this.[29] Much more likely is the possibility of cultures inclining humans away from what may have been an inherited tendency to selfishness. Our biology may encourage us to care only for ourselves and our relatives. What we are taught in the form of culture may grant a different vision, as for instance in the injunction to love our neighbour, even if he or she is not a relative and is in no position to repay our kindness. Sociobiology may explain why this is often difficult for us, and why we may just not want to because of our genetic inheritance. Saying it is an impossible demand requires further argument, since this involves denying that culture is a formative influence on human behaviour, although paradoxically the very denial might have the effect of making people more selfish. Unselfish behaviour has been advocated in many cultures, and if it is impossible a significant element of culture has been exposed as a sham. The real influences on human beings, it seems, must lie elsewhere.

If we accept this conclusion, we have to face the question why this kind of ineffective exhortation should have ever been incorporated in culture. Why do we possess forms of culture at all? The mere ability to create culture certainly gave mankind an evolutionary advantage. It is only a short step from this to seeing that different cultures may themselves vary in their biological effects on their members. Even if some individuals may do worse by being unselfish, the benefits to the majority will outweigh the disadvantages. The culture is not sowing the seeds of its own destruction by encouraging all its members on a course which is destructive of reproductive advantage. Sociobiological misgivings about this can only arise if it is assumed that even the content of effective moral exhortation has to be under genetic control, so that genes encouraging altruism have to be passed on if altruism is to be advocated. Yet this is to reduce the cultural level to the genetic and to refuse to accept that a form of culture can be passed on irrespective of whether genes encourage it or not. In fact, it seems quite likely that the purpose of many cultural norms is to restrain natural human impulses rather than merely to reflect them. The genetic constitution of humans was formed in conditions very different from those of contemporary civilized society, and many societies may find that human nature is not the best guide as to how to co-operate in modern circumstances.

NOTES

1 See my *The Shaping of Man*.
2 Harris, *Cultural Materialism*, p. 127.
3 Ibid., p. 57.
4 Ibid., p. 123.
5 Malinowski, *A Scientific Theory of Culture*, p. 116.
6 Ibid., p. 38.
7 Ibid., p. 206.
8 Ibid., p. 148.
9 Durkheim, *Elementary Forms of the Religious Life*, p. 466.
10 Ibid., p. 474.
11 R. Merton, *Social Theory and Social Structure*, 1968, p. 114.
12 G. C. Homans, 'Bringing Men Back In', in A. Ryan (ed.), 1973, p. 55.
13 R. P. Dore, 'Function and Cause', in A. Ryan (ed.), ibid., p. 67.
14 P. and B. Berger, *The War over the Family*, 1983, p. 202.
15 Ibid., p. 203.
16 Ibid., p. 144.
17 Ibid., p. 90.
18 e.g. by E. O. Wilson, *On Human Nature*, 1978.
19 C. Lumsden and E. Wilson, *Genes, Mind and Culture*, 1981, p. 13.
20 Ibid., p. 13.
21 See P. L. Van den Berghe, 'Human Inbreeding Avoidance: Culture in Nature' *Behavioral and Brain Sciences*, 6, 1983.
22 Ibid., p. 97.
23 Harris, *Cultural Materialism*, p. 132.
24 Ibid., p. 80.
25 Van den Berghe, 'Human Inbreeding Avoidance', p. 99.
26 Ibid., p. 98.
27 Lumsden and Wilson, *Promethean Fire*, 1983, p. 30.
28 Wilson, *On Human Nature*, p. 165.
29 e.g. R. D. Alexander, 'The Search for a General Theory of Behavior', *Behavioral Science*, 20, 1975.

9

Sociobiology and Determinism

I accepted in the last chapter that much of human culture is not under direct genetic control, and have remarked that social scientists feel that they can safely ignore biological theory. It even looks as if cultural norms may be so far from being under genetic control that their purpose might sometimes be to control the desires that still are. How does this match with Lumsden and Wilson's view that the genes hold culture on a leash? Van den Berghe has enlarged on this by picturing genetic evolution as a man taking a dog for a walk, with the dog representing culture. The dog has a certain limited range of choice about its direction, but can soon be pulled back by its master. Van den Berghe comments:

> What many social scientists have long tried to do is to explain the movements of the dog by rubbing out the man and the leash. What the sociobiological paradigm is suggesting is that we regard man, leash and dog as an integrated system in which the motions of the dog are always to be explained by interrelated motions of the man and the dog, mediated by the leash. What we can legitimately argue about is whether we are dealing with a Great Dane held by a toddler, a Chihuahua held by a Sumo wrestler, or some more likely pairing in between.[1]

On occasions, the dog can pull the man, instead of the man controlling the dog, and this accords with the contention of Lumsden and Wilson that culture can itself create an environment in which genetic evolution can take place. Nevertheless, as the leash principle indicates, sociobiology maintains that genetic evolution is the predominant factor in our understanding of culture. The dog does not usually take the master for a walk.

Natural selection does not merely provide the stage on which the drama can take place, but it influences the course of the play. A sociobiologist must cast doubt on the wisdom of social scientists who ignore the findings of biology. The fact that human cultures can only vary within limits provides an underpinning for our assumption that we can understand the members of alien cultures.[2] Cultural relativism is challenged by human sociobiology, since all cultures can ultimately be measured by the success or failure with which they respond to the basic human genetic constitution. The leash is slack enough to allow for different kinds of cultural development, but if some serve the demands of human biology badly it can be sharply pulled in.

We have already seen how a culture which does not allow its members to survive and have healthy offspring will not itself survive long. No culture could advocate youthful suicide and last, while a tribe too given to making war may find itself exterminated. More complicated elements in culture may have more subtle effects. Even living in high-rise flats might have an eventual biological cost. Certainly the type of diet favoured by a culture is relevant to its survival. Nevertheless, whatever the validity of particular examples, different forms of culture do make a biological impact, which will eventually become manifest. Cultures can become so debilitated that they change or die, while other cultures may allow their members to flourish, and in consequence become more firmly rooted.

Is nothing, then, beyond the scope of sociobiology? E. O. Wilson thinks not. While accepting that religion appears to offer the greatest challenge to sociobiology, he tries to show that even that can be explained in terms of its biological effects.[3] He finds it difficult to see how religion could be such a widespread human phenomenon if it had not proved advantageous to people. His conclusion is that 'the highest forms of religious practice . . . can be seen to confer biological advantage.'[4] He suggests in a quaint phrase that 'above all they congeal identity' In this he is following functionalist explanations of religion, such as that of Durkheim, although he differs from functionalism in so far as he is not talking of societies or systems, but traces the benefits of religion back to the individual biological organism. There are clear reductionist and materialist overtones. He argues that 'sociobiology can account for the very origin of mythology by the principle of natural selection acting on the genetically evolving material structure of the human brain.'[5]

The biological effects of religion can be examined by sociobiology, just as the social sciences can investigate its social effects. Some religions could go beyond the limits of what is biologically acceptable, by advocating complete celibacy or mass suicide. Such positions cannot be maintained for very long. Conversely, just because of the central biological importance of such questions as abortion, contraception and the regulation of sexual relations, religion could be expected to offer guidance on such matters. Religious rules which adversely affected the biological fitness of individuals must eventually be changed. Any religion would itself begin to lose ground if its members failed to flourish. From a theological standpoint, indeed, this is not surprising. It would be strange indeed if any religion which preached the love of God for mankind championed a code of conduct which in the long run actually harmed its adherents.

Wilson, however, is *only* concerned with questions of biological advantage. He brushes aside questions of the truth and falsity of beliefs to the extent that, like some functionalists, he classifies together systems of belief which directly contradict each other. Yet, once a role is given to culture and the contents of consciousness, one cannot deny that truth matters and concentrate attention on the biological consequences of belief. Wilson even argues that, as in the case of communist commitment, 'the blinding force of religious allegiance can operate in the absence of theology'.[6] Even if we suppose that communism and different religions can ultimately have similar biological effects, this only illustrates the fact that biology, even in the guise of sociobiology, can only have a limited usefulness. The role of culture has to be emphasized because the substance of beliefs is important. The basic question must be not whether a religion is biologically advantageous – any more than whether it has been produced by a particular kind of society or fulfils an important social role – but whether it is true or not.

Sociobiology and reductionist views of culture themselves involve beliefs that are entertained for reasons, good or bad. They are themselves part of the variegated pattern of human culture, and are not held merely as a result of some biological process. Dismissal of questions of truth and falsity can only be accomplished from the standpoint of a position that implicitly claims truth regardless of the ultimate biological consequences. What sociobiology can assert is that, however widely human reasoning may range, its results as laid down in culture must interact with human genes.

OPPOSITION TO SOCIOBIOLOGY

Many would hold that the existence of sociobiology as a discipline itself demonstrates that society is the major influence on human reasoning. They would say that it merely applies the presuppositions of the society which produced it. There is a remarkable similarity between some of the basic assumptions made in economics about the nature of human rationality and those made about the behaviour of biological organisms in sociobiology. Both are attracted by the view that forms of egoism constitute the most intelligible type of behaviour. The economist considers that people merely seek to satisfy their desires or fulfil their preferences, and can easily slip into thinking that these must be selfish. Indeed, there appears to be no reason why they should not be. The sociobiologist thinks that all action must ultimately further biological fitness. Both find the spectacle of people deliberately going against their own interests to help others difficult to explain. Sociobiologists tend to dismiss pure altruism towards non-relatives as an impossible state of affairs. They sometimes cloak this by redefining the term, but their notion of reciprocal altruism would be familiar to any economist espousing egoism.

The sociobiologist would partially deal with the 'free-rider problem' by assuming that evolution inhibits animals (or humans) from helping a second time those who have deliberately refused to return favours. This presupposes the ability to remember, and so it is not an account that could be applied to lower forms of animals. It is easy to see how resentment towards those who receive advantages without contributing may be natural. There would have been an evolutionary advantage in encouraging co-operation and in refusing to allow some to benefit from the contribution of others. Parasitical behaviour has to be restrained, since parasites would flourish at the expense of those contributing, because they would receive benefits without the cost of taking their share of the burdens. All the individuals in the group would begin to be weakened, because the parasites would become too numerous to receive proper benefits, and there would not be enough contributors left. It could recover its equilibrium only if those contributing tried to ensure that only those who gave their labour received advantages. A minority might always try to exploit the situation, and research into animal behaviour shows how this can happen. Nevertheless this type of reasoning shows how evolution, through natural selection, can restrain the development of uncooperative behaviour.

Thus the problem which economists raise at the level of what it is rational to do is dealt with by sociobiologists at the level of the evolution of social behaviour. Their perspectives, however, are remarkably similar, since each sees society in exclusively individualistic terms. The problem then is inevitably raised as to why individuals should contribute to society. Since society can be built up only by the efforts of individuals, explanations have to be found as to why it is in their interests to strive to this end. The egoist flavour is also significant. Not only is a community conceived as being constituted by atoms, but the atoms tend to be colliding with each other. There is bound to be conflict because each person is concerned only with his or her own interests, whether consciously or not.

One of the interesting aspects of animal behaviour is ritual conflict, where animals fight to find a winner but rarely mortally wound each other. They thus achieve the benefit of conflict without incurring the losses. A willingness to retreat can clearly be passed on genetically as the animal is likely to produce offspring on another occasion even if it fails to mate on this one. An 'all or nothing' strategy, however, is likely to result in an animal dying before it can pass on its genes to its offspring. If human behaviour is looked at in this way, in terms simply of costs and benefits to the agent, the result will be a picture of strongly competitive society. It may even appear that some people will naturally 'know their place'. Social relations will be described in terms suitable for the behaviour of stags in the rutting season. Each individual has to adopt the strategy which will gain the most advantage. The strong will grab what they can, and the weak will try to pick up whatever crumbs are left. Such an account may be appropriate for animal behaviour, which is not complicated by the intervention of culture. For example, one zoologist writes about the current stress on individual strategies in animal behaviour:

> The emphasis is now on selfish individuals competing to maximize their gene contribution to future generations. If some males are attracting females by calling, then we now expect to find other males parasiting their efforts and behaving as satellites.[7]

He goes on to give an example of how old male elephant seals, as well as red deer, can fight successfully to defend groups of females. Younger, smaller males that cannot hope to obtain a harem for themselves 'hang around the edge of the harem and attempt to sneak copulations'. Among animals strategies can evolve which trade on the behaviour of the majority, but checks and balances have had to develop to ensure that the underlying 'selfishness' of each animal is not disastrously destructive in its consequences.

There are obvious dangers in extrapolating from the animal world to human social reality, but critics of sociobiology are making a more profound point. The nub of the matter is where the categories of sociobiology come from. Their similarity with those of economics might arouse a suspicion that they are derived from the economic conditions of the society in which sociobiologists happen to live. Might they not even be projecting those categories on to animal societies? Moreover, the allegation continues, are they not then using the apparent types of animal behaviour as an actual justification for what happens in Western capitalist society? If certain forms of behaviour are made to appear 'natural', nothing will be done to change them, because it seems that nothing can be done.

This criticism typically comes from those Marxists who are able to demonstrate to their satisfaction that, far from being science, sociobiology is mere ideology. It is seen as disguising the true conditions of capitalist society and serving as a legitimation of the existing structures of society. Indeed, Marxists have no alternative but to view sociobiology as a product of capitalism, since their emphasis on holism cannot coexist with the rampant individualism of sociobiology. Paradoxically, however, both espouse different versions of materialism.

It could be significant that sociobiology originated in America. Perhaps the conditions of their society, with its emphasis on the individual, will predispose many Americans to look favourably on the discipline. That is a sociological question, and unless we are ready to embrace relativism we should hold it to be strictly irrelevant to questions of truth. The roots of sociobiology are very firmly in biological theory, since it is above all an application of Darwinism to social behaviour. Mixed with the insights of modern genetics, this produces the very emphasis on individual selection which many find objectionable. No doubt some are tempted to grant that animal behaviour can be understood in sociobiological terms, but refuse to accept that this has any bearing on human behaviour. The distinctiveness of human society could then be guaranteed. Many in the social sciences will make just such a stand, and claim the irrelevance of biology. Unless, however, social science is willing to make use of biology it is going to be completely cut off from the physical sciences. Instead of merely adopting the *methods* of the physical sciences, the social sciences may well find themselves considerably helped by using some of the *knowledge* gained by biology. Understanding those human needs and interests which have developed through natural selection will help us to understand the societies which have grown up to deal with them.

Sociobiology has sometimes tended to make extravagant claims to have superseded the social sciences. This view is particularly attractive to those who believe that the physical sciences set the only standard for knowledge.[8] As a result, social and cultural categories have to be reduced to terms which exclude reference to anything mental. The meaning of actions to the agents has to be ignored. It is hardly surprising that sociobiology has aroused fierce opposition for its uncompromising reductionism. The acceptance by Lumsden and Wilson that mind and culture have to be taken into account appears at first to remove this spectre: 'Culture is not just a passive entity. It is a force so powerful in its own right that it drags the genes along. Working as a rapid mutator, it throws new variations into the teeth of natural selection.'[9]

This appears to allow plenty of scope for the study of culture in its own right, rather than as a by-product thrown up by our genes. Advocates of 'gene–culture co-evolution' must be wary, though, of laying too great an emphasis on the effects of culture on genes. Culture may have had an effect on human genetic evolution over many thousands of years, particularly if the environment was stable enough. It seems very dangerous, however, to correlate cultural variation with genetic variation in the contemporary world. Mobility and intermarriage over the centuries serve to keep the human gene pool from being partitioned into separate compartments. Significantly Lumsden and Wilson themselves admit this and give as an example the Indian caste system, which I referred to earlier. They say that, despite its rigidity and the fact that it has persisted for two thousand years, it is maintained by cultural conventions. They continue:

> So far as is known (although the matter has never been thoroughly studied), members of different castes differ from one another only slightly in blood type and other measurable anatomical and physiological traits.[10]

It seems safe to assume that much the same mixture of genes is likely to be present in any human society. Sociobiology seems to emphasize the essential oneness of mankind, rather than giving comfort to any brand of racialism. Cultural differences will never become very great before they are sharply pulled back by the leash. They are, however, real enough, and cannot be explained by biologists. No doubt the interaction of the same genes with different environments will suffice to explain some differences. The thesis of 'gene–culture co-evolution' entails, however, that some cultural differences are inexplicable in biological terms.

DETERMINISM

The assumption that causal explanation is the only proper kind of explanation can lead to a desire for a simpler scheme of causal explanation. Sociobiology seemed to offer just such a scheme with its original tendency to favour a biological determinism which claimed that everything can be explained in terms of genes. Others look for causal explanations in other directions and adopt some form of environmental determinism, looking to society or economic systems as their source of explanation. Marvin Harris, for instance writes:

> In its commitment to the rules of scientific method, cultural materialism opposes strategies that deny the legitimacy or the feasibility of scientific accounts of human behavior – for example, humanist claims that there is no determinism in human affairs.[11]

Assuming that determinism is the thesis that every event has a cause, a belief in determinism embraces the claim that all human behaviour is causally explicable. Even the adoption of the belief in determinism is the product of some causal chain, and those who advocate determinism have to accept that their own commitment to it is itself causally explicable. Determinism is thus a global doctrine making very strong claims. They are metaphysical since they go far beyond any available empirical evidence. A belief in determinism may even have been an important factor in scientific progress, since one will never discover causal chains unless one is prepared to look for them. For that reason metaphysical determinism is sometimes distinguished from the methodological sort. One can look for causes while not necessarily believing that they must be there to be discovered. Sometimes apparent scientific difficulty may stem from alleged indeterminism in the world. Battles have raged in quantum mechanics because of apparent indeterminism at the sub-atomic level. The problem has been whether quantum mechanical description has to be regarded as incomplete because it still allows for indeterminism.[12] Is that because of our continuing ignorance or because of the nature of the reality being investigated? There is always a difficulty, since saying it is because of the nature of the reality may mean we give up too easily in our scientific investigations. On the other hand, refusing to allow for indeterminism may involve a stubborn refusal to see reality as it is.

These considerations are equally vital when the reality being studied is human rather than merely physical. Does an inability to predict action stem from present ignorance, which the onward march of science will rectify, or does it demonstrate something about human freedom? Since all we are certain of is our failure to make successful predictions, our answer will depend on our metaphysical presuppositions. Any social science which wishes to model itself on the physical sciences is likely to be deterministic (even though modern physics is not), since it wants to produce firm explanations of action. It will not allow for any unpredictability in principle, since it holds a much stronger thesis than the commonplace view that human action can be influenced by all kinds of factors. No one doubts that biological or environmental factors can incline people to some courses of action rather than others. They may argue about which are the most influential, but everyone would agree that human action does not take place in a vacuum. It takes place in a particular social and cultural context and is perhaps constrained by human biology. What is controversial is whether these factors, taken together or severally, are sufficient to explain human behaviour or just illuminate tendencies.

The argument between sociobiologists and their opponents has to some extent cut across the issue of determinism, with one side tracing the springs of human action to genes and the other to our social being. Yet both are happy to talk in terms of causation and to apply scientific categories of explanation to human behaviour. Their disagreement is not so much over determinism but over the kind of causes which should be invoked as explanations in human contexts. We have already come across instances of specialists who are ready to claim omniscience for their discipline, with little left for other disciplines. Social scientists become redundant if biology can explain all human behaviour. Conversely, biology is not needed to illuminate social behaviour if the social sciences can give adequate explanations on their own. It is one of the attractions of the notion of 'gene–culture co-evolution' that it may leave room for both biological and social scientists. The purposes of culture can be a fit topic for biological research, while its independence of direct genetic control could allow the social scientist to study it in its own terms. Yet at the same time a link is established between the physical and human sciences. They can complement each other, without isolating themselves for each other.

Does sociobiology, though, have to be deterministic in its assumptions? At first sight a reductionist programme attempting to explain human behaviour in terms of the evolution of the human brain is thoroughly determinist. It assumes that the physical structure of the brain can provide a satisfactory explanation for what people do. Lumsden and Wilson do seem very ready to slide from the contents of the mind to the structure of the brain. They refer, for instance, to 'the association between symbols in the brain'. In defining 'symbol' they say that 'the physical basis of a symbol in the brain is thought to be a network or cluster of neurons'.[14] Yet symbols are part of the contents of minds and are associated with questions of meaning. Locating them in the brain turns them into something very different. Lumsden and Wilson talk about node-link structures, and it is never clear whether these are part of the content of memory or part of the physical brain. If they have been directly fashioned through evolution, they are going to be the latter, but it is important for a thesis about culture that they are the former. It is very tempting for anyone wanting to make the leap from genes to the meaningful contents of culture to minimize the distinction. The problem is highlighted by the fact that Lumsden and Wilson define 'node' as 'an abstract representation of a symbol, or elementary unit in the brain'. It does matter, however, which it is, since the mental grasp of a symbol is, on many views, utterly distinct from whatever processes occur in the brain. Refusing to notice the distinction is in itself tantamount to reducing the social to the physical sciences.

Nowhere is the reduction of the mental to the physical clearer than when Lumsden and Wilson refer to sex and deny that its main purpose is to give pleasure. Saying the reverse is the case, they remark that 'the feeling of pleasure in the brain makes the performance of sex more likely'.[15] While it is possible to accept their thesis that the pleasurable nature of sex has evolved to encourage reproduction, it is hard not to observe that, wherever pleasure may be felt, it is certainly not in the brain. Once again they confuse the contents of one's mind, in this case felt sensations, with the brain processes which may underlie them. They can be identified only as a result of an explicit materialist theory, and Lumsden and Wilson do refer approvingly to the central-state identity theory of mind, which identifies particular mental events with particular physiological events in the brain.[16] They are thus able to say:

> The mind springs from a machinery of neurons created according to the genetic blueprint, but it grows in an environment created by the pre-existing culture, which is a particular history embedded in the memories and archives of those who transmit it.[17]

Culture is interpreted in a thoroughly individualist manner, existing only in so far as it can be identified with particular brain deposits, or in archives which will then be referred to by individuals. It becomes a matter for psychologists or even neurophysiologists, so that its development and transmission would appear to be totally explicable by physical laws. Their reductionism leaves little room for any notions of culture or of mind which can themselves act on the brain as well as be constrained by the physical characteristics of the brain.

Lumsden and Wilson mention several principles which they believe are inherent in science. They insist first of all that 'all domains of human life, including ethics, have a physical basis in the brain and are part of human biology'.[18] They go on to say that 'none is exempt from analysis in the mode of the natural sciences'. This seems consistent with their reductionist and materialist assumptions, and appears to leave little room for the social sciences. They even describe sociobiology as 'the embattled spearhead of the natural-science advance'. Yet they also wish to emphasize the role of mind and culture in ways which suggest that a crude reductionism is inadequate. One of their other principles, which is supposed to be inherent in human science, is as follows: 'The biases in mental development are only biases: the influence of the genes, even when very strong, does not destroy free will.'[19] They insist that 'the genes create and sustain the capacity for conscious choice and decision'.

SOCIOBIOLOGY AND FREEDOM

It is usual to regard a belief in free will as incompatible with determinism, even though attempts are sometimes made to show their compatibility. There is normally a clear distinction between those who hold that all explanations of human action must ultimately be causal and invoke scientific laws and those who rely on conceptions of rationality, believing that rational action does not have a cause. Arguments certainly rage over whether reasons can be causes, but ultimately it seems that choices and decisions are either themselves at the end of a causal chain or they are not. One's confidence in science to explain human behaviour will stem very largely from how far one views people as in principle predictable in what they do. There may be statistical regularities, but many scientists would hope to explain individual action as well as general trends. Lumsden and Wilson appear to want the advantage of being on both sides of the argument. Whatever they mean by 'free will', their reference to the concept cuts right across their desire to explain culture in terms of the working of the brain. It suggests that culture may be partly the result of free decisions by individuals as well as of the programmed processes of their brains. It certainly does not seem possible easily to talk of choice and will, at the same time as invoking neurophysiological concepts. Certainly a very sophisticated theory would be needed to harmonize the two, even if that were possible.

It is difficult to affirm any form of rigid reductionism with consistency, not least because of the difficulty of applying it to itself. The theory seems to demand a validity which it should not lay claim to if it is itself to be identified with the predictable workings of particular brains. Yet on this issue hangs the fate of the social sciences. If some of the remarks quoted are correct, the neurophysiologist will be able to explain the origin and nature of culture better than any social scientist. If, however, it is accepted that culture may be a powerful force in its own right, acting on brains as well as being produced by them, it is unsatisfactory to identify it with brain processes; it must be studied in its own right. Even if it is accepted that culture can only affect individuals through the functioning of their brains, that does not mean that research into the nature of the brain is a sophisticated form of social science. The fact that the characteristics of the human brain provide a necessary condition for the development of culture, and may predispose humans to some types of culture rather than others, still does not add up to an argument for the identification of the two. Ideas and other contents of the mind may have a more positive role than as mere concomitants of physical processes.

Lumsden and Wilson are quite happy to posit the independence of each other of genes and culture. It would be impossible to talk of them 'co-evolving' if culture could be reduced to genes. The trouble seems to come with the identification of culture with memories laid down physically in brains and with physical 'archives'. Thus when they say that people 'are neither genetically determined nor culturally determined' they continue by claiming 'they are something in between'.[20] They are still able to think in terms of physical determinism, and what is at issue for them is whether the springs of human behaviour lie in genetic programmes or environmental stimuli. Both will be understood in terms of the functioning of the brain.

The role of the social sciences is created through the assumption that such categories as the social and the cultural cannot be adequately studied in the terms appropriate to the natural sciences. The difficulty about attempting to build a bridge between the physical and social sciences is illustrated only too clearly by the work of Lumsden and Wilson. Once it is accepted that biology is relevant to understanding the contours of human society, it seems hard to avoid being dominated by biological and, ultimately, physical categories. The quest for the unity of the physical and social sciences often seems to end in reductionism, and the jettisoning of whatever concepts cannot be dealt with by physical science. The alternative seems to be the total independence of the two types of science. Unless, however, the social sciences are able to develop different methods, they are reduced to being the poor relation, never quite able to live up to the rigorous standards demanded.

Yet the sociobiological concept of 'gene–culture co-evolution' may suggest a way in which the discoveries of the natural sciences can be used to illuminate the social sciences. The recognition that biology puts con-

straints on the kind of society which can be sustained for long is important, and it is also crucial to realize that human nature does influence the
choices made in societies. The biggest single contribution which sociobiology can make to the social sciences is to give some empirical content
to the notion of human nature. It has been all too apparent that the
study of society can only result in a self-destroying relativism if the concept is not given any substance.

Lumsden and Wilson are themselves full of confidence about the prospects for the scientific study of human nature, claiming that it seems the
appropriate way 'to create value-free social sciences': 'When the roots of
ethics and motivation are fully exposed, political science, economics and
sociobiology can be more easily uncoupled from the genetic and cultural
biases of the specialists who originate them.'[21] This is all part of the view
that, if we can only discover the forces controlling us, we shall somehow
be able to control them. If we only know the values which bias us, we
shall be able to shake ourselves free of them. Yet it by no means follows
that this is so, if some form of determinism is assumed. Knowledge may
be itself a determining factor, but, on the other hand, knowing the evolutionary origin of our taste for sweet things may not stop us wanting
them. The point about genetically determined biases is that we have to
make the best of them. We may not always give in to them, but we cannot eradicate them at will. The whole message of the doctrine of 'gene–
culture co-evolution' is that culture ignores the demands of our genes at
its peril. Sociobiology may help us to understand the situation we are in,
but it gives us little power to alter it (unless we have sinister plans for
genetic engineering). Knowing we are selfish does not of itself give us the
power to cure our selfishness. Similarly, mere knowledge of cultural bias
may not enable us to alter our culture. We may not want to change it if
our desires themselves have been produced by it. If, for instance,
sociobiology is a typical product of a capitalist society, accepting this will
not necessarily spur sociobiologists to purge their work of prejudice and
bias. They may either shrug their shoulders and reflect that they cannot
help being what they have been conditioned to be, or they could give up
sociobiology completely if they concluded that it was *merely* the expression of a culture and not genuine science.

The opposition between a 'scientific' study of human nature and
value-laden social sciences is in any case a false one. We have already
seen that the aim should be not to create value-free social sciences, but to
ensure that the values inherent in them are appropriate for their subject-
matter. The question is how far sociobiology can illuminate human
nature, and how far its own assumptions and values result in a

misleading picture. The more ambitious it becomes and the less room it allows for the social sciences in their own right, the more suspect it becomes. If, however, it makes modest claims and recognizes that it cannot hope to explain all the quirks of human society, then it can provide a valuable underpinning to the social sciences. They themselves must use the insights of the physical sciences into human nature, because that is the foundation of society.

Social scientists have themselves often made the same kind of global claims that sociobiologists make. Both claim to hold the fundamental insight into the explanation for human behaviour, and as a result each has seen itself in competition with the other. Lumsden and Wilson saw the problem as being one of either genetic determinism or cultural determinism, but their flirtation with the concept of free will reintroduces a further element into the argument. Perhaps human societies cannot ultimately be fully understood by any brand of scientist, since the quest for causal explanations may prove fruitless long before all human behaviour is explained. Since arguing for the reality of human freedom, even of a limited kind, restricts the scope of social science, many social scientists may not take kindly to the possibility. Yet the fact remains that the inability of the social sciences to make exact predictions may not stem from any faults in the techniques being adopted, but have everything to do with the nature of what is being investigated. If we do possess a significant degree of freedom to choose what we do, an increased knowledge of the forces inclining us to one course of action rather than another will give us greater ability to control our fate. Lumsden and Wilson may believe that increased knowledge gives greater independence, but this can only be true if we are free to resist or control the basic tendencies of our nature. Their view of the power of sociobiology to bring enlightenment and an enhanced ability to control our lives itself depends on an assumption concerning human freedom which must limit the scope of that discipline.

HUMAN FREEDOM

The possibility of human freedom is not just a complication for sociobiology; it haunts the social sciences. Very often the problem is dealt with by being ignored. For example, W. G. Runciman, writing on social theory, says: 'the practising sociologist, anthropologist or historian can safely disregard the suggestion that any behaviour which he has observed, or has been reported to him, is beyond the reach of causal explanation altogether.'[22] He not only remarks that otherwise there would be no point in engaging in research but also flatly asserts that there is no convincing argument that any event 'does not depend on any antecedent condition at all holding true'. Runciman suggests that practising social scientists should sidestep 'old debates' about the freedom of the will 'with all possible speed'.[23] His view is that social science must assume that human decisions *are* 'explicable and not merely justifiable'. In other words, causal explanations can be elicited. He admits that this presupposition itself cannot be conclusively demonstrated, but he is clearly still under the spell of positivist assumptions about the world. He refers to 'the ultimate presupposition of all science, that everything is indeed explicable'.[24] It would follow from this that, to be successful, social science must itself search for causal explanation.

Once, though, it is accepted that human social reality may be different from physical reality, causal explanation seems more dubious as a goal. One point often made is that, whereas attempts at predicting aspects of physical reality do not normally have any effect on that reality, predictions about human behaviour can easily themselves alter the course of events, assuming they become known. Even in the case of sub-atomic particles there is a problem about the way in which the mere act of measuring the state of a system can itself alter the system. There is the added factor of human consciousness, in the case of the social sciences. Humans can take account of predictions in deciding what to do, and can indeed even set out deliberately to falsify them. A candidate in an oral examination is said to have been questioned about free will, and one examiner claimed that they all knew he was not free to walk out of the examination that minute. Whereupon the candidate immediately got up and left, thus proving the point he wished to make. Knowledge of what other people expect us to do can induce us to alter our behaviour, sometimes out of sheer perversity.

Whatever might be said about the constraints on human freedom, human action must be distinguished from merely bodily movements. The former involves choice and decision, whereas the latter, like an involuntary twitch, just happen to us. Many argue that this itself is sufficient to distinguish human action from what can be predicted by the physical sciences. The bank clerk threatened by a gunman may decide there is no reasonable alternative to handing over the money. He is, however, in a significantly different position if a bank robber grabs hold of him and forces him to do what he has been refusing to. In the former case he is an agent, but in the latter his body is no longer under his own control. Many determinist views appear to ignore the distinction. They might discriminate between different types of causes, but all seem equally compelling. The upshot is that the influences of society can seem as inexorable as the physical force exerted on the bank clerk. It is easy to drift into a position according to which impersonal forces at work in society hold individuals at their mercy. This is not unlike the position attacked by Sir Karl Popper and which he dubs 'historicism':

> I mean by 'historicism' an approach to the social sciences which assumes that *historical prediction* is their principal aim, and which assumes that this aim is attainable by discovering the 'rhythms' or the 'patterns', the 'laws' or the 'trends' that underlie the evolution of history.[25]

Popper, however, is still ready to embrace the notion of sociological laws or hypotheses analogous to those in the natural sciences. While admitting that their existence has often been doubted, he gives examples, claiming that they provide a parallel to physical laws.[26] Antony Flew has commented that Popper's suspicions ought to have been aroused when he found that he was having to provide his own candidates, and certainly the examples do not have the well-known character of physical laws as laid out in a physics textbook.[27] Popper gives as one example: 'You cannot have full employment without inflation.' No doubt belief in this as a law will have significant political consequences, but it is hard to see why it should be a law. Flew himself finds it the 'most persuasive' of Popper's examples, since there will tend to be a measure of wage-push inflation in conditions of full employment, but he comments 'however strong and well-grounded our confidence that we will never in fact suppress our unrelenting desire to better the condition of ourselves and our families, we do nevertheless all know equally well that we could.'

The point is that, although we may be only too ready to exploit economic conditions to our temporary advantage, according this commentary on human short-sightedness the status of a law ignores one simple fact. If we were all ready to sacrifice short-term gain, we might all benefit in the longer term by avoiding the bad consequences of inflation. The tendency of economics to assume the worst about human selfishness makes this state of affairs hard for some economists to comprehend. Yet inflation only accompanies full employment because of people's reluctance to accept less money when they know they could obtain more. This is far from being irrational if the wider consequences of wage-push inflation are taken into account. More to the present point, it is certainly not impossible for anyone to choose less money, rather than more, and it is perfectly intelligible to act with one's eye on the longer term and even on the general good. The situation is not unlike the prisoners' dilemma. It is apparently rational for each wage earner to try to obtain higher wages whenever possible. After all, if you do, I must attempt to keep up, but, if you do not, I have the chance of getting ahead. This kind of reasoning leads to runaway inflation. The paradox is that giving up thinking of one's own interests will not only be in the general interest but may actually prove to be in one's interest too.

It is possible to make generalizations about human nature, relying upon the insights of sociobiology. The issue, however, concerns not what people are likely to do but what they must do. Water does not generally boil at 100°C at sea level, or have a tendency to do so; it always does. A comparable law about human social behaviour would seem to have to deal with comparable regularities. We are all imprudent and selfish at times, but the opinion we each hold that we could do better and that we are capable of improving need not be mere illusion. Perhaps reference to sea level in the case of the boiling point of water concedes the conditional nature of laws. Other factors such as the purity of the water will also be relevant. A law would maintain that water boils at 100°C in certain conditions. May not conditions be similarly specified in the case of human action? A law about wage-push inflation will then state among its conditions that people are going to look after their short-term interests. If they do not always behave in this way, the law fails to apply. It is not invalidated. This proposal seems somewhat specious, and may even reduce the law to the truism that people are going to behave selfishly except when they do not. The question is whether humans are normally selfish in the way that water normally boils at 100°C. Even if laws are interpreted in terms of the constant conjunction of events, as an empiricist such as Hume would, it is unduly cynical to assume such widespread selfishness.

Instead of merely correlating phenomena, we may give a different interpretation to laws and think in terms of mechanisms in nature giving rise to the phenomena.[28] In that case sociobiological explanations in terms of human genetic constitution will be relevant, in that an appeal is being made to an apparent cause of much human behaviour. Yet talking in terms of a law would still seem to be claiming too much. The boiling-point of water can be explained in terms of its chemical constitution. Can we explain human selfishness simply in terms of our genetic constitution? That may explain a natural concern for our own interests, but it hardly allows us to make any firm predictions about whether people will act in accordance with those desires or not. We are able to resist selfish impulses, however real they may be.

Some of the other examples Popper gives of putative sociological laws seem curious. One is: 'You cannot introduce agricultural tariffs and at the same time reduce the cost of living.'[29] It may be trivially true that, other things being equal, you cannot reduce the cost of living if you raise tariffs. Presumably, however, Popper means his law to be a substantive one, and it is by no means obvious that a government would not be able to compensate for the raising of tariffs by making reductions in prices of other items. Another of Popper's suggestions is brusquely swept aside by Flew. Popper holds that 'you cannot introduce a political reform without strengthening the opposing forces, to a degree roughly in ratio to the scope of the reform.' Flew says that 'this one is simply not true'.[30] He points out that 'there are plenty of reforms which, once implemented, win the more or less grudging acceptance of those previously opposed'.

To take a final example from Popper's list, it is suggested that 'you cannot in an industrial society organize consumers' pressure groups as effectively as you can organize certain producers' pressure groups.' Since Popper wrote that, the power of consumers' organizations has risen markedly. It may be arguable who possesses the most influence, but it seems questionable that there is anything to prevent consumers' groups being organized as effectively as any other. In this example, as in the others, the proper response always seems to be to go on trying, whatever the obvious obstacles. Human societies are not run according to inexorable laws of nature. The pressures and even the apparent necessities encountered in them are created directly or indirectly by human beings. Because of this they can be influenced and changed by human beings. It is true that people's actions can have unintended and unforeseen consequences, and one function of social science is to show how this fact can affect the nature of society. Popper gives an example of how the liking of some people for mountains and solitude can be explained psychologically. He goes on to point out that 'the fact that, if too many people like the mountains, they cannot enjoy solitude there, is not a psychological fact'.[31] He remarks that this kind of problem is 'at the very root of social theory'. Nevertheless even these unintended consequences do not take on the character of inexorable laws. Popper's attack on historicism should also have led him to be much more suspicious of anything in sociology which appeared to be a law of nature, constraining human freedom.

One reason Popper gave for refusing to accept psychology as the basis of social science was that he believed it was itself 'just one of the social sciences'.[32] He argued that ' "human nature" varies considerably with the social institutions, and its study therefore presupposes an understanding of those institutions.' This brings us back once more to sociobiology, since Popper's assertion is at total variance with the whole basis of that discipline. Anyone who believes that individuals are the creation of their society is bound to be tempted by the notion that social science can discover laws, or at least present hypotheses, which show how society works. Yet, once it is accepted that human nature can sometimes explain the character of social institutions rather than be explained in terms of them, social science can no longer glory in its independence. It must be willing to use the insights of other disciplines, such as sociobiology. More attention has to be given to individuals than to their social context. However powerful an influence the latter may be, the fact remains that the individual's decisions will help to determine the character of the society. While society may not be ignored, the scientific enterprise has to start with the individual. How much human behaviour it can hope to explain depends on the extent of human freedom.

This is perhaps an answer to those who wish to argue against Popper and say that the human and the natural sciences are fundamentally dissimilar. Flew argues this on the basis 'that there could not be any laws of human action as such'.[33] He is right to resist the attempt to construct sociological laws on analogy with physical laws. Yet what if physical science in general, and biological science in particular, can illuminate the springs of human action? In that case, the social sciences would be neither analogous to the physical ones, nor totally dissimilar. Their credibility would depend very largely on their ability to apply the insights of physical science to the functioning of society. To those who fear reductionism, the reply need only be that it is by no means certain that human action can be totally explicable at any level by scientific means.

We seem to be caught between the Scylla of determinism and the Charybdis of being unable to explain anything. On the one hand, every event, including human action, may have a cause, and the job of science seems to be to discover the relevant causal chains, in order to explain past occurrences and predict future ones. On the other hand, if causal explanation is to be ruled out and prediction thereby becomes impossible, does not that undermine the whole task of the social sciences? The answer must be that it only does if the social sciences are understood to be treating the behaviour of humans in the same way as the physical sciences deal with that of physical objects. It is all too easy to conclude that they should adopt different techniques and goals, and ignore the physical sciences completely. The reaction against positivism has too often meant that social science has felt free not merely to invent its own methodology but to ignore any advances made by the physical sciences. Perhaps human sociobiology has pointed out a way of building the social sciences upon the physical ones without being reduced to them.

NOTES

1 Van den Berghe, 'Human Inbreeding Avoidance', p. 101.
2 See my *The Shaping of Man*, ch. 9.
3 Wilson, *On Human Nature*, p. 175.
4 Ibid., p. 188.
5 Ibid., p. 192.
6 Ibid., p. 184.
7 N. B. Davies, 'Competition for Scarce Resources' in *Current Problems in Sociobiology*, Cambridge, 1982, p. 363.
8 See, for example, Alexander Rosenberg, *Sociobiology and the Pre-emption of Social Science*, 1981.
9 Lumsden and Wilson, *Promethean Fire*, p. 154.
10 Ibid., p. 151.
11 Harris, *Cultural Materialism*, p. ix.
12 See my *Reality at Risk*, p. 165 ff.
13 Lumsden and Wilson, *Genes, Mind and Culture*, p. 376.
14 Ibid., p. 383.
15 Lumsden and Wilson, *Promethean Fire*, p. 28.
16 Ibid., p. 76.
17 Ibid., p. 77.
18 Ibid., p. 181.
19 Ibid., p. 182.
20 Ibid., p. 84.
21 Ibid., p. 174.
22 Runciman, *A Treatise on Social Theory*, Vol. 1, p. 198.
23 Ibid., p. 201.
24 Ibid., p. 183.
25 Karl Popper, *The Poverty of Historicism*, 1957, p. 3.
26 Ibid., p. 62.
27 A. Flew, 'Human Choice and Historical Inevitability' *Journal of Libertarian Studies*, 5, 1981.
28 See, for example, Roy Bhaskhar, *A Realist Theory of Science*, 1978.
29 Popper, *The Poverty of Historicism*, p. 62.
30 Flew, 'Human Choice', p. 348.
31 Popper, *The Poverty of Historicism*, p. 158.
32 Ibid.
33 Flew, 'Human Choice', p. 346.

10

Philosophies of Social Science

At the end of the last chapter we saw the problems faced by those who wish to model explanation in the social sciences on that in the physical sciences. The assumption of determinism certainly might make this task easier, but, with or without it, plausible sociological laws are hard to find. In the end, the doctrine of determinism is more a gesture of faith that causes are operating than the result of any significant discoveries. Those who feel that the narrowly scientific goal of causal explanation leaves out of account all that is most characteristic of human action may react vigorously to attempts to treat humans as physical objects. Indeterminism at the microscopic level still leaves room for ordinary determinism at the macroscopic level, and faith in the behaviour of particles as a justification for human freedom may seem misplaced. Laws about human behaviour seem hard to come by, and physicalist views of human behaviour only serve to dehumanize people. The impact of post-positivist philosophy of science has not only served to point out the limitations of science but has undermined its authority to the extent that many feel free to reject its claims.

This has sometimes resulted in grandiose claims being made for the sociology of science, but that is still heavily influenced by notions of causal explanation derived from physical science, and tends to be deterministic. It emphasizes that the causes of belief are social rather than, say, psychological, but it still talks in terms of causes. It is far in spirit from the work of Winch, with his emphasis on rule-governed ways of life instead of causal explanation. His work marks a switch to the notion of meaning as central to an understanding of human activity, and, as we have seen, it gains its inspiration from the later Wittgenstein. David Bloor, however, sees an affinity between his own work in the sociology of knowledge and the views of Wittgenstein, and claims there is a gap between Wittgenstein's ideas and those of Winch. He finds a 'natural continuity between the Wittgensteinian and positivist traditions'[1] and takes particular exception to the way in which Winch conceives of human activity as totally distinct from animal behaviour:

> By placing all the emphasis on the differences between human and non-human animals Winch flies in the face of Wittgenstein's quite proper sense of the biological basis of social life. Concepts and rules have their roots in a natural community of judgement.[2]

An understanding of society cannot merely be a matter of participants' own understanding, if society's character depends on the biology of its members. Winch himself has seen the need for those 'limiting concepts', such as birth, sexual relations and death, which clearly have a biological base. Even so there is a fundamental distinction between the view that human society is built upon human biology and the view that society floats free. There is a contrast between views which separate humanity from animal species and those which see some continuity. It is no coincidence that those which stress the distinctness of humanity and hence of human society have no room for the methods of the natural sciences as ways of investigating society. On the other hand, any position which considers the study of animal behaviour to be relevant to the understanding of human society cannot make a sharp distinction between the human and non-human sciences.

The connection between the human and the natural sciences, and between humanity and animals, often seems to be made a matter of a very clear-cut choice. Either one can reduce human categories to a level at which they can be dealt with by the physical sciences, or one cannot. Either humans are like other animals, or they are not. Yet the issue need not be put in as extreme a way. Why should there not be both continuities and discontinuities between humans and, say, chimpanzees? Just because humans possess language, we should not conclude that everything worth knowing about human social behaviour must be understood through the category of language.

Winch's position separates humans from animals, since only the former learn the relevant language and grasp the meaning of what is being done. Bloor, however, is worried about how the process of social learning can ever get started. He proposes that there is continuity between 'social shared concepts and our innate sense of the groupings of things'. He thus by implication begins to suggest a way in which connections could be made even between some of the insights of the sociology of knowledge and those of human sociobiology. He further boldly claims: 'that culture depends on such shared orientations to the world is what Wittgenstein assumed all along.'[3] I have already referred to Wittgenstein's ambivalence on this issue. He may well accept that our shared orientations are integral to a particular culture. The big question is who 'we' are. Are we just members of a particular society, with shared orientations as the expression of that membership? Alternatively, are we above all human, with all human societies taking these same orientations as their starting-point? According to the first viewpoint, any orientations are the outcome of culture, and nothing about the culture can be explained by them. From the other perspective, the orientations would instead be pre-cultural, and could well explain not only how a culture can be learned, but how different cultures can be correlated with one another.

Wittgenstein was in fact very quick to identify social phenomena with the possession of concepts, and concepts in their turn with words in a language. Without concepts we could make no adequate discrimination between one type of activity and another, or even one type of entity and another. Yet concepts are acquired, he held, through the acquisition of language. For example: 'You learned the concept "pain", when you learned language.' In a similar vein, he poses a question about how we know a colour is red and responds: 'It would be an answer to say I have learnt English.'[4] In fact this is a translation of Wittgenstein's German: what he really asked was how we know a colour is 'rot' and the answer was 'Ich habe Deutsch gelernt'. This accords with Wittgenstein's other views that we learn to recognize a colour through the acquisition of a language. It does, however, leave unanswered the question how we come to translate the term we have learnt into another language. There is no problem if we assume that Germans perceive the same world in the same way as the English. In that case we can teach a child the word 'red' or 'rot' just as easily. If the child is human like us with the same sensory organs, and is looking at the same objective world, we need only point out red objects of different shapes to be sure that the child will fairly quickly realize their similarity. Wittgenstein makes this much more difficult by stressing the priority of the public and the social over private experience. As a result language is given a position of great importance.

What basis is there for assuming that Germans and English, not to mention the members of radically distinct cultures, see the same world in the same way? If language forms their respective worlds, and moulds their experiences, there is no reason to assume that the worlds need necessarily coincide or that the languages can be translated into each other. If concepts are wholly linguistic in origin, there seems to be nothing left beyond language to which we can appeal. The understanding of language seems to provide the key to the social sciences. Indeed the mere possibility of learning a language seems hard to explain. Language apparently determines both social and physical reality, rather than reality determining language, and we cannot therefore appeal to what language is about. We cannot appeal, either, to any notion of a shared human nature, since that too is apparently defined by our linguistic categories. Thought without language becomes impossible, and different languages will produce different thoughts.[5]

The belief in the absolute priority of language does not just make learning or translating a strange language problematic, but, as we saw in chapter 4, it makes it remarkable that one can even teach and learn one's own. When Wittgenstein talks about teaching language concerning pain, he relies heavily on the notion of shared behavioural responses. The child we teach can be expected to cry when it falls and hurts itself. Yet the assumption that others are going to be like us in particular circumstances, whether 'others' are just humans or are fellow members of a particular culture, is crucial. It trades on the idea of a common nature and that of a situation being the same for them as for us. Both must be pre-social, because, if they become the product of society rather than a partial explanation for it, society becomes in principle inexplicable. The transmission of a culture seems to be a miracle, since there seems to be no way one individual can learn it from another. Any society, whatever its complexity, must be seen as the product of human nature confronted with objective reality. Otherwise we are left in a situation where we have to assume the categories of a society in order to explain how they can be passed on. Both the society and the language which defines it become free-floating phenomena, themselves creating the only categories which might somehow explain them.

STRUCTURALISM

The identification of language and culture has become very common in several philosophical traditions. This is not very surprising, as any stress on the priority of language serves to demonstrate the distinctiveness of mankind and, as a result, the separate nature of the social sciences. It leaves little scope for understanding culture or society in terms of anything else. In particular, two major philosophical movements, structuralism and hermeneutics, which both stress the central importance of language, have been major influences on the social sciences. Both are hostile to any attempts at explaining human society in terms of human nature. Jürgen Habermas has noted the revival of 'biologistic approaches' to social science, such as sociobiology. He considers that they, along with other tendencies, are 'indicators of the same syndrome, expressed as the widespread belief that whatever is universal in culture, if anything, is due more to the natural state of man than to any rational infrastructure of human language, congnition and action, that is of culture itself.'[6]

Structuralism would disagree with sociobiology over this, since it is prepared to examine culture in just the same way as linguistics studies language. Unlike phenomology, it is not interested in the individual consciousness, and indeed questions the whole antinomy between subject and object. The importance of individual thought can be minimized if a close connection between thought and language is insisted on. Structuralism stresses instead the importance of language, and also of culture, as systems. Saussure, the founder of modern linguistics, asserted: 'Without language, thought is a vague uncharted nebula. There are no pre-existing ideas, and nothing is distinct before the appearance of language.'[7]

If this is true, it follows that we must look at the existence of language as a system rather than at the thoughts or activities of individuals. Saussure distinguished between language as a system (*la langue*) and the actual use of language by individuals in speech and writing (*la parole*). While he accepts that speaking is an 'individual act', he says: 'Language is not a function of the speaker; it is a product that is passively assimilated by the individual.'[8] This idea of a system existing independently of individuals and exerting a dominant influence on them, even when perhaps unrecognized, has proved very powerful. The picture of language thus presented may pose questions about the status of the individual, but it certainly provides a model of analysis which can be applied in other areas. Claude Lévi-Strauss comments:

> Linguistics presents us with a dialectical and totalizing entity but one outside (or beneath) consciousness and will. Language, an unreflecting totalization, is human reason which has its reasons, and of which man knows nothing.[9]

The ensuing search for underlying structures in language and, by analogy, elsewhere embodies a clear reaction against the idea of man as conscious subject and source of all meaning. Phenomenology and existentialism are both decisively rejected. This kind of structuralism offers a threat to any idea that man is the centre of the universe. The very categories of human thought are given to us. Traditional classifications of 'world' and 'subject' are discarded, since we can no longer be understood as subjects thinking about an independently existing world and devising language to describe it. We are not the source of language or of culture. Being human involves living in a world which has already been determined. It has not, however, been determined by its own character, and the objective nature of the world is discarded. What is left is a world constituted by culture which logically precedes and makes possible the subjectivity of human beings. This subjectivity is, it seems, merely the internal representation of forces over which we have no control and of which we may be totally ignorant.

The nature of language and culture, viewed as systems, cannot be discovered at the level of the subject. Any concept of human nature as pure subjectivity, such as that favoured by Sartre and arising from the Cartesian tradition, is discarded. Lévi-Strauss makes appeal to a social unconscious. He conceives of the unconscious activity of the mind as 'imposing forms upon content' and he claims that these forms are 'fundamentally the same for all minds'.[10] Thus he says that 'it is necessary and sufficient to grasp the unconscious structure underlying each institution and each custom, in order to obtain a principle of interpretation valid for other institutions and other customs.' He interprets myths and symbols in this way, saying that 'the world of symbolism is infinitely varied in content but always limited in its laws'. The form of myth takes precedence over its content.

Lévi-Strauss analyses kinship systems in a similar way, viewing them as languages. His focus of interest is not so much the terms of a language but the relations between them. He notes that no kinship is universal, although he does accept 'the universal presence of an incest taboo'.[11] He explains that prohibitions on incest result in women being cast from their own groups and assigned to husbands from other groups. Thus bonds of alliance between these natural groups are cultural, 'the first ones', he says, 'which can be called social'.[12] He concludes that the incest prohibition is the basis of human society and, 'in a sense, it *is* the society'. This explanation is very different in kind from sociobiological explanations. Lévi-Strauss speculates that in advanced societies we may be attached to the taboo because of 'a later discovery of the harmful consequences of consanguinal unions', but he prefers the view that our society, like others, depends for its coherence and existence on a network of ties between different families.

There is no suggestion that this view of systems, such as kinship systems, can be based on biological discoveries. Lévi-Strauss denies that the biological family, real though it may be, provides the foundation for any system. Kinship, he believes, is sociocultural in character, and he concentrates not on biological families but on the relations between them. He says:

> A kinship system does not consist in the objective ties of descent or consanguinity between individuals. It exists only in human consciousness; it is an arbitrary system of representations, not the spontaneous development of a real situation.[13]

The whole emphasis in this is on the search for objective laws underlying human activity. These are not the product of human consciousness, since the way in which terms are related, whether they are the parts of a language or the units of kinship, must be traced back to unconscious processes. The human subject, as source of meaning, is destroyed, and it is difficult to see what function is left to man as such. This conclusion is explicitly drawn, and Lévi-Strauss provocatively says that he believes that 'the ultimate goal of the human sciences is not to constitute, but dissolve man'.[14] The search for invariant features underlying human societies leads him to reject any thought of combining 'particular humanities into a general one'. He is concerned not so much to discover human nature as to uncover the systems, whether of kinship or language, which are built by the mind, as he puts it, 'on the level of unconscious thought'. Language, for instance, is viewed as an entity in its own right, rather than as merely the product of conscious minds.

What is the explanation for the character of such unconscious processes? Lévi-Strauss himself seems ready to link it up with questions concerning the nature of the human brain. He looks forward to what he terms 'the reintegration of culture in nature, and finally of life within the whole of its physico-chemical conditions'.[15] This suggests that structuralism could be combined with scientific views about the development of the human brain. In this context, it may not seem fanciful to suppose that biological theories of evolution could supply explanations of why the brain makes the discriminations it does. It is striking that Lévi-Strauss puts so much emphasis on the incest taboo, when there are also powerful biological reasons for its existence. Nevertheless this is somewhat speculative, and sociobiology would assert the validity of its own theories in a way which is bound to suggest that structuralist explanations are of secondary importance. The *real* reason for an incest taboo is biological, it would be held, whatever may be its consequences in forming society. Lumsden and Wilson, however, seize on structuralism as a

192 PHILOSOPHIES OF SOCIAL SCIENCE

possible ally for their own position. They remark that Piaget, Lévi-Strauss and Chomsky, while using methods which are largely non-experimental, do postulate 'the existence of innate constraints of a kind which are more or less consistent with gene–culture co-evolution theory'.[16] Yet the emphasis in modern biology on individual selection is perhaps more easily combined with some form of methodological individualism than with a structuralist view of systems.

The search for 'deep-level' universals underlying the varieties of human culture forces attention on the mechanisms at work, however they may be ultimately explained. Man is dehumanized in a way that becomes ever more explicit. The traditional dichotomy of a human subject confronted with an objective world is destroyed. The systems of signs have their source neither in the world confronting the subject nor in the subject. Language neither reflects the objective characteristics of the world nor expresses the independent thought of separate consciousness. It rather creates the conditions in which it is possible to be a subject, just as it creates the world as it is presented for intersubjective experience. Human cultures as systems are explained in terms which are intended to bypass questions about the way the world 'really' is, or the way individuals attempt to find it intelligible.

Structuralism can explain how it is possible to understand one culture from the standpoint of another, since all are the outcome of the same unconscious activity of the human mind. The symbolism thereby produced not only makes the world for man but also produces man. Human beings must be understood in terms of the invariant and impersonal structures of thought expressed in language. Similarly the objective world disappears. An emphasis on the logical priority of language and other systems of signs inevitably produces a concentration on the structures of language and thought rather than on the features of the objective world. The world as mediated by language becomes instead the pale reflection of language. The thought, the word and the thing can no longer be regarded as three separable elements in our attempts to describe and interact with the world. Language becomes of central importance.

THE VIEWS OF FOUCAULT

Michel Foucault cannot perhaps be regarded as a typical structuralist, but he has been strongly influenced by structuralist thought. He has argued that what he terms the modern 'episteme', or framework of knowledge, which has existed for the last two hundred years, has been bound up with the emphasis on objectivity rather than on language as an end in itself. Now that the role of language is being emphasized, he asks whether 'man is in the process of perishing as the being of language continues to shine ever brighter upon our horizon'. He asks further:

> Ought we not rather to give up thinking of man, or, to be more strict, to think of this disappearance – and the ground of possibility of all the sciences of man – as closely as possible in correlation with our concern for language?[17]

With his interest in the different historical forms of what he terms 'discursive practices', Foucault is not searching for a universal theory of language. As a result, his conclusions must be relativist. He will have nothing to do with any realist understanding of the world, or with any notion of a conscious subject existing prior to language. We must all be trapped in the assumptions of our own society. Foucault explains that his objective 'has been to create a history of the different modes by which, in our culture, human beings are made subjects'.[18] He further asserts that conceptualization 'should not be founded on a theory of the object', but that 'we have to know the historical conditions which motivate our conceptualization'.[19] Thus the notion of a subject, according to Foucault, is very much the product of a particular society, and for this reason he investigates the forms of power which can apparently impose their categories on individuals. His view is that the task of philosophy is to be a 'critical analysis of our world', and he suggests: 'Maybe the most certain of all philosophical problems is the problem of the present time, and of what we are, in this very moment.'[20]

There is something very ironic about any attempt to understand human society which ends up by enquiring who we are now. Yet it is an inevitable question if every basis for understanding is knocked away and all our assumptions are shown to be culturally conditioned. When no knowledge appears possible, and we are barely conscious of the historical conditioning which has produced us, we are bound to wonder who or what we are. We are creatures of our time and place but even our understanding of that is historically conditioned. Once Foucault turned away from the possibility of invariant structures underlying all language and hence all culture, he was bound to be faced with the question of what, then, produced our ways of thinking. He would also be struck more by the differences between cultures than by any possible underlying structural similarities. As a result, he has been drawn to analyse the power relations in society which lead us to reason as we do and to make the distinctions we do.

This type of product is fraught with danger. The more the distinctiveness of particular practices of power is stressed, and the more, for example, it is shown how our own culture has made a world composed of subjects and objects, the more the question must be raised how Foucault himself can be immune to these practices. The problem of reflexivity reappears. If reality is defined by a culture in a particular way, how can individual members of that culture distance themselves from its effects? The project of discovering who we are is undertaken by 'us'. Once, however, the practices of our culture are laid bare, and we see objectification and subjectification for what they are, we have already abstracted ourselves from the culture. It seems that we are able to withdraw from the very practices that apparently made us what we are. The project of philosophical enquiry demands that 'we' or 'I' can reflect on features of our society in such a way that we can refuse to allow ourselves to be conditioned by them. I am more than the social influences upon me. Foucault himself remarks that 'maybe the target nowadays is not to discover what we are, but to refuse what we are'.[21] It is banal, but perhaps appropriate, to add that it must be *we* who refuse what we are. The distinction between the way things are, in this case in society, and ourselves is still crucial.

We may or may not understand the true state of affairs in society. Foucault suggests we can and offers an analysis of it. Historical conditioning cannot, therefore, be crucial if we can abstract ourselves from it and even reject it. Foucault's whole enterprise has to presuppose the distinction between subject and object which he wishes to supersede. We cannot understand our own society and reject its influences without discriminating between ourselves as the possessors of knowledge and the culture we come to know. As soon as we stop taking the presuppositions of our society for granted and can no longer accept as real what our society has conditioned us to accept, we thereby reaffirm our allegiance to a distinction between how things are and how we conceive them to be. We may realize that our unquestioning acceptance of certain categories, our 'objectification', is merely the outcome of a particular set of power relations. If this is to be a reason for rejecting what we are, it must be because we realize that reality may not be as we have been conditioned to view it. If the concept of objective reality is rejected, there can be no reason to take exception to whatever way we have been conditioned. Any way is then as good as any other.

Any philosophical position has to accept that there is a difference between what is and what is not the case. Without this distinction, there seems little point in a philosopher trying to convince anyone of anything.

Silence is the only proper outcome. Once the distinction is accepted, we are almost bound to acknowledge that our understanding of what is the case, whether in physical or social reality, may in fact be deficient. We may be wrong. Thus it seems that any argument must presuppose the distinction between subject and object, the person with a belief and the reality which the belief purports to be about. Even the structures which structuralism tries to uncover are presumably located in reality and are to be distinguished from the thought of those positing them. Foucault would presumably wish to distinguish the historical facts he purveys about, say, prisons or sexuality from his own views about them. He is attempting to write a form of history, not autobiography. Reality and conceptions of it can never collapse into one another without disastrous consequences.

HERMENEUTICS

Structuralists have not been alone in trying to transcend the distinction between subject and object. Whereas they have concentrated on structures which are impersonal and perhaps in the last resort arbitrary, those in the tradition of hermeneutical philosophy have emphasized the importance of meaning. They refuse to follow phenomenologists in locating it in the individual consciousness, but typically locate it in the language of a tradition. Once more the role of language is stressed in such a way that subjects are held to be what they are because of the linguistic world they inhabit. Thus the attitude of a physical scientist in investigating how things *are* is contrasted with that of an interpreter of some aspect of the human world who has to understand what is *said*. Interpreters cannot then claim a privileged position, because they are themselves located in a tradition and must therefore acknowledge that their interpretation is dependent on the context in which it is made. Hermeneutics began as a discipline attempting to interpret biblical and legal texts. Now, however, it has been given a much wider application, so that the problem of interpretation is seen by many as being of central importance in the social sciences. Habermas comments:

The main arguments of philosophical hermeneutics have become more or less accepted, not in terms of a philosophical doctrine but as a research paradigm *within* the social sciences, within anthropology, sociology and social psychology.[22]

The main emphasis in hermeneutics is on understanding and communication. It aims to arrive through language at a common understanding or shared view. The paradigm for hermeneutics is the interpretation of a traditional text, where the problem must always be how we can come to understand in our own context something which was written in a radically different situation. At first we may feel we do not properly understand a particular text, and this may be because we are bringing to bear the assumptions of our society, and making no allowance for the social context in which it was originally written. A proper interpretation has to allow for the mutual interplay of the two contexts. H. G. Gadamer refers to this as the 'fusion of horizons'. However, understanding appears to become impossible, the more that hermeneutics roots whatever is said in its own context. Both the text being studied and the interpreter have to be related to their own backgrounds. The doctrine of the historical nature of understanding seems to imprison us within our own tradition while the text recedes into its own, and hermeneutics must show how this gap can be bridged. Yet the problem is one of its own making: the initial strangeness of an ancient text has been elevated into an argument about the separateness of traditions. Gadamer's attempt to fuse horizons is only necessary because he has split different traditions apart, largely because of his insistence on the priority of language. He refers to the 'indissoluble unity of thought and language' and concludes that linguistic tradition forms us and our thoughts:

> The interpreter does not know that he is bringing himself and his own concepts into the interpretation. The linguistic formulation is so much part of the interpreter's mind that he never becomes aware of it as an object.[23]

When language creates the categories with which we think, any attempt to understand those writing at a different time in a different language is fraught with difficulty. Their thoughts must be conditioned by their historical situation, just as ours are by ours. Again and again, Gadamer emphasizes the primacy of language. Tradition is, he says, 'linguistic in character',[24] and he stresses, in a manner reminiscent of Wittgenstein, that 'all forms of human community of life are forms of linguistic community'.[25] Because language creates our world, there will in a sense be a succession of different worlds as human society and language change:

> The historical 'worlds' that succeed one another in the course of history are different from one another and from the world of today; but it is always, in whatever tradition we consider it, a human i.e. a linguistically constituted world that presents itself to us.[26]

Gadamer's argument is that the possibility of translation shows that the linguistic world in which we live is not a barrier, but that our own insights can be expanded. We can gain contact with the writers of a previous generation as our world can take in theirs. Yet this begs the question how translation is possible. If we see the world so differently from those who have been brought up in a different linguistic and cultural tradition that it is plausible to talk of them living in different worlds, understanding is bound to be a major problem. Our world is created by language, and Gadamer seems to have a picture of it being constantly widened as our horizons are widened. He explicitly repudiates a realist understanding of language, and inverts realism so that while agreeing that one can talk of an objective world he insists that this is in itself part of our linguistic understanding. Language is about 'the world' only in so far as this is a presupposition *within* discourse. He makes the obvious point that the world can exist without human beings but immediately denies any realist conclusion, since he says: 'This is part of the meaning in which every human, linguistically constituted view of the world lives.'[27] Rather than being a presupposition which makes language possible, it is thus reduced to the status of a thought which can be constituted only in linguistic terms. 'The 'world' is part of language, rather than its basis. As a consequence, he denies any notion of a 'world in itself' against which different views of the world can be set. Instead, understanding can only develop as we use our own concepts to try to interpret a historical text. We cannot escape the prejudices of our own tradition, and the most that we can hope to do is to include another vision of 'the world' within our own. Gadamer writes:

> The criterion for the continuing expansion of our own world-picture is not given by a 'world in itself' that lies beyond all language. Rather, the infinite perfectability of the human experience of the world means that, whatever language we use, we never achieve anything but an ever more extended aspect, a 'view' of the world.[28]

The question must inevitably be asked: what are we viewing if there is no 'world in itself'? It seems as if our world is extended as our aspect on 'it' is. This loss of grip on the notion of an objective world can easily result in the world, as we view it, appearing to be merely the product of our viewing. Certainly the inability to grasp the world as it is results in the hermeneutic stress on the historical nature of understanding. The world of the ancient Greeks or of the Romans seems sealed off from ours before the task of interpretation begins. We cannot assume any congruence between their 'world' and ours on the grounds that we have each been confronted with the same objective reality. Once the latter is subordinated to the demands of language, its nature too becomes historical. Roman reality may not be ours, and we can make it meaningful to us only by a supreme effort of interpretation. There is a sense, indeed, in which we can never enter their world since we have to use our own concepts for the task. It is no wonder that the hermeneutic stress on the way human understanding is historically conditioned can lead to an apparently insoluble dilemma. Either we are simply trapped in our own linguistic world, or we must base our interpretations on concepts which are bound to render them inappropriate.

For Gadamer, one possible solution would be to invoke a strong concept of human nature. Perhaps a similarity between ourselves and the inhabitants of the ancient world would provide the basis for our understanding of them. Yet the emphasis on language should warn us Gadamer believes that human uniqueness is bound up with human linguistic ability. What man is depends on it. Man's world is linguistic in character and Gadamer uses this fact to distinguish man from other beings. Only for human beings does the world exist 'as a world'. Because of the linguistic constitution of the world, humans have a certain freedom from what Gadamer calls their 'habitat'. This is a reason, he thinks, for the wide variety of languages, and he contrasts this freedom of humans to rise above whatever habitat they find themselves in with the predicament of animals: 'Animals can leave their habitat and move over the whole earth without severing their environmental dependence.'[29] The human and the linguistic are explicitly identified, but language is deprived both of any foundation in reality, and of any constraints offered by human nature. Gadamer dismisses any idea of similarity between different human beings in different historical contexts. No such connaturality, he believes, unites the creator and interpreter of a work.[30]

One of Gadamer's purposes is to transcend the distinction between subject and object, and he also wishes to contrast the human with the physical sciences. Hermeneutic philosophy stresses the distinction between the human world and the physical world. The concentration of hermeneutics on language seems to make the distinction true by definition. The physical world may be thought to exist in itself in a way that the linguistically constituted worlds of humans do not. Yet this contrast is entirely spurious, since the physical world as investigated by the physicist is as much a linguistically constituted world as that of the historian. Gadamer can claim that there is no such thing as a 'historical object' existing in itself, since what appears as an object of investigation to historians must itself be partly the product of their own tradition.

Sociologists of science, however, are ready to make similar claims about the investigation of physical rather than social reality. The categories we use to theorize about physical reality are, it may be argued, as much the outcome of a particular tradition as are those of historians. Gadamer, however, does not accept this line of reasoning but tends to take the progress of the natural sciences as self-evident. He accepts that tradition can play a part in determining that, for example, particular lines of research are preferred in particular places. He continues:

> But scientific research as such derives the law of its development not from these circumstances, but from the law of the object that it is investigating. It is clear that the human sciences cannot be described adequately in terms of this idea of research and progress.[31]

The view that the natural and human sciences can be sharply distinguished from each other inevitably trades on an assumption that the natural sciences can set a standard of objectivity which the human sciences cannot reach, and therefore should not attempt. Gadamer has a very straightforward view of the way in which the natural sciences proceed. They have, he believes, an object of research, and that is what would be known if we had perfect knowledge of nature. It is not, on the other hand, possible to talk of an object of history towards which research is directed, because it is senseless, Gadamer thinks, to speak of a perfect knowledge of history. Objects can only be posited, it seems, if it is possible to have knowledge of them. This inverts a realist position which would maintain that we can gain knowledge, in whatever area, precisely because there is a reality to be known.

Just as Gadamer tries to remove the concept of an 'object' in the human sciences, he attempts to show that the notion of a 'subject' has no application. Any idea of subjectivity is secondary to that of the tradition in which we find ourselves. Individuals are placed firmly in their social context, and the subject does not give meaning to his or her activities. Instead, meaning is generated by tradition, and self-reflection must be parasitic on it. Gadamer asserts that 'history does not belong to us, but we belong to it'. He thinks that we come to know ourselves in the context of our family and society long before we can abstract ourselves from our social environment and be aware of our 'subjectivity'. He continues:

> The form of subjectivity is a distorting mirror. The self-awareness of the individual is only a flickering in the closed circuits of historical life. That is why the prejudices of the individual, far more than his judgements, constitute the historical reality of his being.[32]

We are conditioned by society and become what we are through its agency. Our reasoning is not so much the outcome of our own efforts as a reflection, even if unintended, of our historical situation. A sociologist of knowledge could not have expressed the matter better. The result is that any Cartesian notion of the self is squeezed out. Our attention is focused not on the individual in his or her 'life-world', but on the tradition of a society. The trend of Gadamer's thought is holist.

THE REACTION FROM POSITIVISM

The replacement of the notion of reason with that of tradition, and the deliberate rehabilitation of the concept of prejudice, carries its price. Without the possibility of rationality, abstracted from its social context, there can be no room for any objectivist notion of truth, and there is nothing for us to be right or wrong about. We cannot escape from our prejudices and can understand the members of other traditions only from the standpoint of our present situation. Gadamer's denial of historical objects removes all possibility of dispassionate or disinterested reason aspiring to objectivity. Everything is certainly seen from a point of view, but, as so often in the philosophy of the social sciences, this somewhat banal point is made to appear an important insight.

Hermeneutic philosophy may seem an attractive alternative to the rigours of positivism, because it pays greater attention to the humanity of agents. Its emphasis on language draws a decisive distinction between humans and physical objects, and also humans and other animals. For that reason it would take little notice of attempts to use biology as a means of understanding mankind. Yet even though it allows room for systems of meaning, in a way that structuralism does not, there is the same subordination of the individual to a wider whole. Humans as such do not disappear into a configuration of apparently chance structures, but are created by the tradition into which they are born. We can never abstract ourselves from our situation in a particular society, whatever modifications or extensions may be made to it.

The intriguing fact, however, is that hermeneutics does not replace positivism. It merely re-asserts the importance of the human world in comparison with a positivist understanding of the natural world. Gadamer's picture of natural science progressing in a way that is largely free from the influence of social context stems from an acceptance of traditional views in the philosophy of science. Physical science can grasp neutral facts about 'objects' and so sets a standard for objectivity.

Because social and human sciences self-evidently do not meet this standard, the task of hermeneutic philosophy has been to show that they have a different function. Rather than suggest that they are 'unscientific', Gadamer has tried to show that talk of objects and objectivity is misplaced, so that truth in the human sciences is not the same creature as truth in the natural ones. Maintaining that research in history is not only research but 'the transmission of tradition', Gadamer says that 'we do not see it only in the terms of the law of progress and verified results.'[33] He does see natural science in just this way. Natural scientists can, it seems, free themselves from prejudice and the assumptions of tradition in order to verify experimental results in a way that owes nothing to historically conditioned views of what constitutes 'truth' or even an 'experiment'. Language, it appears, is no constraint for physical scientists.

Once this notion of physical science is queried, physical scientists are likely to appear subject to the tradition of their discipline in at least the same way as historians. If we cannot approach 'the world' from an independent standpoint in the human sciences, why should we be able to in the natural sciences? The work of Kuhn and Feyerabend only serves to remind us that questions about truth and objectivity are as problematic in natural science as elsewhere. The problems highlighted by hermeneutics, in particular the historically conditioned nature of our thought, are real ones, but they are general philosophical ones affecting all human endeavour. The natural sciences cannot claim some kind of diplomatic immunity, because they are as embroiled in the difficulties as any branch of human understanding. They may be attempts to uncover the nature of an objective world, but they are *human* attempts. Indeed, the alleged problems of understanding one scientific theory from the standpoint of another precisely mirrors the problem of understanding one tradition given the assumptions of another. Kuhn and Feyerabend have to admit that different theories are incommensurable. Perhaps Gadamer's wish to achieve a 'fusion of horizons' and to allow the possibility of tradition is unduly optimistic, given his rejection of the concepts of objective reality and of human nature.

Without holding to a realist conception of the world, and without a substantive belief in human nature, it becomes miraculous that the members of one culture should understand those of another. Indeed, no possible basis for understanding has been left, and the only conclusion is that we must be doomed to mutual incomprehension. Social science itself is rendered impossible in so far as it involves the comparison of cultures and detachment from the assumptions of any particular one. Different philosophies have all come to grief on this issue. Phenomenology, with its emphasis on subjective meanings and different 'life-worlds', can easily collapse into subjectivism, if not solipsism. Wittgenstein's emphasis on the priority of the social only serves to underline the differences between societies. The sociology of knowledge makes reality something constructed by particular societies and offers no basis on which it can itself be validated.

All too often the social has been emphasized as a reaction from empiricist theories of knowledge, which build up our knowledge of the world on the contents of individual sense-experience. The modern approach to the philosophy of the social sciences has been coloured by an acceptance or explicit rejection of the positivist view of science. As a result, the social sciences have been portrayed either as a pale imitation of physics or, as in the case of hermeneutical views, as something so entirely different that normal scientific conceptions of objectivity can no longer apply. Yet the situation is transformed when positivist conceptions are completely rejected. The question becomes not whether they are proper sciences but whether science as traditionally understood is even possible. As we have seen, the practice of physical science can be seen merely as a social institution. Human intellectual endeavour rapidly becomes pointless without the realist assumption that there is an independent reality for us to investigate. The demise of positivism with its strong notion of verification must not lead us to deny the possibility of truth.

CONCLUSION: THE IMPORTANCE OF PHILOSOPHY

What physical and social science must hold in common is not an empiricist methodology. Instead they must each hold fast to their aim of discovering the nature of whichever reality they are investigating. Physics must find out the workings of the physical world in the most appropriate manner, and the social sciences must do the same for social reality. Yet difficulties creep in at this point because the concept of physical reality seems less problematic than that of social reality. One of the most vexed issues facing the social sciences is whether there is a reality to be discovered at the social level or whether everything of significance must be dealt with at the level of the individual. The whole nature of sociology, and its relations with psychology and biology, depends on this question. Arguments about the relevance of sociobiology rage because many look for social explanations for social phenomena and feel they can disregard issues concerning the common biology of individual members of a society.

All this suggests that philosophical arguments about the nature of the reality to be investigated are of prime importance for the social sciences. Their claim to be scientific must rest not on their ability to copy the methods of physical science but on their adoption of those best fitted to obtaining knowledge about the nature of human society.

The constitution of social reality is highly controversial, even at a philosophical level. Those who hold Marxist assumptions may see nothing incongruous in a specifically Marxist social science. This is because they believe Marxism to be correct in its estimation of the nature of social reality. On the other hand, those who hanker after a value-free social science which allegedly discovers neutral facts about society themselves prejudge important issues. They are not being as objective as they think, since for them objectivity involves adopting the stance of the physical scientist looking in a detached manner at a separate world. This picture begins to break down in quantum mechanics, but it certainly is inapplicable to social science. We cannot abstract ourselves from all societies and divest ourselves of all presuppositions. The repudiation of positivism has usually begun with this insight. We can only investigate reality by means of a conceptual framework or theory, and we are products of a particular society in a particular time and place. We cannot acquire facts by discarding all our values.

The rigid separation of fact and value in the name of science has itself been held to be a characteristic of a particular kind of society. It is suggested that science has been invoked as a defence against religious dogmatism and arbitrary political authority. Thus it seems that, although values were apparently proscribed, modern science has actually operated with a lively sense of the kind of society which was desirable. An introduction to one book about social science describes the rise of science as follows:

> Modern science became a central part of the ideology of modern society, a promise to liberate the individual from the whims of nature or powerful men. In time science would help to legitimate both the capitalist economy and the democratic politics that came to characterize distinctively modern societies.[34]

Yet revealing science as ideology can have devastating consequences. Modern social science may expose some of the social roots of contemporary science, but, once it suggests that all knowledge is the product of society, we shall be dragged down in the quagmire of relativism. The assertions of social science themselves purport to convey knowledge about society. A reflexive social science applying its findings to itself will soon destroy itself. Whatever our presuppositions, we are not thereby prevented from investigating how far they help or hinder us in our quest for knowledge. We must consciously adopt those values which are appropriate to the task in hand.

The notion of a value-free social science may itself be ideological, since it conceals the values with which we do operate. An obvious result is that we treat humans as physical objects whose behaviour is to be predicted. Much that is characteristic of mankind is thereby ignored. Behaviourism and physicalism take this approach to its logical conclusion. Yet those who react against the positivist picture of human beings sometimes over-react by emphasizing what positivism leaves out to the exclusion of all else. Language is given special status because it seems to be character-istically human. It is often made the vehicle of meaning, so that the inter-pretation of human activity becomes a matter of translating language. Yet the study of language abstracted from the reality it purports to be about can itself become a self-defeating task. Language is rooted in human societies and expresses their conceptions of the world. It cannot be understood without a firm conception of human nature. Any scien-tific view of human society cannot investigate 'meaning' in a vacuum, but must take into account the modern biological understanding of man.

Just as an attack on a narrow 'scientism' can seem to involve an attack on all notions of objectivity, it also sometimes appears to be an attack on the possibility of rationality. The latter has so often been identified with the austere standards of physical science that it has sometimes seemed as if any belief that is not corroborated by science is thereby irrational. This is one reason why such great problems have arisen over the interpretation of 'pre-scientific' cultures. The classification of the majority of the human race as 'irrational' has been exposed as itself the prejudice of one form of society. The great problem has been to rescue the rationality of those with apparently 'primitive' beliefs without having to accept that one belief is as good as another.

In a different context, the desire to assimilate rational behaviour with self-interested behaviour has proved just as questionable. Both economic theory and biological theory have tended to talk of individuals maximiz-ing advantage for themselves. The assumption that this is so no doubt makes prediction easier in principle, because people are held to have fixed desires and act to implement them. It seems as if they could never act out of moral conviction to help others at a permanent cost to themselves. Yet, if this is possible and even happens, any social science which pretends it does not is going to be unsuccessful in its own terms. It will, for instance, fail to predict some human behaviour. It may even so powerfully influence action through its portrayal of the possibilities open that I do not believe, for instance, that I can be unselfish; I have a powerful reason for doing what I want to do anyway.

The basic belief of some social science is that its purpose is to predict and control the workings of society in the same way that natural scientists attempt to predict and control the physical world. Yet this itself alters people's expectations of what is possible, and further shows how assumptions about the function of social science inevitably involve a commitment to one picture or another of human society. It is vitally important that we see society as it is and not as we might wish it were. We cannot begin to study it without making up our minds about what it is we are studying. Because we are ourselves human, we will find that our most basic conceptions about human needs and interests are involved. We cannot look at human society without some conception of human nature. I cannot become a social scientist without facing the question who 'I' am. This constitutes a radical difference from physical science. It is possible to study the behaviour of material objects without being constantly brought face to face with myself. This cannot happen in social science, and it is hardly surprising that it is riddled with controversy. The illusion that it could investigate 'facts' was an attempt to avoid this unpalatable conclusion. Yet, once we recognize that the practice of social science cannot be detached from philosophical assumptions about people's nature and their role in society, we should not despise it for this. Far from being an inadequate copy of 'proper' science, it is wrestling with some of the most important questions facing mankind. Empirical social science must start from a properly articulated philosophical base if it is to be successful. The philosophy of the social sciences cannot be an optional activity for those reluctant to get on with the 'real' empirical work. It is the indispensable starting-point for all social science.

NOTES

1 Bloor, *Wittgenstein: a Social Theory of Knowledge*, p. 168.
2 Ibid., p. 175.
3 Ibid., p. 176.
4 Wittgenstein, *Philosophical Investigations*, I, § 384.
5 See further my 'Thought and Language'.

6 Habermas, 'Interpretative Social Science vs. Hermeneuticism', in N. Haan et al. (eds), *Social*, p. 253.
7 F. de Saussure, *Course in General Linguistics*, 1974, p. 112.
8 Ibid., p. 14.
9 Claude Lévi-Strauss, *The Savage Mind*, 1966, p. 252.
10 Lévi-Strauss, *Structural Anthropology*, p. 21.
11 Ibid., p. 46.
12 Lévi-Strauss, *Structural Anthropology*, Vol. II, 1977, p. 19.
13 Lévi-Strauss, *Structural Anthropology*, 1963, p. 50.
14 Lévi-Strauss, *The Savage Mind*, p. 247.
15 Ibid.
16 Lumsden and Wilson, *Genes, Mind and Culture*, p. 35.
17 Michel Foucault, *The Order of Things*, 1970, p. 386.
18 Foucault, 'The Subject and Power' in *Michel Foucault: Beyond Structuralism and Hermeneutics*, 1982, p. 208.
19 Ibid., p. 209.
20 Ibid., p. 216.
21 Ibid., p. 216.
22 Habermas, 'Interpretative Social Science vs. Hermeneuticism', p. 225.
23 H. G. Gadamer, *Truth and Method*, 1975, p. 364.
24 Ibid., p. 351.
25 Ibid., p. 404.
26 Ibid., p. 405.
27 Ibid., p. 406.
28 Ibid., p. 405.
29 Ibid., p. 403.
30 Ibid., p. 277. See my *The Shaping of Man*, p. 55 ff.
31 Gadamer, *Truth and Method*, p. 252.
32 Ibid., p. 245.
33 Ibid., p. 253.
34 N. Haan et al. (eds), *Social Science as Moral Inquiry*, 1983, p. 2.

Glossary

The definitions are not intended to be exhaustive, but merely indicate how the terms are used in this book.

adaptation Any physical structure, or behaviour, that aids an organism's ability to survive and reproduce.

alienation A term used in Marx's early writing to denote the dehumanization of people confronting the products of their social activity. Their labour becomes a commodity, apparently independent of the producer.

altruism Serving the interests of others, without any regard to the cost to the agent.

anti-realist Any position which denies the realist claim concerning the logical independence of reality from human minds and concepts.

atomistic Any view holding that persons or events must be understood separately rather than merely as part of a wider whole. Opposed to holism.

behaviourism The analysis of apparently private mental phenomena, such as pain, in terms of publicly observable behaviour.

causal law The correlation of two independent types of events so that the occurrence of one is explained by the occurrence of the other.

causation The process whereby an event is produced by another independent one.

collectivist Anyone treating people in groups and not as individuals.

concept The way we think of something and pick it out. Concepts can be shared and are sometimes identified with words in a language.

conceptual relativism The view that the nature of our concepts depends on the particular society we belong to. The concepts of one society cannot be translated into those of another.

conceptual scheme The whole set of our concepts. Arguments rage over whether humans can have different schemes, or must all share the same one.

consciousness The private awareness of the world, directly accessible to the person possessing it in a way that is not available to others.

contextualist Someone who emphasizes the social background of any practice as the source of its meaning.

counterfactuals They posit what would have occurred if circumstances had been different in some significant way. They are relevant for the establishment of causal laws.

culture Whatever is passed by teaching from one generation to the next and is not inherited.

cultural determinism The view that culture is the sole influence on humans.

cultural materialism The grounding of culture in a material base, so that its features can be explained in terms of, say, economic factors.

cultural relativism The stress that everything can be judged only by the standards of its own culture. An African culture, for example, should not be judged by European standards.

deduction The logical derivation of a conclusion from premises. One would not be able to assert the premises and deny the conclusion without self-contradiction.

determinism The view that every event has a cause.

dualism The view that the physical and the mental are distinct kinds of events, so that one cannot be reduced to the other.

egoism The evaluation of everything solely in terms of one's own interests.

emergent properties Characteristics that are possessed by an entity or collection of entities, but not by the parts which compose it.

empirical Pertaining to human experience. An empirical science produces knowledge from experience such as observation and experiment.

empiricism The view that all knowledge is obtained from human experience.

epiphenomenon An experience or feature of one which has no causal influence.

epistemology The philosophical study of the basis of our knowledge.

ethnomethodology An attempt to examine empirically the ways in which meanings are produced in social practice. It holds that all knowledge is a social creation, even itself.

ethology The study of animal behaviour.

eugenics A science, later discredited, which stressed the importance of biological inheritance, and wished to improve human genetic constitution.

evaluation A term often distinguished by empiricists from description, so that whatever is evaluative is non-factual. It implies the making of a value-judgement.

evolution The process by which different species acquire their characteristics through evolution.

existentialism A philosophical position which emphasizes the central importance of the individual subject or self as the source of meaning and values. All understanding has to derive from experience of one's own self and situation.

expressive Revealing an attitude to the world as opposed to saying anything about the world.

fact Something that is the case. Often opposed to value on the grounds that facts are part of the fabric of the world, and values are not.

false consciousness The misapprehension of features of a society, so that one does not perceive social reality as it is.

falsificationist The stress on the importance of being able to refute a theory rather than conclusively verify it.

fitness A biological term referring to an organism's capability to survive and reproduce. The kinds with greatest fitness become more prevalent in a population.

form of life Wittgenstein's term for the way in which words are embedded in particular practices and cannot be understood apart from them.

foundationalist An epistemological position resting knowledge on an incorrigible and certain basis.

free-rider Anyone who receives the benefits of a collective policy while avoiding the costs of contribution.

free will The ability to make uncaused, but rational choices.

functionalism The explanation of human institutions in terms of their contribution to the good of society as a whole.

gene The basic unit of heredity, composed of DNA.

gene–culture co-evolution The thesis that genes and culture can act on each other.

genetic determinism The view that important features of society can be explained solely by reference to genes.

group selection The controversial alternative to individual selection. It is the biological process by which one group of individuals leaves more descendants than another group. Kin selection is one accepted form of group selection.

hermeneutics The attempt to elucidate meaning, first in ancient texts and, by analogy, in all human activity.

holism The insistence that societies must be understood as wholes and not in terms of their parts. Thus individuals, and particular events, can be understood only in their social context.

humanist Someone opposed to naturalism, who stresses the separate nature of the human.

hypothesis In science, a possibility which is entertained and put to empirical test.

idealism The view that existence depends logically on perception by a mind.

ideology A system of ideas justifying the vested interests of a group. The term normally assumes their falsity, but it can be used, more generally, to refer to any definition of reality.

incommensurability The inability to compare, or interchange, the terms of one theory with those of another.

individualism The stress on the individual rather than society as a whole, so that the latter must be understood in terms of its members.

individual selection The biological process whereby an individual and its direct descendants are favoured through evolution.

infrastructure Whatever underlies and causes the manifest features of society.

kin selection The biological process whereby relatives, who probably share the same genes, are favoured by the behaviour of an individual. Thus even self-sacrifice can encourage the spread of one's genes, if relatives are thereby kept from harm.

language-game Wittgenstein's term for the manifold, rule-governed ways in which language is embedded in human activity.

legitimation A social process whereby institutions are explained and justified.

materialism The doctrine that everything, even the apparently mental, is composed of matter or totally dependent on it.

metaphysical Anything beyond the scope of physical science which is accessible to reason. Positivists would deny the possibility of metaphysics.

methodology The theory of the aims and procedures of a discipline.

natural selection The biological process whereby different genetic types produce more or less offspring, and the fittest come to predominate.

naturalist In the context of social science, someone who believes that society can be studied in the same way as the physical world. Often, but not necessarily, linked with positivism.

nihilism The possibly incoherent view that nothing matters and that there is no such thing as truth. It is therefore a matter of indifference what one believes or does.

objectivity The property of being the case whatever human conceptions

GLOSSARY 211

of the matter may be. Also used to signify detachment from all particular points of view.

ontology The theory of what there is.

paradigm Used by Kuhn to signify examples of scientific practice in 'normal science' that provide the starting-point for traditions of research.

phenomenology The analysis of human consciousness or subjective experience, 'bracketing-off' questions of truth.

phylogeny The evolutionary history of a group of organisms or species, contrasted with 'ontogeny', referring to the development of a single organism in its lifetime.

physicalism The doctrine that everything can be explained in terms of physical laws.

pluralism The view that different theories and ways of life have to be accepted as they are, and one should not seek supremacy or domination.

positivism The view which considers scientific method the only path to truth. Opposed to any form of metaphysics.

private language A language which can only be understood by one person. The possibility was attacked by Wittgenstein, who stressed the social character of language.

public good A benefit available to more than one person (such as street-lighting).

rationality The ability to reason to what one considers true conclusions. Mere ignorance is not a sign of irrationality, but inconsistency is.

realism The view that reality is objective and logically independent of all beliefs and conceptions of it.

reciprocal altruism The performance of acts beneficial to others so that similar benefits may be received in return.

reductio ad absurdum An argument which refutes a position by demonstrating the absurd consequences necessarily following from it.

reductionism The attempt to demonstrate that statements about one kind of entity are in reality about a different kind – for example, that statements about minds are really about bodies.

reflexivity The application of a statement, or theory, to itself. If all beliefs beliefs are socially conditioned, then so must be the belief that they are.

reification The viewing of human products as if they were entities independent of man.

relativism The view that there are different, possibly self-contained, traditions and ways of life, each to be judged only in accordance with its own standards.

ritual A practice performed for its own sake, regardless of any beliefs accompanying it.

scepticism Doubt about whether we can obtain knowledge.

science In general, any form of knowledge, but more particularly that body of empirical knowledge obtained through observation and experiment.

scientific revolution Kuhn's term for a major change in scientific outlook as one theory is discarded in favour of another.

sense-data The basic elements of sense-experience, according to many empiricists. They were supposed to be neutral in respect of differing theories and interpretations and to form the foundation of empirical knowledge.

social reality The humanly constructed environment, formed by beliefs and expectations, and contrasted with physical reality.

society A group of individuals co-operating with each other. Arguments rage over whether emergent properties can be attributed to it.

sociobiology The biological study of the development of social behaviour in all organisms including man.

sociology of knowledge A discipline which attempts to uncover the social origins of belief.

solipsism The denial of any reality beyond myself and my experiences.

structuralism The view, derived from linguistics and applied to other fields, that phenomena should be understood in terms of invariant underlying systems of organization.

subjective Used in opposition to 'objective', and referring to what is accessible to only one person or has validity for only one person.

symbolist In anthropology, a stress on what is expressed by behaviour such as a rain-dance, as an alternative to viewing it as a means to the achievement of a desired end.

tabula rasa 'A blank slate'. Refers to the empiricist belief that we are born without any inherited tendencies.

theory In science, a system of laws and hypotheses which attempts to explain and predict observable phenomena.

theory-laden Any word or concept which can only be understood within the context of a particular theory. It could not normally be used within another theory without a significant change of meaning.

underdetermination A term used, particularly by Quine, pointing out that a theory may not be deducible from empirical evidence but may go far beyond it.

universal A property attributed to all the individuals of a certain kind. The universal, redness, is thus predicated of all red objects.

utility maximizing A procedure to achieve the best possible outcome in a situation. Utilities (namely, whatever is preferred) are estimated, together with the probability of obtaining them. The rational action is considered the one with the maximum expected utility.

values Often thought to be matters of personal choice and preference, and contrasted with 'facts' about which agreement can be obtained.

value-freedom The ideal of making judgements about facts without the intrusion of values.

verificationism The adoption of the positivist view of the link between verification and meaning.

verification theory of meaning The doctrine that the meaning of a statement consists in our knowledge of the way its truth can be ascertained.

Verstehen Term used by Weber to denote what he considered to be the practice of social science, namely the interpretative understanding of human agents and of the meaning they themselves attached to their actions.

Bibliography

Alexander, R. D., 'The Search for a General Theory of Behavior', *Behavioral Science*, 20, 1975.

Barnes, B., *T. S. Kuhn and Social Science*, London, 1982.

Beattie, J., *Other Cultures*, London, 1964.

Berger, P., and Berger, B., *The War over the Family*, London, 1983.

Berger, P., and Kellner, H., *Sociology Reinterpreted*, London, 1982.

Berger, P., and Luckmann, T., *The Social Construction of Reality*, London, 1967.

Bhaskhar, R., *A Realist Theory of Science*. Hassocks, Sussex, 1978.

Bloor, D., *Knowledge and Social Imagery*, London, 1976.

—— *Wittgenstein: a Social Theory of Knowledge*, London, 1983.

—— 'A Sociological Theory of Objectivity', in S. C. Brown (ed.), *Objectivity and Cultural Divergence*, Cambridge, 1984.

Bloor, D., and Barnes, B., 'Relativism, Rationalism and the Sociology of Knowledge', in M. Hollis and S. Lukes (eds), *Rationality and Relativism*, Oxford, 1982.

Braithwaite, R. B., 'An Empiricist's View of the Nature of Religious Belief', in I. T. Ramsey (ed.), *Christian Ethics and Contemporary Philosophy*, London, 1966.

Buchanan, A., 'Revolutionary Motivation and Rationality', *Philosophy and Public Affairs*, 9, 1979–80.

Cohen, R. S., and Wartofsky, M. W. (eds), *Epistemology, Methodology and the Social Sciences*, Dordrecht, 1983.

Cupitt, D., *Taking Leave of God*, London, 1980.

—— *The World to Come*, London, 1982.

Davies, N. B., 'Competition for Scarce Resources', *Current Problems in Sociobiology*, King's College Sociobiology Group, Cambridge, 1982.

Dore, R. P., 'Function and Cause', in A. Ryan (ed.), *The Philosophy of Social Explanation*, Oxford, 1973.

Durkheim, E., *Elementary Forms of the Religious Life*, New York, 1965.

—— *The Rules of Sociological Method*, ed. S. Lukes, London, 1982.

Evans-Pritchard, E., *Witchcraft, Oracles and Magic among the Azande*, Oxford, 1937.

Fay, B., and Moon, J. D., 'What Would an Adequate Philosophy of Social Science Look Like?', *Philosophy of the Social Sciences*, 7, 1977.

Feyerabend, P., *Science in a Free Society*, London, 1978.

—— *Philosophical Papers*, Vol. I, *Realism, Rationalism and Scientific Method*, Cambridge, 1981.

—— *Philosophical Papers*, Vol. II, *Problems of Empiricism*, Cambridge, 1981.

Flew, A., 'Human Choice and Historical Inevitability', *Journal of Libertarian Studies*, 5, 1981.

Foucault, M., *The Order of Things*, London, 1970.

—— 'The Subject and Power', in *Michel Foucault: Beyond Structuralism and Hermeneutics*, ed. H. Dreyfus and P. Rabinow, Brighton, 1982.

Frazer, J., *The Golden Bough*, London, 1922.

Freeman, D., *Margaret Mead and Samoa: The Making and Unmaking of an Anthropological Myth*, Harvard, 1983.

Gadamer, H. G., *Truth and Method*, London, 1975.

Garfinkel, H., and Sachs, H., 'On Formal Structures of Practical Actions', in J. C. McKinney and E. A. Tiryakin (eds), *Theoretical Sociology*, New York, 1970.

Graham, L., *Between Science and Values*, New York, 1981.

Grandy, R., 'Reference, Meaning and Belief', *Journal of Philosophy*, 70, 1973.

Grene, M., 'Dogmas in Empiricism', in R. S. Cohen and M. W. Wartofsky (eds), *Epistemology, Methodology and the Social Sciences*, Dordrecht, 1983.

Haan, N., Bellah, R., Rabinow, P., and Sullivan, W. M. (eds), *Social Science as Moral Inquiry*, New York, 1983.

Habermas, J., *Knowledge and Human Interests*, London, 1972.

—— 'Interpretative Social Science vs. Hermeneuticism', in N. Haan et al. (eds), *Social Science as Moral Inquiry*, New York, 1983.

Harris, M., *Cultural Materialism*, New York, 1979.

Hempel, C., *Philosophy of Natural Science*, Englewood Cliffs, NJ, 1968.

Hesse, M., *Revolutions and Reconstructions in the Philosophy of Science*, Brighton, 1980.

Hirsch, F., and Goldthorpe, J. H., *Political Economy of Inflation*, London, 1978.

Hollis, M., and Lukes, S. (eds), *Rationality and Relativism*, Oxford, 1982.

Holmstrom, N., 'Rationality and Revolution', *Canadian Journal of Philosophy*, 13, 1983.

Homans, G. C., 'Bringing Men Back In', in A. Ryan (ed.), *The Philosophy of Social Explanation*, Oxford, 1973.

Hume, D. *Hume's Ethical Writings*, ed. A. Macintyre, New York, 1965.

Kahn, V. Saifullah, 'Pakistanis in Britain: Perceptions of a Population', *New Community*, 5, 1976.

Kuhn, T. S., *The Structure of Scientific Revolutions*, Chicago, Ill., 1962.

―― *The Essential Tension*, Chicago, Ill., 1977.

Lévi-Strauss, C., *Structural Anthropology*, New York, 1963.

―― *The Savage Mind*, London, 1966.

―― *Structural Anthropology*, Vol. II, London, 1977.

Luckmann, T., *Life-World and Social Realities*, London, 1983.

Lukács, G., *History and Class Consciousness*, London, 1971.

Lumsden, C., and Wilson, E., *Genes, Mind and Culture: the Co-evolutionary Process*, Cambridge, Mass., 1981.

―― *Promethean Fire: Reflections on the Origin of Mind*, Cambridge, Mass., 1983.

MacDonald, G., and Pettit, R. *Semantics and Social Science*, London, 1981.

McPherson, M. S., 'Want Formation, Morality, and Some Interpretive Aspects of Economic Inquiry', in N. Haan et al. (eds), *Social Science as Moral Inquiry*, New York, 1983.

Malinowski, B., *A Scientific Theory of Culture*, Chapel Hill, NC, 1944.

Mannheim, K., *Ideology and Utopia*, London, 1936.

Marx, K., *Capital*, New York, 1967.

―― *A Contribution to the Critique of Political Economy*, New York, 1970.

―― *Early Texts*, ed. D. McLellan, Oxford, 1971.

―― *Grundrisse*, ed. M. Nicolaus, Harmondsworth, 1973.

Mead, M., *Coming of Age in Samoa*, 1928, reprinted London, 1943.

Mehan, H., and Wood, H., *The Reality of Ethnomethodology,* London, 1975.

Meltzer, B. N., Petras, J. W., and Reynolds, L. T., *Symbolic Interactionism, Genesis, Varieties, Criticism,* London, 1975.

Merton, R., *Social Theory and Social Structure*, New York, 1968.

Neurath, M., and Cohen, R. (eds), *Otto Neurath: Empiricism and Sociology*, Dordrecht, 1973.

Passingham, R., *The Human Primate*, Oxford, 1982.

Phillips, D. Z., 'Primitive Reactions and the Reactions of Primitives', Marett Lecture, Exeter College, Oxford, 1983.

Popper, K., *The Poverty of Historicism*, London, 1957.

Quine, W. V., *Word and Object*, Cambridge, Mass., 1964.

Rawls, J., *A Theory of Justice*, Oxford, 1972.
Reynolds, V., and Tanner, R., *The Biology of Religion*, London, 1983.
Rorty, R., 'Method and Morality', in N. Haan et al. (eds), *Social Science as Moral Inquiry*, New York, 1983.
—— *Philosophy and the Mirror of Nature*, Oxford, 1980.
Rosenberg, A., *Sociobiology and the Pre-emption of Social Science*, Oxford, 1981.
Rubinstein, D., *Marx and Wittgenstein: Social Praxis and Social Explanation*, London, 1981.
Runciman, W. G., *A Treatise on Social Theory*, Vol. I, Cambridge, 1983.
Ryan, A. (ed.), *The Philosophy of Social Explanation*, Oxford, 1973.
Saussure, F. de, *Course in General Linguistics*, London, 1974.
Schutz, A. *Collected Papers,* Vol. I, *The Problem of Social Reality*, and Vol. II, *Studies in Social Theory*, The Hague, 1962.
Sen, A., 'Rational Fools', *Philosophy and Public Affairs*, 6, 1977.
—— *Choice, Welfare and Measurement*, Oxford, 1982.
Stigler, G., and Becker, G., 'De Gustibus non est Disputandum', *American Economics Review*, 67, 1977.
Taylor, C., 'Rationality', in M. Hollis and S. Lukes (eds), *Rationality and Relativism*, Oxford, 1982.
Trigg, R. *Pain and Emotion*, Oxford, 1970.
—— *Reason and Commitment,* Cambridge, 1973.
—— 'Thought and Language', *Proceedings of the Aristotelian Society*, 79, 1978–9.
—— *Reality at Risk: A Defence of Realism in Philosophy and the Sciences*, Brighton and Totowa, NJ, 1980.
—— *The Shaping of Man: Philosophical Aspects of Sociobiology*, Oxford, 1982, and New York, 1983.
—— 'The Limits of Science', in H. P. Duerr (ed.), *Science and the Irrational,* New York, 1984 (also in H. P. Duerr (ed.), *Der Wissenschaftler und das Irrationale*, Frankfurt, 1981).
—— 'The Sociobiological View of Man' in S. C. Brown (ed.), *Objectivity and Cultural Divergence*, Cambridge, 1984.
Turner, D., *Marxism and Christianity*, Oxford, 1983.
Van den Berghe, P., 'Human Inbreeding Avoidance: Culture in Nature', *Behavioral and Brain Sciences*, 6, 1983.
Weber, M., *Theory of Social and Economic Organization*, trans. A. Henderson and T. Parsons, London, 1947.
—— *Selections*, ed. W. G. Runciman, Cambridge, 1978.
Wilson, E. O., *Sociobiology: The New Synthesis*, Cambridge, Mass., 1975.

—— *On Human Nature*, Cambridge, Mass., 1978.
Winch, P., *The Idea of a Social Science*, London, 1958.
—— 'Understanding a Primitive Society', *Ethics and Action*, London, 1972.
Wittgenstein, L., *Philosophical Investigations*, Oxford, 1958.
—— *On Certainty*, Oxford, 1969.
—— *Remarks on Frazer's Golden Bough*, ed. Rush Rhees, Retford, 1979.

Index

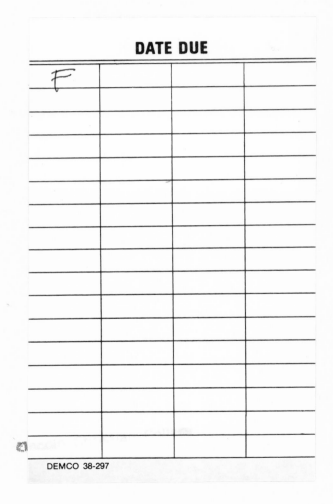